Praise for *The Jesus Fractal*

Metaphors are primary for the joining of visible with invisible. As such, they are essential parts of speech in communicating the Christian faith, for most of what we deal with is invisible. "No one has seen God at any time…" So David, and all the rest of us, use metaphors to clarify: "God is a rock."

Those of us who use words to write about the Christian faith are always on the lookout for a fresh metaphor. Elizabeth Frykberg has introduced me to a new one: "Fractal." It comes from the vocabulary of science and mathematics, but it also gives fresh insight to the invisibles involved in following Jesus.

Perchoresis is a word introduced by the seventh century theologian, John of Damascus (literally, Father, Son and Holy Spirit *Dancing Around*). It has been my favorite for dealing with the Trinity, a notoriously difficult term for the Christian imagination to come to terms with.

I grew up in square-dance country (Montana) and, having learned the meaning of *perchoresis*, every mention of the Trinity brings to mind a weekend square dance in the barn: the partners joined hands, the violins playing, the caller giving directions, "change your partners," "dos e dos," – faster and faster until the partners (Father, Son and Holy Ghost) could no longer be identified.

But, no longer in square-dance country, I find *Fractal* much more useful in the world I now inhabit. Thank you, Elizabeth! Now in conversation with friends and parishioners, I find myself in much larger company.

Eugene H. Peterson
Professor of Spiritual Theology, Regent College
Author of *The Message*

Now and then someone comes along and provides you with a new lens for life. Suddenly you are able to see details and patterns to the miracle of existence that somehow you'd missed. At first they stun you. Then they inspire you. Finally, they reshape your experience of daily life. Such is the influence of Elizabeth Frykberg's, *The Jesus Fractal*. With breathtaking sweep and insight, Rev. Frykberg reveals the genius of divine creation, human community, and a strategy for progress in personal character. This book will not just fascinate you. It will change you for the good.

Dan Meyer
Senior Pastor, Christ Church of Oak Brook
Author of *Witness Essentials* and *Leaderhip Essentials*

It's no mean feat to bequeath the Christian community with a fresh perspective on Jesus – who he was and is, why he came to earth, and how we should follow him now – but Frykberg has done just that. From her elucidation of the fractal concept to her useful appendices, *The Jesus Fractal* is a terrific book for anyone seeking to fine-tune their daily walk with God.

Rev. John R. Landgraf, Ph.D.
The Center for Ministry
Author of *Singling*

For centuries Christians have discovered images of the three-in-one God in nature. Consider the many sermon illustrations inspired by the three-leaf clover...
Now Beth Frykberg introduces us to the fractal: a powerful new image for perceiving the loving, relational nature of God. Just as Jesus Christ ushered in the redemption of the whole cosmos, Jesus' own fractal pattern graciously permeates every corner of Creation.
Thanks to Beth Frykberg for this gift of love and encouragement to the church.

Don C. Richter
Associate Director, Louisville Institute

This highly original thesis, wherein the Divine is seen as a fractal, provides a fresh insight into the mystery surrounding the Holy Trinity and how it might be perceived using a different modern paradigm. Dr. Frykberg suggests there are dimension to the Christian life experience that can be best described as: being part of the whole and yet, one with the whole itself—as exampled by Jesus Christ in his earthly ministry. Her training in both Physics and Theology make her insights all the more cogent. Her book, *The Jesus Fractal*, is a profound and enjoyable read.

Dr. William J. Amend, MD

Although this work can be used in churches both by lay and clergy, Frykberg is clear to point out that the "seven dimensions of faith" are lived out in the life of every believer. *The Jesus Fractal* will bring renewal in the church as well as motivate and inspire individuals who are tired of the linear approach in much of Christendom and who seek a broader foundation for understanding spiritual life and practice.

Dr. Kim Engelmann
West Valley Presbyterian Church
Author of *Running in Circles* and *The Joona Trilogy*

This book is a remarkable tour de force by a veteran pastor and professor. Useful in preaching, parish small groups, for individual spiritual development, as well as, seminary coursework, Dr. Frykberg blends theological insight with practical spirituality. This combination personal workbook, devotional guide and ground-breaking text explores God's love (and God's gift of our love for God and others) from unique angles that are exciting for a pastor or any serious Christian to explore.

Paul Watermulder
pastor of First Presbyterian Church of Burlingame

Informative and challenging, practical and accessible, *The Jesus Fractal* is a great tool for Christians seeking to deepen their relationship with God. With clarity and insight, Rev. Frykberg takes the reader on a journey that will not only strengthen their faith, but will also expand their understanding of and relationship with God.

Rev. Libby Vincent, Ph.D.

THE
JESUS
FRACTAL

THE JESUS FRACTAL

SEVEN DIMENSIONS OF FAITH

REV. ELIZABETH A. FRYKBERG

elevate

Copyright © 2016 by Elizabeth Frykberg

Published in Boise, Idaho by Elevate. A division of Elevate Publishing. For more information please go to www.elevatepub.com or email us at info@elevatepub.com.

All rights reserved. No part of this publication may be reproduced, distributed or transmitted in any form or by any means, including photocopying, recording, digital scanning, or other electronic or mechanical methods without the prior written permission of the publisher, except in the case of brief quotations embodied in critical reviews and certain other noncommercial uses permitted by copyright law.

For permission requests, please contact Elevate Publishing at info@elevatepub.com

Editorial Work: Dave Troesh and AnnaMarie McHargue
Cover Design: Bradford Foltz
Interior Design: Kiran Spees

This book may be purchased in bulk for educational, business, organizational or promotional use. To do so, contact Elevate Publishing at info@elevatepub.com

ISBN-13: 978-1943425-1-29

Ebook ISBN: 978-1943425-5-49

To Franklin and Marie,
God's Gracious and Best Gifts EVER!
I love you both!

Contents

Acknowledgments 1

Introduction: What is a Fractal? Why is it Important? 7

Part 1: The Jesus Fractal Explored

1. The Jesus Fractal in the Life of Jesus 21

2. The Jesus Fractal Unfolds in A Contemporary Faith Story . . 49

Part 2: The Seven Dimensions of the Jesus Fractal

3. Listening Dimension:
   Hearing and Experiencing the Word of God 67

4. Listening Dimension: Ministry Implications 81

5. Community Dimension:
   Following Jesus Christ in Community 91

6. Community Dimension: Ministry Implications:
   Role Structure Stumbling Block 105

7. Desiring Dimension: Desiring to Do the Will of God 111

8. Desiring Dimension: Ministry Implications:
   Transforming Bible Study 123

9. Humble: Humbled in Faith 129

10. Humbled Dimension:
    Ministry Implications: Transformational Process 141

11. Grace Dimension: Graced by God's Love 149
12. Grace Dimension: Ministry Implications 159
13. Empowered Dimension: Empowerment in the Spirit 165
14. Sending Dimension: Sent into the World. 189
15. Sending Dimension: Ministry Implications:
    Flowing Fountain of the Seventh Dimension 203

Part 3: So What?
16. Spiritual Practices for Each Dimension 213
17. Spiritual Practices for the Seven Dimensions 241

Epilogue 251
Appendixes:
  A. Chart: Characteristics of Persons
     in Each Jesus Fractal Dimension 253
  B. Worksheet for Telling Initial Faith Story 257
  C. Worksheet for Telling Ministry Story 261
  D. Assessing Present-Day Spiritual Practice
     in Light of Jesus's Spiritual Practice 265
  E. Open-Ended Questions to Assess Present Engagement
     in the Seven Dimensions 269
  F. Multiple Choice Questions to Assess Current
     Engagement in the Seven Dimensions 271
  G. Bible Study:
     The Seven Dimensions in Peter's Life of Faith 285
  H. The Kenosis Passage as Example 293
  I. Martin Luther and Having no Shame in the Gospel 297

Acknowledgments

Writing this book has been a seven dimensional faith project. It began in Princeton listening to the wisdom of learned professors, especially James E. Loder, my Ph.D. advisor, and seminary President Thomas W. Gillespie, who shepherded me in faith long before he took that prestigious position. I love them both and thank God for their being in my life and ministry.

I am part of a wonderful faith community. Many in this community have contributed significant insights. Chief among them are my colleagues in ministry at the First Presbyterian Church of Burlingame: Paul Watermulder, Henry Hansen, Linda Galligan, Alex Bootzen, and Sonja Tappen. For two years under the leadership of Vince Siciliano, this group sought to hone and implement the seven dimensions into our church's DNA. We learned so much as a team. Thank you!

I am also so grateful to Patti Pierce, Teri O'Neel, Russ Ikeda, Paul Dumesnil, and Eff and Patty Martin for the gift of Soul Care. God spoke powerfully through the time we shared together at Singing Wood. My understanding of spiritual practices and direction grew under your gracious leadership. Thank you!

Conversations with Susan Siciliano, a wonderful spiritual director at our church, have been key in bringing the final chapter on spiritual practices into being. She acted as my primary dialogue partner and content critic during the process of creating the

Spiritual Practices Chart. She is an amazing gift from God. Thank you, Susan! You are a blessing!

I am grateful to our church session for adopting the seven dimensions as our church strategy. I also greatly appreciate the time and financial support to write while on sabbatical which was handled so graciously by Joan Cleary, our Director of Administration and Finance.

The congregation as a whole listened patiently to the original sermon series on the life of Peter and another on the Jesus Journey. Program staff added input and insight, especially Cort Bender, our choir director. The church's support staff through the years has been helpful in so many ways: Jane Sherfy, Jackie Gainer, Jon Berryman, Sonu and Onkar Sharma, Adrienne Pryor, and Heather Thompson.

There are so many more particular people to thank!

I am so grateful for the graphic designs of Scottie Prusko.

Those who contributed their stories: Deb, Henry, Paul, Leonard, Nancy, Annette, Louise, Man, and Chantielle. Thank you!

My small group Bible study consisting of Barbara Lowe, Judy Kell, Dana Ayoob, Ann England, Marie Frykberg, and Jodi Lowery, supported me with prayer, love, and encouragement. You are the best!

Various classes and groups listened and interacted with the material at various stages in its development, thank you! I am especially grateful for the love and support of the members of Faith Seeking Understanding, Watch, Stephen Ministry and Women Together. The leadership of those groups have been so supportive: Deb Concklin, Martha Mertz, Ann and Dick Darling, Ross and Janice Lunan, Cheryl Toliver, Jill Goodman, Mathew Koshy, Joanne Stodgel, Sara Prusko, Donna DerAshotean, Jan Fox, Connie Amend, Ellen Howard, Pat Carlson, and Kurt Pappenhause.

When I would get discouraged there were those who helped me see that God wanted me to get this paradigm onto paper for others. In this regard John and Laura Landgraf were key in rekindling the fire that was smoldering under the tyranny of the immediate.

There are also those who graciously read and critically commented on different versions of the manuscript along the way:

Nancy Nelson and Kim Engelmann both made helpful and valuable suggestions regarding structure and content. I cannot thank them enough for giving of their time and spiritual insight in amazing ways. I love you both!

Connie and Bill Amend graciously and meticulously read and proofed the final manuscript! You are the best! Thank you for being my partners in ministry for over forty years!

Anna McHargue, Dave Troesh and the whole team at Elevate have been amazing. Their critique was both gentle and right on. You have made my manuscript a book. Thank you!

Last, but not least, there is family to thank for all they have been and done for me in my life: Mom and Dad, the best parents any kid could ever have; sisters who have been my partners in so many ways; a daughter and her family (Wayne, Zoë, and Xander) for all their help with pictures, stories and love; a son I love more than life itself; nieces and nephews whom I love and pray will be edified as they read these pages; family friends like Julie O'Leary, Jon Berryman and the Engelmann clan; all the young adults who congregate in our family room each night, in particular Jeremy, Kevin, and Jordan; and a step-mother who is becoming more and more gracious as the years go by.

Thanks to all of you for being in my faith community! I love you!

Seven Dimensions of the Jesus Fractal

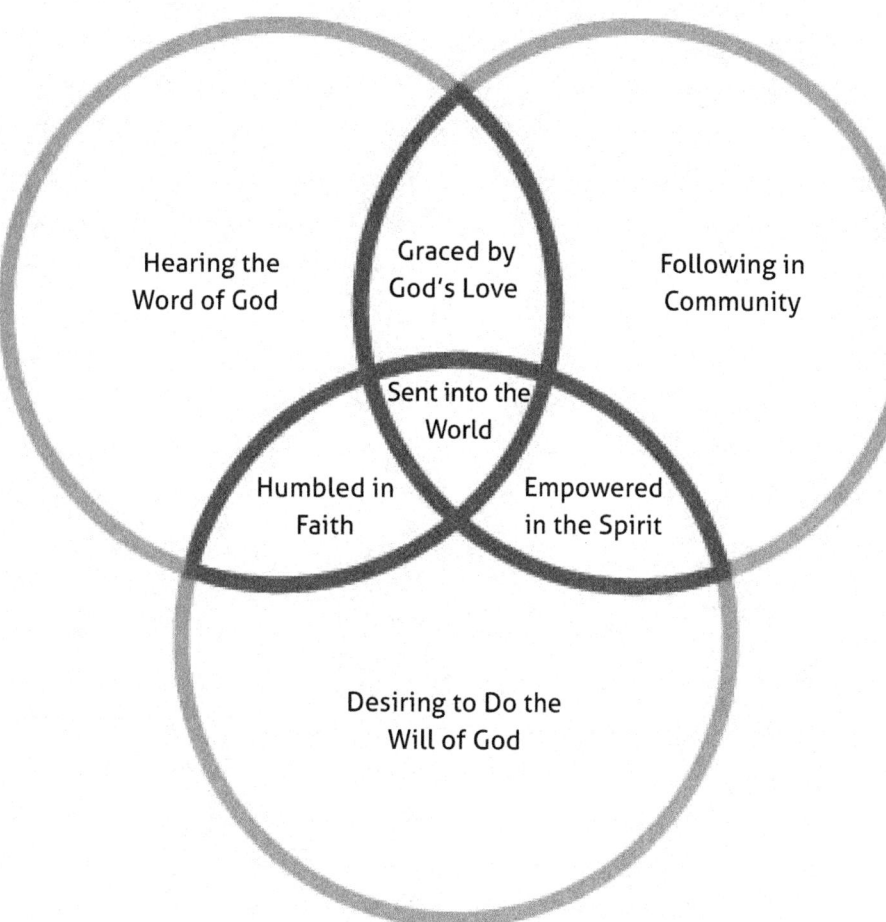

INTRODUCTION
What Is A Fractal?
Why Is It Important?

"Clouds are not spheres, mountains are not cones, coastlines are not circles, and bark is not smooth, nor does lightning travel in a straight line," so said brilliant French American mathematician and thinker Benoit Mandelbrot. Nature's beauty is not equated to the intertwining smoothness of the Euclidean geometry—the geometry learned in school. To the contrary, the magnificence of nature bursts forth in the splendor of irregular surfaces, asymmetrical shapes, uneven edges, and rough corners.

Rarely, if ever, does one find a perfectly formed symmetrical geometric shape in the natural realm. It would be wrong, however, to infer from the irregularity and roughness of nature that there is therefore no grand design, no blueprint. For imbedded in the seeming irregularity and roughness of nature is the regularity of "the fractal patterns" discovered by Mandelbrot. To validate and demonstrate his innovative and pioneering thinking Mandelbrot invented a whole new field of geometry called, "Fractal Geometry." This is the geometry that lies behind the computer-generated artwork that is remarkably beautiful, but neither smooth nor symmetric.

Elizabeth A. Frykberg

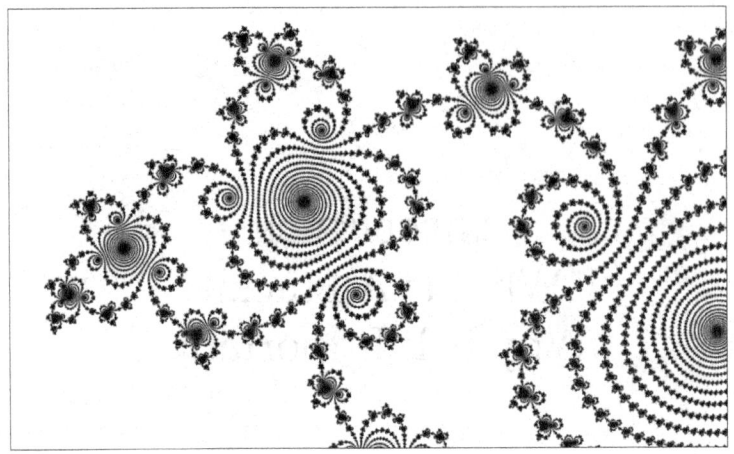

To gain a better grasp of the concept, it may be useful to look systematically at an ordinary cauliflower. Cauliflowers are rough, ball-shaped vegetables. To create a series of measurements to describe a cauliflower, one could easily weigh the vegetable. But how would you measure its three dimensional surface? That isn't so easy! The surface is bumpy and irregular. But if one examines the cauliflower in greater detail, what one will discover is scaled regularity embedded in the roughness.

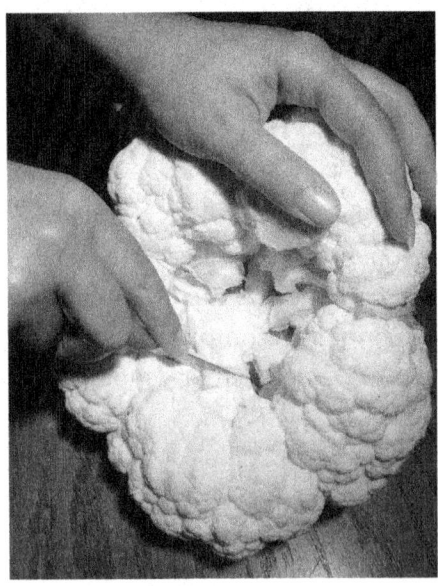

Cut off the florets, and you will see in the smaller pieces of cauliflower, miniature versions of the whole cauliflower in all of its irregularity.

The same is true if you cut the sprigs off the florets.

What you now have are even smaller pieces of cauliflower, themselves also miniature versions of the whole cauliflower. The same is true of the even

The Jesus Fractal

smaller pieces cut from the sprigs. The smaller pieces replicate the whole cauliflower at a smaller scale.

With this in mind, consider this definition: *When the whole has the same shape as one or more of the parts, what you have is a "fractal."* Isolate a piece of a fractal and you see the whole, and vice versa: observing the whole, you see the image of every constituent part—the minute and the infinite reflecting one another. By definition, then, a fractal is a pattern that manifests "self-similarity" across scale. Nature is full of fractal patterns of "self-similarity" of this kind. Perhaps, the one that is easiest to see is the fern.

Elizabeth A. Frykberg

The seeming irregularity of nature is *not haphazard*, but follows simple rules generating complex patterns that may appear chaotic, but are actually ordered. The roughness of nature isn't a mess but instead a repeating of fractal patterns.

Trees are fractal: The shape of the whole tree, trunk and branches, is repeated in the larger branches, and again in the smaller branches, then again in the twigs. Each small part reflects what the whole looks like. The whole is a grand version of the part.

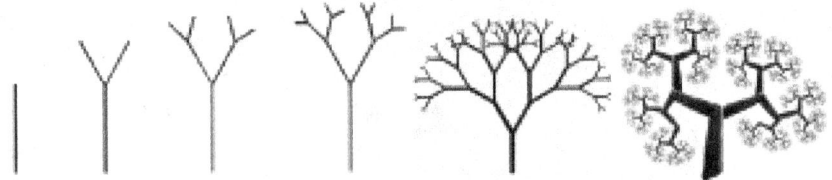

Change the design and you change the tree created.

Great, but so what? What do fractals and this "self-similarity" across scale have to do with faith, God, or theology? A great deal, because God is a relational love fractal. God is Father, Son, and Holy Spirit—three in one a dynamic communion of love. God's being is the mutual sharing of life among Father, Son, and Holy Spirit. The three persons of the Trinity are not separate selves living in isolation from one another. Rather, they are so intimately united that they "indwell" each other in a society of love. Their personhood is defined in terms of their relationship with each other.

In their religious art, Christians from the Eastern Orthodox Church picture Father, Son, and Holy Spirit as three figures sitting around a table together sharing a meal. The advantage of viewing the Trinity as a circle as opposed to the triangle (a symbol often used in Western churches) is that the circle mutes the temptation to see the persons of the Trinity in hierarchical relationship with each other. Picturing the Trinity as three persons gathered together around a circular table in conversation allows the egalitarian nature of the communion to come more easily into focus.

In the seventh century, Greek theologian John of Damascus advanced an understanding of the

Trinity that captures the dynamics of inner Trinitarian relations. The concept is called *perichoresis*—"peri" meaning *around;* "choresis" meaning *dancing*. Father, Son, and Holy Spirit are like dancers holding hands dancing around together in harmonious and joyful freedom. This image depicts the very essence of the Trinity as a "loving, dancing community."

The oneness of the Trinity is, therefore, not the oneness of some distinct, self-contained individual; it is the unity of a community of persons who love each other and live together in harmony. They are what they are only in relationship to each other. Each exists in relationship and would not exist apart from it. Father, Son, and Holy Spirit are one social person, for each is with and for the other so intimately that they can be said to live in and through each other. This is what the Apostle John means when he writes, "For God is love."

This dynamic relational fractal that describes the inner life of God is imprinted on all of creation. God used this relational fractal when in the beginning God created the world. The universe God created is a collection of interconnected fractal communities on the grandest to the minutest scale from smallest atom to largest galaxy. Scripture asserts that in and amongst this relational universe God created humankind as the crown of creation.

In the beginning, God replicates Inner-Trinitarian relational existence (Father, Son, and Holy Spirit) in the creation of humankind as family (mother, father, child.) Let us look at how this happens. First, we are told that humankind is created in God's own image, male and female. God the "relational us," says to God's self,

> Let us make humankind in our image, according to our likeness; . . . So God creates humankind in God's own image, in the image of God he created them; male and female.
> *Genesis 1:27, New Revised Standard Version*

That is two in relationship. God then tells "them" in Genesis 1:28 "to be fruitful and multiply." A child is born creating family, three in community—growing the relational love fractal. Thus, human creation in the image of God replicates Inner-Trinitarian relational existence (Father, Son, and Holy Spirit) in the relational dynamic of the family (mother, father, child.) It is this intimate relational love fractal of human community (the family) that God designed to grow beyond itself to extended family, clan, tribe, and nation.

But the love fractal is broken. That is why there is dissension, divorce, hostility, war and rumors of war, and incidents where family members seek each other's destruction. Human community created to reflect and embody the life of the Trinity, doesn't. That is why Jesus came. Jesus the Christ came to restore the love fractal. To enable and empower us to re-form our communities so they reflect and embody the life of the Trinity—and to build new communities that reflect the quality of life shared by Father, Son and Holy Spirit.

What is the nature of this Trinitarian love fractal community? What can we learn from Jesus about being a loving community? At least three things:

First, the heart of Jesus' relationship with God the Father is an ongoing conversation. Conversation and quality time with God punctuated Jesus' days and occupied his nights. The whole of John 17 is Jesus in conversation with the Father. Trinitarian community involves conversation marked by deep listening. Thus, Christian community in the image of the triune God will also involve an ongoing conversation marked by deep listening—conversation with one another, God, and ourselves.

Second, the Trinity is a relational web that integrates while preserving difference: Jesus is the Father's only Son who is close to the Father's heart. *(John 1:14,17)* The Father is Jesus's Abba. The Spirit is the Spirit of God, the Spirit of Jesus who is sent by Father and Son. In Christian community identity is also knit together in unity and commitment. Note that I didn't say *uniformity*. The Father is not the Son; the Son is not the Spirit. Unity is not sameness. Difference, not sameness, is at the base, the core of creation. Unity is deep integration. The universe exists because God apparently wanted something to be that was not God—something different, something other. God created the universe inviting difference into being. God created humankind in God's own image in similarity and difference. Human beings are not God; but like God, humans are created to celebrate and enjoy difference.

Third, Trinitarian community was not devised simply as a means for division of labor. The ancient creeds confess that each divine person is fully God. But they are fully God only because the others "dwell within" each one. The image of Russian nested dolls gives a vague sense of this indwelling. Divine diversity suggests that difference in deep loving relationship has enormous creative potential. But when difference is structured into hierarchical pyramids, power struggle will inevitably result, even in loving relationships. Here again the Trinity shows us the way:

> Christ Jesus,
> who, though he was in the form of God,
> did not regard equality with God
> as something to be exploited,
> but emptied himself . . .
> and became obedient to the point of death —
> even death on a cross.

In response the Father highly exalted the Son.

> God . . . gave to him the name
> that is above every name,
> so that at the name of Jesus
> every knee should bend,
> in heaven and on earth and under the earth,
> and every tongue should confess
> that Jesus Christ is Lord,
> to the glory of God the Father.
>
> *Philippians 2:5-12*

Thus, Inner-Trinitarian relations are marked by self-giving service, not self-aggrandizing entitlement. The love fractal calls upon us to have the same mind that was in Christ Jesus. Accordingly, the Apostle Paul instructs us:

> If then there is any encouragement in Christ, any consolation from love, any sharing in the Spirit, any compassion and sympathy, make my joy complete: be of the same mind, having the same love, being in full accord and of one mind. Do nothing from selfish ambition or conceit, but in humility regard others as better than yourselves. Let each of you look not to your own interests, but to the interests of others.
>
> *Philippians 2:1-4*

So how do we get this self-giving "mind of Christ?" How is the love fractal restored? The short answer is through the seven dimensions of faith, a dynamic pattern of relationship, evident in the creation of humankind in the image of God, made manifest in the redemptive work of Jesus Christ, and still accessed in faith today through the sustaining work of the Holy Spirit. We are calling this fractal pattern the "Jesus Fractal" because in the New Testament this fractal pattern can be seen structuring all of Jesus' relational interactions. It structures the dynamics of his relationship with God, self, and others. The intent here is to gain an understanding of how the seven dimensions of the fractal play out in the lives of persons in the Christian tradition, so as to facilitate human cooperation with God's desire to restore us to the image of God through Jesus Christ. Exploring the seven dimensions of the fractal will help us to see God's activity in our life of faith in the past and in the present, as we seek to discern what God wants and wills in our future.

The seven dimensions are:

Listening: Hearing and experiencing the Word of God spoken from outside of the self, God speaking to us.

Following in Community: Seeking in community with others to experience and understand what it means to be in relationship with God, taught in dialogue with those who know God.

Desiring: Wanting, desiring, and willing to do God's will.

Humbled: Recognizing one's human condition, limited in what one can do, being human not divine.

Graced: Experiencing God's love in the midst of one's limited human condition.

Empowered: Being empowered by the Spirit to do what is humanly impossible, because the Spirit is at work in and through the person.

Sending: Going into the world with the Spirit to fulfill God's will.

These seven dimensions of the Jesus Fractal are the dynamic that binds the love fractal together. How do human beings relate to God and one another in community? We relate via the seven dimensions of the Jesus Fractal. In the chapters that follow, this dynamic, relational, faith fractal will be defined and explored.

Chapter One will define and describe the seven dimensions of the Jesus Fractal, as they refract in the narrative of Jesus' life: in his growing up years, ministry, spiritual practices, conversations, and last words spoken from the cross.

Chapter Two will illustrate how an understanding of the seven dimensions of the fractal can help Christians sort through the intricate details, twists and turns of their faith story into a coherent journey.

Chapters Three through Fifteen will then describe each of the dimensions in greater detail. In these chapters, the story of Peter's seven-dimension transformational interactions with Jesus will be told and used as a paradigm case, contemporary illustrations presented, characteristics and ways people grow in the dimension described, and a picture of a ministry engaging people in the dimension explained.

Chapters Sixteen and Seventeen will then parallel seven spiritual disciplines with the seven dimensions to produce a matrix of spiritual practices that may be utilized by persons seeking to grow spiritually.

PART 1:
The Jesus Fractal Explored

CHAPTER ONE
The Seven Dimensions of the Jesus Fractal

As it unfolds over time, Jesus' life story gives defining expression to the seven dimensions of the Jesus Fractal. Jesus listens, participates in community, desires to do the will of God; Jesus is humbled, graced by God's love, empowered by the Spirit; Jesus was sent and then sends the Holy Spirit into the world. Jesus lived, died, and ministered to people out of the seven dimensions of the fractal.

In this chapter, the narrative of Jesus' life will be used to define the dimensions and establish the pervasiveness of the fractal pattern in Jesus' life and ministry. We will discover the pattern as Jesus grows up; in the story of Jesus' life, death, and resurrection; his spiritual life; and the give and take of a single faith engendering conversation. Perhaps the most compelling place we will see Jesus living out of the seven dimensions of the fractal is on the cross; as the last seven words Jesus spoke from there give impassioned expression to the dimensions. In Part 2 that follows, the way Jesus lived out of a particular dimension while interacting with Peter will be examined in some detail. Those interactions will be key to understanding how Jesus works through the dimensions to re-create individuals in the image of God.

As we see the pattern repeat in all of these different ways, its fractal nature will become more and more apparent. The pattern seen again and again in the life of Jesus establishes its importance for believers. If one wants to know, follow, and be like Jesus Christ, living a humble, grace filled, empowered life of service to God, then understanding the fractal pattern that structured Jesus' relational interactions during his earthly ministry is crucial. It is crucial because this pattern continues to structure the Spirit of Christ's interaction with believers today. Recognizing and learning to live out of the dimensions is thus important to the life of faith, not just an interesting academic exercise. So let's get started. What follows is a chart that summarizes the fractal pattern in Jesus' growing up years, life story, spiritual practices, and the last seven words he spoke from the cross. It summarizes the content of this chapter:

The Seven Dimensions of the Jesus Fractal in Jesus' Life

Seven Dimensions	In Jesus' Youth	In Jesus' Life Story	In Jesus' Spiritual Practices	Jesus on the Cross
Listen to the Gospel	Born into Jewish Community, where children are taught by Oral Tradition. *(Luke 1-2:20)*	Goes to the synagogue, reads Scripture, hears God's call to ministry through the Prophet Isaiah. *(Luke 4:14-30)*	Goes to the synagogue where the Torah is read and studied *(Luke 4:16.)*; Jesus' teachings exhibit fresh understanding, "You have heard it said... but I say unto you."	Proclaims the Gospel, "Father, forgive them, for they know not what they do." *(Luke 23:34)*
Follow in Community	Raised in Jewish family by Mary and Joseph. *(Luke 2:21-52)*	Calls and teaches disciples in community for three years while in dialogue with God. *(Luke 4:31-18)*	Born into a Jewish family; calls twelve disciples; selects a small group of three within the community; goes to the synagogue, the community center in Jewish towns in the first century; lives in community with God in all these communities.	"Truly, I say to you today, you will be with me in paradise." *(Luke 23:43)*

Seven Dimensions	In Jesus' Youth	In Jesus' Life Story	In Jesus' Spiritual Practices	Jesus on the Cross
Desire to Do the Will of God	At the Temple at age 12. *(Luke 2:41-52)*	Enters Jerusalem allowing Messianic identity to be revealed; submits at Gethsemane, "Not my will but your will be done." *(Luke 22:42)*	States desire in the Lord's Prayer: "Thy kingdom come, Thy will be done on earth as it is in heaven." *(Matthew 6:10)* Also, "I only do what I see the Father doing." *(John 5:19)*	"Woman, behold your son. Behold your mother." *(John 19:26-27)*
Humbled in Faith	Submits to baptism; "Fulfills all righteousness." *(Luke 3:21-23)*	Submits to arrest, trial, and death on the cross. *(Luke 22, 23)*	By living as the incarnated Son of God, Jesus practiced humility. He did not regard equality with God "as something to be exploited." *(Philippians 2:5-11)* Jesus' humility was an everyday practice.	"My God, My God, why have you forsaken me?" *(Matthew 27:46 & Mark 15:34)*

Graced by God's Love	"This is My beloved son." *(Luke 3:22)*	Resurrection *(Luke 24)*	At the transfiguration Jesus shares a "lonely place" experience with Peter, James, and John. God is there and speaks of Jesus, "This is My Son, the Beloved; listen to him." *(Mark 9:7)* This is evidence of Jesus' experience of being loved by the Father as is the intimacy of their relationship as described in John 14-17.	"I thirst." *(John 19:29)*
Empowered by the Spirit	Dove descends. *(Luke 3:22)*	Ascends to the Father becoming highly exalted. *(Acts 1)*	Jesus is empowered to teach, to preach, to heal and to perform miracles like the stilling of the storm and raising the dead.	"It is finished." *(John 19:30)*
Sent into the World	Temptations in the wilderness. *(Luke 4:1-13)*	Sends the Holy Spirit at Pentecost. *Acts 2)*	Jesus relates to the outcast and shunned persons of the world. *(Mark 7:24-30; Matthew 15:21-28)*	"Father, into your hands I commit my spirit." *(Luke 23:46)*

Elizabeth A. Frykberg

Listening Dimension:

The Listening Dimension is hearing and experiencing the Word of God speaking to the self, but coming from outside of oneself. Jesus lived in this dimension growing up in a Jewish community, where the acts of God were preserved in the Torah, the Septuagint, and handed down in their Oral Traditions. The Jews were the people of God. Jesus would have been told family stories, like those of Abraham, Isaac, and Jacob, of Moses and the Exodus, of the Judges, the Kings, and the Prophets. He would have sung the Psalms and heard the prophecies of a coming Messiah, the hope of Israel.

As a child, Jesus at the age of five or six, would have gone to the synagogue school to learn from the Torah with other children. A first spiritual discipline Jesus would have been engaged in there would have been the memorization of prayers and Scripture. As children grew and moved in the synagogue from primary to secondary school education, instruction took on the form of question-answer discussions of Torah and Oral Tradition interpretation.

We see Jesus engaged in this kind of dialogue in the Temple at the age of 12: "After three days they found him in the temple, sitting among the teachers, listening to them and asking them questions. And all who heard him were amazed at his understanding and his answers." *(Luke 2:46-47)* So Jesus as a child listened and studied the Word of God.

As an adult, Jesus still listens. In the synagogue in Nazareth, where he had studied, memorized and heard the Word of God for years, Jesus' ministry begins. That day in the synagogue Jesus reads and hears God calling. It is a call to ministry through the Prophet Isaiah.

> [14] Then Jesus, filled with the power of the Spirit, returned to Galilee, and a report about him spread through all the surrounding country. [15] He began to teach in their synagogues and was praised by everyone.
> [16] When he came to Nazareth, where he had been brought up, he went to the synagogue on the Sabbath day, as was his custom. He stood up to read, [17] and the

scroll of the prophet Isaiah was given to him. He unrolled the scroll and found the place where it was written:

[18] "The Spirit of the Lord is upon me,
   because he has anointed me
      to bring good news to the poor.
He has sent me to proclaim release to the captives
   and recovery of sight to the blind,
      to let the oppressed go free,
[19] to proclaim the year of the Lord's favor."

[20] And he rolled up the scroll, gave it back to the attendant, and sat down. The eyes of all in the synagogue were fixed on him. [21] Then he began to say to them, "Today this scripture has been fulfilled in your hearing." [22] All spoke well of him and were amazed at the gracious words that came from his mouth. They said, "Is not this Joseph's son?"

Luke 4:14-30

Throughout his ministry, Jesus is found in the synagogue where the Torah is read and studied. His teaching exhibits fresh understanding, "You have heard it said...but I say unto you...." This is because Jesus really listened to the Word of God. Jesus didn't simply adopt the teachings of the Scribes and Pharisees. He was not merely socialized into the traditions of the Jewish community. By listening, hearing, and interacting with the Word of God, Jesus created new traditions. Active listening, hearing and experiencing the Word of God afresh, is the listening dimension of the Jesus Fractal.

Follow in Community Dimension:

The community dimension of the Jesus Fractal is living with God together with others in a teaching learning community. In these communities, God is the primary teacher and authority.

The first community Jesus lived and learned in was the Jewish family of Mary and Joseph. This was the family chosen by God to care for the Son of God during the days of his youth. Mary and Joseph were remarkably open to God's teaching and authority. They both listened to God through angels. When the angel Gabriel appears and tells Mary how she is to give birth to the Messiah, even though she is unmarried, she responds faithfully saying, "Here am I, the servant of the Lord; let it be with me according to your word."

On four separate occasions, God communicates with Joseph through dreams. Joseph may not utter one single word in the New Testament, but four of his dreams are fully related. The first dream happens when Joseph resolves to quietly break his engagement to Mary, unwilling to expose her to public disgrace. An angel of the Lord appeared to him in a dream and says, "Joseph, son of David, do not be afraid to take Mary as your wife, for the child conceived in her is from the Holy Spirit." When he awoke, Joseph did as the angel of the Lord commanded, taking Mary as his wife, but having no marital relations with her.

In the second dream the angel of the Lord appears to Joseph and says, "Get up, take the child and his mother, and flee to Egypt." How did Joseph respond to this dream? He immediately obeys. "Joseph got up, took the child and his mother by night, and went to Egypt." The third dream comes when Herod dies. An angel of the Lord appears to Joseph, again in a dream, this time saying, "Get up, take the child and his mother, and go to the land of Israel, for those who were seeking the child's life are dead." How does Joseph respond to the dream? Again, he obeys. The fourth dream happens on the journey back to Israel. This time Joseph is told not to make his home in Judea. How does Joseph respond to the dream? He obeys.

Mary and Joseph also performed the rights required in the law at Jesus' birth. They journeyed each year to Jerusalem for the Passover. All of this suggests that living in the community of this faithful family (the family chosen by God), was the perfect place for the child Jesus to learn to follow God.

The community dimension of the Jesus Fractal is also apparent throughout Jesus' ministry. From the very beginning, Jesus lives in community. He is first and foremost in community with God. Jesus describes this communion with God, saying, "I am in the Father and the Father is in me. The words that I say to you I do not speak on my own; but the Father who dwells in me does his works." *(John 14:10)* This mutual indwelling in community is what Jesus wants with all of his disciples. "Jesus answered him, 'Those who love me will keep my word, and my Father will love them, and we will come to them and make our home with them.'" *(John 14:23)*

Out of this relationship and dialogue with the Father, Jesus chooses twelve disciples, those selected for intensive, intimate mentoring in a teaching-learning community.

> [12] Now during those days he went out to the mountain to pray; and he spent the night in prayer to God. [13] And when day came, he called his disciples and chose twelve of them, whom he also named apostles: [14] Simon, whom he named Peter, and his brother Andrew, and James, and John, and Philip, and Bartholomew, [15] and Matthew, and Thomas, and James son of Alphaeus, and Simon, who was called the Zealot, [16] and Judas son of James, and Judas Iscariot, who became a traitor.
>
> *Luke 6:12-16*

So another community Jesus participated in was the one with the twelve disciples. He traveled, ate, slept and worked with them for the three years of his earthly ministry. From this group Jesus selected Peter, James, and John as a small group within the community for more intimate face-to-face instruction. We will see in Peter's faith story that Jesus engaged in all seven dimensions of the faith fractal with these disciples.

Jesus creates community in conversation with individuals, with the crowds who hear him preach, thus with the larger Jewish faith community. Jesus goes often to the synagogue, which was not just the place to worship and learn, it was the community center of Jewish towns. So Jesus lived in the larger Jewish community perceiving his call to ministry to be among those from the house and lineage of David. This is the larger teaching-learning community in which Jesus participates.

In the midst of all of these communities, Jesus is with God. Jesus explains the nature of his communion with God the Father to the disciples saying, "Believe me that I am in the Father and the Father is in me." *(John 14:11)* This communion of Jesus with God and the disciples is eternal:

[18] "I will not leave you orphaned; I am coming to you. [19] In a little while the world will no longer see me, but you will see me; because I live, you also will live. [20] On that day you will know that I am in my Father, and you in me, and I in you." *(John 14:18-20)*

So the second dimension of the Jesus Fractal is living with God and others in a teaching-learning community.

Desire to do the Will of God Dimension:

Another dimension of the Jesus Fractal is: Desiring to Do the Will of God.

While still a youth, just 12 years old, Jesus exhibits a strong desire to do the will of God when staying at the Temple after the Passover celebration:

> [43] When the festival was ended and they started to return, the boy Jesus stayed behind in Jerusalem, but his parents did not know it.... [46] After three days they found him in the temple, sitting among the teachers, listening to them and asking them questions. [47] And all who heard him were amazed at his understanding and his answers. [48] When his parents saw him they were astonished; and his mother said to him, "Child, why have you treated us like this? Look, your father and I have been searching for you in great anxiety."
>
> [49] He said to them, "Why were you searching for me? Did you not know that I must be in my Father's house?"
>
> [50] But they did not understand what he said to them.
> [51] Then he went down with them and came to Nazareth,

and was obedient to them. His mother treasured all these things in her heart."

Luke 2:43,46-52

One spiritual practice Jesus observes in the Desiring to Do the Will of God Dimension is fasting. He goes off into the wilderness in solitude for 40 days. This is final preparation before his ministry begins. During the fast, Satan tempts Jesus to desire something other than the will of God. First, Satan tempts Jesus to turn stones into bread to meet his physical needs. The second temptation is to test God by jumping from the pinnacle of the Temple desiring signs and wonders from God over relationship with God. The third is wanting fame and fortune more than God.

Another significant discipline Jesus practices out of the desire dimension is prayer. That Jesus' prayers spoke of desire to do the will of God can be seen in the words of the Lord's Prayer where Jesus taught his disciples to pray, "Thy kingdom come, Thy will be done on earth as it is in heaven." He states clearly that his whole ministry is doing God's will. "The words that I say to you I do not speak on my own; but the Father who dwells in me does his works." *(John 14:10b)* "I only do what I see the Father doing." *(John 5:19)* Thus, the preaching, teaching, and healing ministries are not Jesus' own individual work, but Jesus doing the will of God in daily service.

This third dimension is decisively evident as Jesus enters Jerusalem allowing his Messianic identity to be revealed. Here Jesus demonstrates willingness to do the will of God no matter what the personal cost. Earlier, back up in Galilee, Jesus had told the disciples, "The Son of Man must undergo great suffering, and be rejected by the elders, chief priests, and scribes, and be killed, and on the third day be raised." *(Luke 9:22.)* At that time, he asked the disciples to keep his Messianic identity a secret. But now, Jesus allows the people to acclaim him from the mountaintop:

> As he was now approaching the path down from the Mount of Olives, the whole multitude of the disciples

began to praise God joyfully with a loud voice for all the deeds of power that they had seen, saying,

> "Blessed is the king
> who comes in the name of the Lord!
> Peace in heaven,
> and glory in the highest heaven!"

Some of the Pharisees in the crowd said to him, "Teacher, order your disciples to stop." He answered, "I tell you, if these were silent, the stones would shout out."

Luke 19:34-40

Jesus in life and ministry lived desiring in everything to do the will of God. Jesus wanted and willed to do God's will. This is the desire dimension of the Jesus Fractal.

Humbled in Faith Dimension:

The Humbled in Faith Dimension of the Jesus Fractal is recognizing one's human condition, one's human limitations. Jesus acknowledges his humanity, his being fully human, when submitting to baptism by John. In so doing, Jesus "fulfills all righteousness."

> [13] Then Jesus came from Galilee to John at the Jordan, to be baptized by him. [14] John would have prevented him, saying, "I need to be baptized by you, and do you come to me?"
> [15] But Jesus answered him, "Let it be so now; for it is proper for us in this way to fulfill all righteousness." Then he consented.
>
> *Matthew 3:13-15*

By living as the incarnated Son of God, Jesus lives out of this dimension in everything. He did not regard equality with God "as something to be exploited, but emptied himself, taking the form of a slave, being born in human likeness. And being found in human form, he humbled himself and became obedient to the point of death—even death on a cross." *(Philippians 2:7-8)* Thus, humility was an everyday practice for Jesus.

Not just in the everyday, but at all the extremes, as well, Jesus demonstrates an understanding of his limited human condition. In the Garden of Gethsemane, he pleads in faith with God to "take this cup" from him, yet in the end, in full recognition of his limited human condition, he humbly submits, "Not my will but Thy will be done." He then undergoes the humiliation of arrest, trial, scourging, rejection, and crucifixion. *(Luke 22, 23)* The crown of thorns on the cover of this book symbolizes Jesus' humility, his living and loving out of the humble dimension, his crowning glory:

> Therefore God also highly exalted him
>   and gave him the name
>   that is above every name,
> so that at the name of Jesus
>   every knee should bend,
>   in heaven and on earth and under the earth,
> and every tongue should confess
>   that Jesus Christ is Lord,
>   to the glory of God the Father.
>   *Philippians 2:9-11*

Graced by God's Love Dimension:

The grace dimension of the Jesus Fractal is experiencing God's love in the midst of one's limited human condition.

This dimension is evident during Jesus' baptism, where God's love graces Jesus:

> [16] And when Jesus had been baptized, just as he came up from the water, suddenly the heavens were opened to him and . . . a voice from heaven said, "This is my Son, the Beloved, with whom I am well pleased.
>   *Matthew 3:16-17*

It also is evident on the Mount of Transfiguration, where Jesus shares a "lonely place" experience with Peter, James, and John. God is there on the mountain and speaks of Jesus to these disciples saying, "This is my Son, the Beloved; listen to him." *(Mark 9:7)* Jesus makes it clear that experiencing God's love in this dimension is the source of the love he has for his disciples, "As the Father has loved me, so I have loved you; abide in my love." *(John 15:9)*

God's love for Jesus is definitively revealed three days after Jesus died. The humbled Jesus is taken down from the cross and laid in a borrowed tomb. Then on Sunday morning, God's love breaks through the darkness and Jesus experiences resurrection from the dead. There is no record of Jesus' reaction to the experience itself, but for the next 40 days, Jesus shows forth resurrection love to the disciples in various post-resurrection appearances. *(Luke 24, Matthew 28, Mark 16, John 20-21)* Jesus lives out the Father's resurrection love for him.

The grace dimension is being graced by God's love. This love is the definitive source of all love. It is the love within the love fractal refracted into community beyond the Godhead.

Empowered by the Spirit Dimension:
Being empowered by the Spirit to do what is humanly impossible is the empowered dimension.

During his baptism, the Spirit of God descends upon Jesus like a dove:

> [16] And when Jesus had been baptized, just as he came up from the water, suddenly the heavens were opened to him and he saw the Spirit of God descending like a dove and alighting on him."
>
> *Matthew 3:16*

Following baptism, Jesus is empowered to teach, to preach, to heal, and to perform miracles. In this empowered service, he constantly employs his spiritual empowerment for the edification of others and the building up of the Kingdom of God. Jesus is fully human, but his ministry is divinely empowered. When he needed extra strength, it is available to him. So, Jesus seeks and becomes empowered in the Garden to endure the cross. After he prays, "Father, if you are willing, remove this cup from me; yet, not my will but yours be done. Then an angel from heaven appeared to him and gave him strength." *(Luke 22:41-42)*

He is also empowered as he ascends back to the Father, and sits at the right hand of God, the symbolic place of power. God highly exalts and gives to Jesus the name above all names, at which every knee will bow. In ascending Jesus becomes empowered in relationship both to God the Father and the people of God.

Empowerment in the Spirit allowed the human Jesus to teach, preach, heal, and perform miracles . . . in partnership with God the Father, to do the humanly impossible. This empowerment is still available to humankind today through Jesus. Jesus said to the disciples, "Very truly, I tell you, the one who believes in me will also do the works that I do and, in fact, will do greater works than these, because I am going to the Father. I will do whatever you ask in my name, so that the Father may be glorified in the Son. If in my name, you ask me for anything, I will do it." *(John 14:12-14)* Thus, as the Father empowered Jesus in the Spirit, so Jesus empowers us in the Spirit. Empowerment in the Spirit to do what humankind cannot do without the Spirit's help is the empowerment dimension.

Sent into the World Dimension:

The Sent into the World Dimension is going into the world with the Spirit to fulfill God's will.

This is what Jesus did by becoming incarnate, by being born in human form. It is also what happens immediately following his baptism. Jesus is **sent** into the wilderness. There he grapples with worldly temptations: power, prestige, and wealth. He is led into temptation, but does not sin. By means of confronting that which has been the downfall of humankind since Adam and Eve, Jesus is thereby shown prepared to begin his earthly ministry.

> Then Jesus was led up by the Spirit into the wilderness to be tempted by the devil. ² He fasted forty days and forty nights, and afterwards he was famished. ³ The tempter came and said to him, "If you are the Son of God, command these stones to become loaves of bread." ⁴ But he answered, "It is written,
>
> 'One does not live by bread alone,
>   but by every word that comes from the mouth of God.'"
>
> ⁵ Then the devil took him to the holy city and placed him on the pinnacle of the temple, ⁶ saying to him, "If you are the Son of God, throw yourself down; for it is written,
>
> 'He will command his angels concerning you,'
>   and 'On their hands they will bear you up,
> so that you will not dash your foot against a stone.'"
>
> ⁷ Jesus said to him, "Again it is written, 'Do not put the Lord your God to the test.'"
>
> ⁸ Again, the devil took him to a very high mountain and showed him all the kingdoms of the world and their splendor; ⁹ and he said to him, "All these I will give you, if you will fall down and worship me." ¹⁰ Jesus said to him, "Away with you, Satan! for it is written,
> 'Worship the Lord your God,
>   and serve only him.'"
>
> ¹¹ Then the devil left him, and suddenly angels came and waited on him.
>
> Matthew 4:1-11

Another way the sending dimension is seen is in the way Jesus relates to the outcast and shunned: to prostitutes, tax collectors, sinners, and Gentiles—to those with one or both feet outside the Jewish community. Jesus fellowshipped with people from Samaria, *(John 4)* those Jewish half-breeds whom full-blooded Jews despised. In one of his best-known parables, Jesus paints a picture of the Samaritan traveler being the person with compassion, the one who fulfills the law of loving one's "neighbor," better than those who are considered Israel's finest: the Levites, scribes, and Pharisees. Jesus also makes it clear in interaction with the Syrophoenician Woman *(Mark 7:24-30; Matthew 15:21-28)* that his ministry reaches out to the world far beyond the Jewish community and teaches the disciples to go out into the world and make disciples. *(Matthew 28:19)*

This sending dimension also becomes apparent after Jesus' ascension back to the Father. Jesus now sends the Holy Spirit at Pentecost *(Acts 2)* to empower the disciples to go out into the world witnessing to Jesus. The last words Jesus says to them are, "But you will receive power when the Holy Spirit has come upon you; and you will be my witnesses in Jerusalem, in all Judea and Samaria, and to the ends of the earth." *(Acts 1:8)*

The sending dimension is both the first and the last dimension. It is how Jesus came. He was sent. It is what He does in sending the Holy Spirit, so we are empowered to go into the World.

Elizabeth A. Frykberg

Seven Dimensions on the Cross

We have just seen how Jesus lived out of the seven dimensions throughout his earthly ministry and beyond. Let us now look at the way the seven dimensions frame Jesus' dying breath. Jesus Christ's last words, spoken from the cross, give impassioned expression to the seven dimensions. The Seven Last Words are:

> Father, forgive them, for they know not what they do.
> *Luke 23:34*

> He replied, "Truly I tell to you, today you will be with me in Paradise."
> *Luke 23:43*

> Woman, behold your son. Behold your mother.
> *John 19:26–27*

> My God, My God, why have you forsaken me?
> *Matthew 27:46 & Mark 15:34*

> I thirst.
> *John 19:29*

> It is finished.
> *John 19:30*

> Father, into your hands I commit my spirit.
> *Luke 23:46*

Listening Dimension:

From the cross Jesus declares God's Word of Assurance and Love: Father, forgive them, for they know not what they do. *(Luke 23:32-34)* With these words, people hear the Good News of the Gospel from Jesus Christ's own lips, as he hangs on the cross for them.

The Jesus Fractal

> Two other men, both of them criminals, were also led out to be put to death with Jesus. When they came to the place called "The Skull," they crucified Jesus there, and the two criminals, one on his right and the other on his left.
>
> Jesus said, *"Forgive them, Father! They don't know what they are doing."*

Following in Community Dimension:

Jesus commits to be in community with believers. He speaks to the thief hanging on the cross next to him, the one who is learning from Jesus in the community of the crucified. Jesus tells the thief about his being with Jesus in community in paradise that very day.

> One of the criminals hanging there hurled insults at him: "Aren't you the Messiah? Save yourself and us!"
> The other one, however, rebuked him, saying, "Don't you fear God? You received the same sentence he did. [41] Ours, however, is only right, because we are getting what we deserve for what we did; but he has done no wrong." And he said to Jesus, "Remember me, Jesus, when you come as King!"
> Jesus said to him, *"I promise you that today you will be in Paradise with me."*
>
> Luke 23:35-43 (GNT)

Desire to Do the Will of God Dimension:

The third word from the cross is "Woman, here is your son. Here is your mother." Here, Jesus honors his Mother, doing God's will in keeping the Fifth Commandment. He also connects John and his Mother in a mother-son relationship. John is to love Mary like Jesus loved her. John responds by taking Mary into his own home, thereby demonstrating his desire to do the will of God, to love Mary like Jesus loved her. He loved her as a son loves his mother.

> Meanwhile, standing near the cross of Jesus were his mother, and his mother's sister, Mary the wife of Clopas, and Mary Magdalene.
> When Jesus saw his mother and the disciple whom he loved standing beside her, he said to his mother, *"Woman, here is your son."* Then he said to the disciple, *"Here is your mother."* And from that hour the disciple took her into his own home."
>
> John 19:25–27

Jesus here also reveals desire and submission to do the will of God, because these words are like a Last Will and Testament. By taking care to give these last-minute instructions, Jesus' desire to do the will of God the Father is made clear.

Humbled in Faith Dimension:

Jesus remains faithful in prayer to the Father while humbled by the experience on the cross. Unlike Peter, Jesus' faith does not fail him. Jesus continues in faithful relationship asking for assurance and explanation in the midst of pain. "My God, My God, why have you forsaken me?" *(Matthew 27:46 & Mark 15:34)* Here, we see the total humbling of Jesus. Jesus is here so completely identified with humanity that he reflects our human belief that God has forsaken us.

Graced by God's Love Dimension:

After this, when Jesus knew that all was now finished, he said (in order to fulfill the Scripture), "I am thirsty." *(John 19:28)* With this fifth word, "I thirst," Jesus fulfills verse 21 from Messianic Psalm 69, "They gave me poison for food, and for my thirst they gave me vinegar to drink." But for those who heard Jesus teaching just days before in the Temple, the Parable of the Sheep and the Goats would most likely also have came to mind:

³¹When the Son of Man comes in his glory, and all the angels with him, then he will sit on the throne of his glory. ³²All the nations will be gathered before him, and he will separate people one from another as a shepherd separates the sheep from the goats, ³³and he will put the sheep at his right hand and the goats at the left. ³⁴Then the king will say to those at his right hand, "Come, you that are blessed by my Father, inherit the kingdom prepared for you from the foundation of the world; ³⁵for I was hungry and you gave me food, **I was thirsty** and you gave me something to drink, I was a stranger and you welcomed me, ³⁶I was naked and you gave me clothing, I was sick and you took care of me, I was in prison and you visited me." ³⁷Then the righteous will answer him, "Lord, when was it that we saw you hungry and gave you food, or **thirsty and gave you something to drink**? ³⁸And when was it that we saw you a stranger and welcomed you, or naked and gave you clothing? ³⁹And when was it that we saw you sick or in prison and visited you?" ⁴⁰And the king will answer them, "Truly I tell you, just as you did it to one of the least of these who are members of my family, you did it to me."

Matthew 25:31-40

Thus with this fifth word, Jesus references people abiding in loving relationship with him and entering the Kingdom of Heaven loved by the Father, as they continue to love Jesus by loving one another. The source of all of this love is the love of God given in the grace dimension.

Empowered by the Spirit Dimension:

By saying, "It is finished," *(John 19:30)* Jesus in the midst of what appears to be defeat, declares that God's will has now been accomplished. Jesus also shows that God's will is actually being accomplished as he bows his head giving up his Spirit. In that moment,

Jesus makes it clear that he is in control of his death on the cross, not Pilot, not the Romans, not Caiaphas, nor the Sanhedrin. Jesus gave up his spirit of his own volition and at the right time. Spirit empowered, Jesus stays on the cross until the exact "moment the curtain of the temple was torn in two, from top to bottom. The earth shook, and the rocks were split." *(Matthew 27:51)*

> A jar full of sour wine was standing there. So they put a sponge full of the wine on a branch of hyssop and held it to his mouth. ³⁰When Jesus had received the wine, he said, "It is finished." Then he bowed his head and gave up his spirit.
>
> *John 19:29-30*

Sent into the World Dimension:

In death, Jesus is sent to loose the chains of death. He descends into hell and on the third day rose again. This is where Jesus is sent when he commends his spirit into the hands of the Father:

> It was now about noon, and darkness came over the whole land until three in the afternoon, while the sun's light failed; and the curtain of the temple was torn in two. Then Jesus, crying with a loud voice, said, *"Father, into your hands I commend my spirit."* Having said this, he breathed his last.
>
> *Luke 23:44-46*

Seven Words, seven dimensions, wow!

Seven Dimensions in a Single Conversation

There is yet another way the seven dimensions are manifest in Jesus' life. They are evident in his conversations. Because it is the longest recorded in the Gospels, let's review Jesus' conversation with the Woman at the Well. *(John 4:1-42)* In this one brief exchange, the seven dimensions can be seen guiding Jesus' relational interaction.

In the first century drawing water from the town's well was a daily task made more enjoyable because the women of the town would fetch the water together in the cool of the day—in the early morning hours and then again as evening approached. The well functioned like the water cooler or coffee room at work. It gave women the opportunity to be together socially while doing a necessary, but mundane task. Because of this custom, commentators suspect that the Woman at the Well may have been seeking to avoid social contact with the women of her town by coming to gather her water at noon in the heat of the day.

Plan foiled. When the Woman arrives, Jesus is there. No matter. The cultural norms of the day will dissuade this man from making contact with an unrelated, unaccompanied woman. Besides Jesus is a Jew and she a Samaritan woman. Jews and Samaritans had no use for each other, each considering the other to be ethnically unclean and theologically misguided. So upon seeing Jesus, a man and a Jew, the woman would presume he would avoid and ignore her. Instead, Jesus breaks through these social barriers (both ethnic and gender) asking her to give him a drink of water.

Notice how Jesus approaches the Woman. He comes with a request—not a sermon, teaching, or miracle. This is Jesus exercising what my Ph.D. advisor and friend, Jim Loder, called "The Divine Courtesy." Jesus asks the woman to give to him before bestowing anything upon her. Christian community is a relationship wherein we come bringing something of value with us. Jesus let the Woman at the Well give to him.

With something of value to give to Jesus, the Woman, who was avoiding human interaction, now brashly asks Jesus, "How is it that you, a Jew, ask a drink of me, a woman of Samaria?" In essence she is saying, "Wait a minute! You aren't even supposed to be talking to me. Who do you think you are and what do you think you are doing?"

Jesus answered her, "If you knew the gift of God, and who it is that is saying to you, 'Give me a drink,' you would have asked him, and he would have given you living water." For those outside of the community of the called disciples, Jesus often spoke in parables and riddles. So, the Women at the Well is confused by Jesus' talk of living water.

She says to him, "Sir, you have no bucket, and the well is deep. Where do you get that living water?"

Jesus responds by elaborating on the riddle saying, "Everyone who drinks of this water will be thirsty again, but those who drink of the water that I will give them will never be thirsty. The water that I will give will become in them a spring of water gushing up to eternal life."

Intrigued, the woman expresses desire to have this water that Jesus is offering. She says to Jesus, "Sir, give me this water, so that I may never be thirsty or have to keep coming here to draw water."

Do you see what just happened? Because Jesus freely asked her for physical water, she is free to boldly ask for this "living water." There is reciprocity in relationship, even though she doesn't really know what "living water" is. By the way, she isn't alone. None of Jesus' disciples fully understood who he was or what he was offering until after his death and resurrection, actually not until after Pentecost.

Once the Woman at the Well expresses her desire for what Jesus has to offer, Jesus gets personal. He had already crossed over ethnic and gender barriers to draw the Woman at the Well into relationship. Now he gets personal confronting her on the issue of her gathering water in the heat of the day to avoid social contact. It is a place of shame.

Jesus says to her, "Go, call your husband, and come back."

The woman answers, "I have no husband."

Jesus says to her, "You are right in saying, 'I have no husband';

for you have had five husbands, and the one you have now is not your husband. What you have said is true!"

Over the centuries, commentators and preachers focusing on the woman's marital history have suggested that her marital situation is the consequence of immoral sexual behavior. I would argue to the contrary that her being inspired (as opposed to humiliated) by Jesus revealing knowledge of her marital situation, makes it more likely that she had been widowed or abandoned five times and now finds herself dependent on another man for survival, a man who is not yet her husband. In the first century, all a man needed to do to divorce a woman was to write out a bill of divorce and have it witnessed. But to be in right relationship with their first century community, a woman needed to be married.

The Woman at the Well is not married. Jesus does not chastise or call the Woman to account for that circumstance. Instead he praises her truth telling. She returns the favor calling Jesus "a prophet," a prophet being one who speaks forth the truth. Jesus has intimate knowledge of this woman's personal life, but she is not shamed. Rather she is heartened, as she experiences, not judgment, but the heart of Jesus.

Experiencing the compassionate heart of Jesus, the Woman becomes open to Jesus as a teacher saying, "Sir, …Our ancestors worshipped on this mountain, but you say that the place where people must worship is in Jerusalem."

Jesus now teaches more directly. No more metaphors, riddles, or parables. "Woman, believe me, …God is spirit, and those who worship him must worship in spirit and truth."

She says to Jesus, "I know that Messiah is coming. When he comes, he will proclaim all things to us."

Jesus says, "I am he, the one who is speaking to you."

With this revelation something very profound and empowering happens to the Woman at the Well. She goes back into town and connects with the people telling them about her experience at the well. She says, "Come and see a man who told me everything I have ever done! He cannot be the Messiah, can he?" Many went to see Jesus at the well. Many came to believe in him because of the woman's testimony. Wanting to understand more, these Samaritans now invite Jesus into their community.

Jesus stays two days. Many more believed because of his words, saying to the woman, "It is no longer because of what you said that we believe, for we have heard for ourselves, and we know that this is truly the Savior of the world."

What is clear from this analysis of the story of the Woman at the Well is that in just one conversation all seven dimensions may come into play—the whole Jesus Fractal:

Relating with Jesus (community dimension) and hearing what life with Jesus has to offer in living water (listening dimension), the woman wants some of this water (desiring dimension).

Jesus then proceeds to remind her of her human condition (humbled dimension). She in turn expresses faith in Jesus (listening dimension) while continuing to want the water (desiring dimension) in the midst of her conversation with Jesus (community dimension).

Jesus having knowledge of her humble situation (humbled dimension), enables her to recognize his Messianic identity, which he acknowledges saying, "I am he, the one who is speaking to you." This is a grace bestowing revelation (grace dimension).

That something very profound and empowering happened to the Woman at the Well in her encounter with Jesus is evidenced in her leaving the water jar behind when she returns to her village. She could leave the water jar because in encountering Jesus she became filled with the living water of which Jesus spoke (empowered dimension).

The woman now goes back into town, a new woman, free to talk and interact with the town's people, to tell them the good news she just experienced at the well (sending dimension). She says to the people, "Come and see a man who told me everything I have ever done! He cannot be the Messiah, can he?"

What is apparent from this story of the Woman at the Well is that in just one experience all of the dimensions may be at play in a person's life in various ways. That is why the seven dimensions are a fractal and not stages of faith or a hierarchical faith model. The

Woman at the Well just met Jesus, but after that one encounter she already brings others to Jesus with the result that they too believe. This is a sending dimension experience and action on her part. She does not need to be fully mature in Christ for God to empower her to witness for Jesus Christ. Encountering the heart of Jesus, the Woman at the Well moves back into her Samaritan community in a new way and there helps others to experience the heart of Jesus.

So What?

You may be thinking, "I'm beginning to see it, but so what? Why exactly is this fractal pattern important? What difference can understanding the Jesus Fractal make in my life and ministry?"

Here is a partial answer: Understanding the Jesus Fractal can help people celebrate their faith journey, find their calling, live more holistic and holy lives, become transformed and renewed in faith relationship with Jesus Christ, and grow in love for God and other people. It can assist churches in evaluating and structuring holistic ministries, as well as give spiritual directors and ministers a valuable tool in assessing and structuring spiritual practices for those they counsel. This answer is only partial, because I would not presume to know in total why the Spirit of God has chosen to reveal the pattern, "For now we see in a mirror, dimly, but then we will see face to face. Now I know only in part; then I will know fully, even as I have been fully known." *(1 Corinthians 13:12)*

In the next chapter I will show how the seven dimensions of the Jesus Fractal structured my own chaotic faith journey including some dark moments. I am convinced that the conspiracy of silence amongst Christians regarding these darker moments in our faith journeys is hurting the witness of the church. My depth of sinfulness should have disqualified me from ministry, but by the grace of God, I will celebrate 40 years of ordained Christian ministry in the Presbyterian Church USA on September 11, 2017. Jesus said to the Pharisees, "Those who are well have no need of a physician, but those who are sick. I have not come to call the righteous, but sinners to repentance." *(Luke 5:31-32)* I am one who Jesus came to call to repentance and God isn't finished with me yet.

CHAPTER TWO
The Jesus Fractal Unfolds in a Contemporary Faith Story

Introduction

Jesus experienced all seven dimensions of the fractal pattern growing up, lived out of them in his life and ministry, readied his disciples for ministry through a seven dimensional faith journey, and related to God and others seven dimensionally. To illustrate how the seven dimensions of the Jesus fractal are still unfolding in lives today, I will tell my own faith story by answering seven simple questions, one for each of the seven dimensions. Shared faith stories glorify God for it is God who is at work in and through them. The seven faith story questions are:

Listening Dimension: When and how did you first hear the Gospel of Jesus Christ?

Following in Community Dimension: When and how did you respond to the call to follow Jesus Christ as part of a community of believers?

Desiring Dimension: When and how did you first experience yourself wanting to live and love like Jesus, to do the will of God?

Humbled Dimension: When was the first time you remember

experiencing failure (significant limitations) in your ability to live in accord with God's will after expressing your desire to do God's will with your whole heart?

Grace Dimension: How have you experienced God loving and caring for you in spite of or in the midst of your failure to love God with your heart, soul, strength, and mind and your neighbor as yourself?

Empowered Dimension: What is your first memory of experiencing the Holy, God's Holy Spirit in your spiritual life?

Sent Dimension: To what ministries have you been called and commissioned to serve? How did this come about?

Each of us has a faith story to share. What follows here are my own answers to these seven questions. By reading my story I hope you will see the relevance of the seven dimensions for telling your own faith story. I also hope you will see how the Jesus Fractal is already manifest in your life of faith.

I have used this exercise in a number of different contexts. Participants share their faith stories either by answering all seven questions at the same time or one question at a time. Through this process, many people have been able to more deeply understand and communicate their faith. This was the experience of a covenant group with years of sharing group history, senior members of a church staff who work and pray with each other every day, and even brand new church members who used the questions to construct their own personal statements of faith.

What I describe here happened many years ago. It is the story of how I was initially introduced to each of the seven dimensions. It is the first chapter of my faith story, but only the first.

The Story of My Initial Introduction to the Seven Dimensions

Listening Dimension

The listening dimension is hearing and experiencing the Gospel. The question that can help us see God at work introducing us to this dimension is: *When and how did you first hear the Gospel of Jesus Christ?*

I first heard the Good News of Jesus Christ on television while watching The Billy Graham Crusades. I don't remember accepting Billy Graham's invitation to ask Jesus Christ into my life, but I do remember being positively open and accepting of Graham's preaching. I also heard about Jesus Christ in the feature film, *A Man Called Peter*, which told the story of Peter Marshall's life of faith. Peter Marshall became a kind of faith hero to me. I remember wanting to experience God calling me to do something important, like God called Peter Marshall to be Chaplain of the U.S. Senate. Openness to the Word of God and Jesus Christ continued in high school as I followed my high school chemistry teacher, Chuck Mink, to church one day. Within a year after attending my first youth group meeting, I was baptized and joined the church. At this point, my faith was profession of belief in Christian doctrine, as I understood it at the time, not yet a heartfelt relationship with Jesus Christ.

'Following in Community Dimension

The question that can help us to see God at work introducing us to the following in community dimension is: *When and how did you respond to the call to follow Jesus Christ as part of a community of believers?*

My senior year of college my mother died. I came home to Burlingame after graduation to learn the family business. The death of my mother had rocked my world. She was the center of warmth and love in our family. What would we do without her? I found myself back at the church not looking so much for Jesus, as I was looking for friends. In Seeker's, the church's college and career youth group, I found young people to hang out with. The youth group's advisor was the church's youth minister, Ron Stan. The first time I talked to Ron at group, he remembered me, knew my major and commented that I had lost weight. He was right on about the major and the weight; I was very impressed. The only other time I had met him was at one Bible study he led the summer after my freshman year of college.

A few months after I joined the group, we all went on a weekend retreat together. The speaker challenged us to go home and trust two people. I decided I would put my trust in Jesus and Ron. That was Sunday. Monday after work, I walked from work over to the church. I wanted to tell Ron of my decision. But when I got there before going inside, I paused for a moment to write in eucalyptus leaves on the sidewalk, "Jesus loves you." As I stepped back to read the sign, I suddenly felt excluded. The "you" in the sentence at that moment meant everyone in the world except me. Sadly, I turned and walked away from the church.

For what seemed like hours I walked the streets of Burlingame. It was a powerful time of reflection and prayer. Eventually, I ended up back where I had written "Jesus loves you." This time, the "you" in the sentence meant me. Jesus loves me! I went inside and told Ron all of the reasons I thought Jesus couldn't possibly love me. We prayed. He gave me some helpful suggestions as to how to deal with some unsettled relational issues from college. I left feeling loved, forgiven, and known in the midst of Christian community!

Desiring Dimension

Desiring to Do the Will of God is the third dimension. The question for this dimension is: *When and how did you first experience yourself wanting to live and love like Jesus—to do the will of God?*

The Jesus Fractal

Once I put my trust in Jesus, I began to wonder what God wanted me to do with my life. I majored in physics. People with physics majors were being laid off at that time, so looking for work using my college degree seemed futile. One of the things I was doing for our family's real estate business was appraising properties in my mother's estate. After I finished the appraisal, we gave it to our lawyer to submit to the court. Hearing about my work somehow, a real estate appraisal company came to our office to interview me for a job. They were offering $1500 a month as a starting salary. My Dad was paying me $500 a month, so I was very excited. I was sure this must be God's answer to my prayer for vocational guidance.

I showed the man the 172-page report I had created and talked about the appraisal process. I thought the conversation had gone really well. But at the conclusion of the interview, instead of offering me the job, the man said, "I would love for you to come and work for us, but you would be bored with our job in two months. I can't afford to train you for such a short tenure." I was devastated.

That night there was a Lenten dinner program at church. After dinner, I shared my woes with Tom Gillespie, our Senior Pastor. He asked if I had ever taken any vocational tests. I had. Recalling the results of the tests, I told him, without thinking, that they said I should go into social work or become a minister. His eyes widened with glee and suggested I make an appointment to come in and talk.

Concerned that Dr. Gillespie didn't understand how God wouldn't possibly want someone like me in ministry, I went and talked to Ron instead. Before meeting with Ron, I happened upon my high school yearbook and read under my senior portrait, "Beth's secret ambition is to become a minister." How could this be, when I had never met or seen a woman minister in all my life? When I finally met with Ron, he played down the vocational tests and yearbook and instead had me articulate the pros and cons of various career options from physics to real estate to ministry.

A few days later while reading the story of Jacob wrestling with God, I found myself identifying with the cunning Jacob. I heard the text speaking to me, "You are Israel, no longer Jacob." *(Genesis 32:28)*

I went down to the church almost immediately to let Ron know that I was going to apply to seminary to see whether God could possibly be calling me into ministry. It was like throwing out a Gideon fleece. Soon I was enrolled at Fuller Seminary studying for a Master of Divinity degree.

Not long after that Ron received a new call to serve a church in Washington State as their Senior Pastor. Before leaving he told me that my new mentor in the faith (spiritual director) would be Tom Gillespie. One of the first things Tom did was to give me a Bible. He inscribed Philippians1:6 in it, "He who began a good work in you will bring it to completion in the day of Christ Jesus." Because I was so young in my faith, Tom wanted me to do my seminary fieldwork class at our church in Burlingame. So every weekend, I would fly home. More than anything, I wanted to live the life God wanted me to live. People started calling me "the flying nun."

I was in the same place in my faith as Maria was in the "Sound of Music." The song from that musical that captures to my mind the essence of this third dimension is "Climb Every Mountain." Sister Gregory who taught drama at a Catholic college consulted with Oscar Hammerstein on the musical. He asked her once, "Why do young women choose the religious life?" She responded, "Everyone must find one's own answer to the simple question: What does God want me to do with my life? How does God wish me to spend my love?"

> Climb every mountain,
> Search high and low,
> Follow every byway,
> Every path you know.
>
> Climb every mountain,
> Ford every stream,
> Follow every rainbow,
> 'Till you find your dream.

A dream that will need
All the love you can give,
Every day of your life
For as long as you live.

Climb every mountain,
Ford every stream,
Follow every rainbow,
'Till you find your dream.

Humbled in Faith Dimension

The question that may help us discern God introducing us to the Humbled in Faith Dimension is: *When was the first time you remember experiencing failure (significant limitations) in your ability to live in accord with God's will after desiring to do God's will with your whole heart?*

The first time I remember failing as a Christian and getting in touch with my human condition was when as a seminary intern, I co-led a 3 ½ week mission trip for high school and college-aged youth to Sheldon Jackson College in Sitka, Alaska. On the trip, I kept stuffing my anger instead of giving it expression, because I thought that was the Christian thing to do. A couple of things got me angry. First, I agreed to help lead the trip only after being assured I wouldn't be asked to cook. Well, for the first 10 days of the trip, I was put in charge of preparing three meals a day for 27 people. Only when we finally got to the college in Sitka was I relieved of those cooking responsibilities. The two weeks we worked at the college, I led a crew of four assigned to the task of constructing framing forms for a sidewalk in front of the administration building. It was hard work, digging up the frozen ground and using sledgehammers to set pegs to hold the wood framing in place. Finally, we were finished, ready for the cement truck. At that point the strangest thing happened. The male co-leader of the trip, the one who had assured me I wouldn't be cooking, brought boys from other work sites over to our sidewalk and told me and the high school girl on the sidewalk team that we were no longer needed. He said something like, "This is men's work. It needs to be done fast and right, so the cement doesn't set up before it is properly distributed. You two girls can go back to the dorms to clean up or stand over there and watch."

My response to that chauvinistic statement was to throw my shovel in the direction of my fellow leader before walking off the job. It was literally the first time anyone had ever dared to suggest that I was incompetent because I was female. My big take away from this experience of repressing instead of dealing constructively with my anger was the realization that I was still a sinner, even though I was a Christian. I was dismayed by the revelation. I had failed my Lord.

Fortunately, when I got home I shared my feelings of failure with June Simmons, who was our Christian Education secretary at the time. I would drop by her desk and talk with her about my spiritual confusion and frustration, my imperfection, and inability to do God's will. June told me I wasn't called to perfection. She helped me see that because I wasn't Jesus, I would always need God's grace and forgiveness. I have never forgotten her wise counsel.

I wish I hadn't thrown that shovel. I am grateful it missed its intended target. But I am even more grateful for the deeper understanding of God's grace that the experience gave me. It was the first in an ever-deepening understanding of my sinful human condition and of my complicity in the death of Jesus.

Graced by God's Love Dimension

The question for the Graced by God's Love Dimension is: *How have you experienced God loving and caring for you in spite of or in the midst of your failure to love God with your whole heart, soul, strength and mind and your neighbor as yourself?*

Whether related to hormone treatments taken to lose weight, continued grief over the death of my mother, or my feelings of failure about living up to my own expectations as to how I wanted to live the Christian life, I became very depressed following the trip to Alaska. It felt as if I was falling through a dark tunnel with nothing to hold on to; I couldn't slow my fall into the abyss. One night the agony became so excruciating that I determined that I would end my life. By the way, a classic definition of suicide is: "anger turned inward." The problem was that I had already promised our Pastor Tom Gillespie that I wouldn't do that.

I called to let him know that I couldn't keep my promise. I then said, "But I will let you choose the means. Should I use my Dad's 22 or his 38 revolver?" Wisely, Tom wouldn't choose. I became frustrated and hung up. The phone began to ring and ring and ring. I panicked thinking that somehow the police were going to come. I left the house and started driving. When I got to the freeway entrance to 92 West, I thought maybe I should go say goodbye to my Mom up at Skylawn Cemetery. At that time, I thought suicide was an unforgivable sin, so the choice I was making to commit suicide would mean losing the opportunity to ever see her again. I turned onto the freeway and drove to the cemetery gate. It was late at night, so I parked the car, jumped the fence and walked through the cemetery in the darkness to her grave on the far side. I sat there for a long time talking to her. This calmed me down. Suddenly, I remembered Tom. I ran back through the cemetery, jumped back over the fence, got into my car and drove home to call him. This was way before cell phones. When I got to the house I found one of Tom's calling cards at the front door and another one inside on top of the guns. I called to tell Tom I was okay. I spent the whole next day at the Gillespie home. Tom and his wife Barbara were extremely nice to me that day, especially given the hell I had put them through the night before. Still, Tom made it perfectly clear that this suicide thing had to stop.

The next day was Sunday. I was still working as a seminary intern. During the 9:30 a.m. worship service, I led the congregation in the unison prayer of confession. I was also supposed to pronounce the assurance of pardon. But when I got to the last line of the pardon, "Your sins are forgiven," my voice rose at the end of the statement in essence turning the declaration of pardon into a question, "Your sins are forgiven?" At the 11 o'clock service, I knew I had to do better. So this time preceding the prayer of confession I said, "If we say we have no sin the truth is not in us, but if we confess our sin, God is merciful and just and will forgive us and cleanse us from all unrighteousness." As I finished that sentence, I heard as clear as day the words, "That is true!" With that assurance from behind me, this time I was able to say the words, "You are forgiven," with conviction.

Now I don't know where the words, "That is true!" came from. At the time, I attributed them to the voice of God. I was in worship after all. But the fact is Tom Gillespie was sitting right behind me that morning. The words I heard may very well have been his, I never asked. But in either case, I experienced the grace of God in my life that morning. All thoughts of suicide subsided and have never returned. I knew I was a forgiven sinner. I was loved.

Empowered in the Spirit Dimension

The question for the Empowered in the Spirit Dimension is: *What is your first memory of experiencing the Holy, God's Holy Spirit in your spiritual life?*

I am convinced that when people start wondering about the Holy Spirit, their spiritual relationship with Jesus Christ deepens. At least that was what happened to me. While still at Fuller Seminary and still very young in the faith, I went to a lecture on the Holy Spirit given by Tom Gillespie at St. Peter's by the Sea Presbyterian Church in Palos Verdes. During the lecture Tom claimed that the normative experience of the Holy Spirit was "the experience of being loved by the One who stands outside of you and says, 'I love you.'" As he said those words, he held out his hands as if embracing the shoulders of an imaginary person.

After the lecture, I asked Tom whether I had ever had an experience of the Holy Spirit. I told him I knew God loved me through people like him and Barbara, but I wasn't sure I had had a direct experience of God's love. Tom knew how much God had been working in my life as I dealt with my anger and grief with a Christian counselor. He responded incredulously, "Of course you have!" He then turned immediately if not dismissively to the next person in line.

But I really didn't know God loved me except through my experience of people at church. So on the way back to Fuller Seminary that night, I prayed telling God of my confusion. Fortunately, I wasn't driving, because as I prayed the car filled with a loving presence that embraced and assured me that I was not just loved by the people of God, but I was also loved by the Holy Other, "the one who stands outside of us and says, 'I love you.'"

Sent into the World Dimension

The question that can help us discern God introducing us to the Sent into the World Dimension is: *To what missions or ministries outside of your faith community have you been called and commissioned to serve? How did this come about?*

When I attended Fuller, there were only three women in the Master of Divinity program. So it took a while for me to understand exactly what God wanted me to do with my theological education. Two years into the program my head was full of theological doctrine far beyond my experience of God.

I had come to seminary full of faith, seeking understanding. Taking a course in ethics and another in the Prophets at the same time, I began to ask myself whether I knew how to live a just life, never mind a loving one. The result of this questioning was the development of a ministry to unchurched high school youth in our community. We called it "The Alternative." We went into Washington Park to love kids for Jesus. That was in 1974, three and a half years after my mom died.

I was still in Burlingame, but reaching out to the world in the name of Jesus. In 2014, the first young person who ever walked into The Alternative came back to tell me about how Jesus had touched his life through that ministry and beyond. At lunch, he asked me if he could say grace before we ate. It was an amazing prayer.

Through The Alternative I came to understand that I had been given gifts for ministry. I sensed that God was actually calling me to become an ordained minister. I finished my seminary degree at Fuller and was licensed by the church. Then I took off to Princeton Seminary to get a Master of Theology degree in Christian Education. I wanted to be qualified in the field of Christian Education, since that was probably the area of ministry I would be working as an Assistant Pastor. I had no desire to be a Senior Pastor or to preach. I loved kids and wanted to continue to work with youth. I was ordained as a Presbyterian minister in 1977.

Conclusion

Sharing faith stories using these seven questions may remind people of distant but significant religious experiences and enable them to discern the hand of God at work in seemingly random events. In this way there may be renewed trust in God and God's work in one's life. Using these questions to share our stories with other believers has the added benefit of fostering sacred bonding, connection at a deep spiritual level.

Worksheet: Telling Your Initial Faith Story

Dimension One: When and how did you first hear the Gospel of Jesus Christ?

_____

_____

_____

_____

_____

_____

_____

Dimension Two: When and how did you respond to the call to follow Jesus Christ as part of a community of believers?

_____

_____

_____

_____

_____

_____

_____

_____

Dimension Three: When and how did you first experience yourself wanting to do God's will, to live and love like Jesus?

Dimension Four: When was the first time you remember experiencing failure (significant limitations) in your ability to live in accord with God's will after expressing desire to do God's will with your whole heart?

Dimension Five: How have you experienced God loving and caring for you in spite of or in the midst of your failure to love God with your heart, soul, strength, and mind and your neighbor as yourself?

_____
_____
_____
_____
_____
_____
_____
_____

Dimension Six: What is your first memory of experiencing the Holy, God's Holy Spirit in your spiritual life?

_____
_____
_____
_____
_____
_____
_____
_____

Dimension Seven: To what missions or ministries outside of your faith community have you been called and commissioned to serve? How did this come about?

PART 2:

The Seven Dimensions of the Jesus Fractal

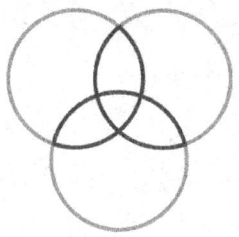

CHAPTER THREE
(PART ONE)
Listening Dimension:
Hearing and Experiencing the Word of God

So faith comes from what is heard, and what is heard comes through the Word of Christ.
Romans 10:17

From the oral tradition of ancient Israel to today, the Good News of God's love has been proclaimed. But with the invention of radio, television, and now the Internet, the telling of God's story no longer demands person to person contact. Sound waves disseminating Bible content are widely accessible through digital media around the world. At some level in the 21st century, exposure to stories from the Old and New Testaments is almost a given, availability a certainty. Much of this proclamation is evangelistic in nature, the people of God going out on sound waves to tell the Good News to the world. This kind of hearing of the Good News of Jesus Christ is preparation for hearing and experiencing the story of God's love communicated personally in face-to-face community with a believer, the kind of communicating Jesus did with people in the first century. Jesus didn't just talk about the Kingdom of God; Jesus lived the Good News he proclaimed.

So, hearing and experiencing the Word is the listening dimension of the Jesus Fractal. In churches around the world, people engage in this dimension each week. Children and youth participate in this dimension as they live and learn in church communities. All ages engage with the dimension in worship when hearing Scripture read and proclaimed. But this dimension isn't just experienced in the church. In coffee houses, sporting arenas, and our homes, whenever the Good News of Jesus Christ is shared person to person, the dimension is encountered. It is the act of paying attention to the Word of God. It requires no formal or public confession of faith, but does involve openness to the message. Engagement with the story is the key element. As such, this dimension can be defined as focused, open, attention to the proclamation of the Word of God heard.

In this and the following twelve chapters, one for each of the seven individual dimensions, the way Jesus interacted with Peter, as Peter matured in faith, will be told within the context of the seven dimensions of the Jesus Fractal. Jesus' interaction with Peter is taken as a paradigm case, because the Gospels describe his faith journey more completely than any of the other disciples. Jesus engages with Peter on his faith journey, beginning with the listening dimension, moving sequentially through all seven. Movement through the dimensions does not need to take place sequentially, but in Peter's case it does. Maturing in faith over time is just one way the Jesus Fractal manifests itself, but an important way.

Peter Hearing and Experiencing the Word of God
Question: When and how did Peter first hear the Gospel of Jesus Christ?

After being baptized in the Jordan River and spending 40 days in wilderness, Jesus began to teach in the synagogues of Galilee. He went to Capernaum, a village on the Sea of Galilee. The people were surprised and impressed, because Jesus' teaching was forthright, confident, and authoritative, not like that of the Scribes and Pharisees. The people of Capernaum watched in wonder as Jesus commanded unclean spirits to leave possessed people. The spirits obeyed.

With regard to the specific content of Jesus' teachings in

The Jesus Fractal

Capernaum, Scripture does not inform us. We know, however, from his teaching in Nazareth that Jesus was anointed to preach Good News to the poor, release to the captives, recovery of sight to the blind, and liberty to the oppressed. *(Luke 4:16-20)* We also know that at the beginning of his ministry Jesus announced a new era, "The time is fulfilled, and the kingdom of God has come near; repent, and believe in the Good News." *(Mark 1:45)* It is reasonable, therefore, to presume that Peter, who lived in Capernaum, heard these teachings.

One day after leaving the synagogue, Jesus entered Peter's house. Peter's mother-in-law was running a high fever. Jesus was asked if he could do something for her. Jesus responded by telling the fever to leave and it left. Before long, Peter's mother was up and about getting dinner ready. As news of the healing spread, those in the town who were sick were brought to Jesus. One after another Jesus placed his hands on them and they were healed. Demons left in droves, screaming, "Son of God! You're the Son of God!" Jesus rebuked the spirits refusing to let them speak concerning his being the Messiah.

Thus, before Simon Peter was asked (called) to follow Jesus in community as a disciple, he was exposed to the teaching and healing of Jesus. Peter's openness to this new teacher and his teaching is evidenced by Peter bringing the Rabbi into his home. More than this, Simon Peter gives expression to some degree of belief in Jesus by asking Jesus to heal his mother-in-law. Peter doesn't just hear Jesus' teachings, he experiences Jesus' ministry personally. This is the listening dimension of faith: hearing and experiencing the Word of God, the Gospel of Jesus Christ.

It is logical to assume that Peter's synagogue education prepared Peter to hear Jesus' preaching. When Jesus came to Capernaum preaching and teaching concerning the Kingdom of God, Peter listened to Jesus in light of what he had already heard and experienced as a member of the Jewish community. Just like people today hear and experience the Gospel of Jesus Christ presented in face-to-face community in light of what they have already heard and learned through the media in our culture.

Once this listening dimension is engaged by a person of faith it is repeatedly engaged in worship as the Good News is proclaimed from pulpits, in prayer, song, and Bible reading each week. Following his initial encounter with Jesus, Peter remained immersed in the listening dimension throughout his life while interacting with Jesus and the community of disciples. Similarly, adults today remain immersed in the listening dimension all of their lives.

Henry's Story of Engagement in the Listening Dimension

As a child I spent a lot of time at my grandfather's church not only on Sunday mornings, but also throughout the week. My grandfather was the pastor of the church and lived in the manse behind the main church building. My earliest recollections of hearing the Gospel were quite simply anytime my grandfather spoke. My granddad's words were, as they say "gospel." He could do no wrong. Whatever he said or did I heard as being in direct relationship to God and the church. Turns out I wasn't the only one so deeply impacted by my granddad. Once when a teacher asked one of my Sunday School peers where he thought God lived, the boy answered with confidence, "In that green house with the red brick right behind the church!"

My grandfather's Gospel message was simply this: "God loves you and we know this best through the person of Jesus Christ who came to redeem us from our sins so that we could experience God's presence now and have life eternal." I heard this message through the songs learned at Vacation Bible School like "Jesus is the Way to a Brand New Day; He's the Truth, He's Life, He's the Way." I heard it in Bible stories like Zacchaeus taught with hand motions and great joy by his Sunday school teachers who loved the Bible. I heard it in the lines learned each year for the Christmas pageant, in memorizing the Ten Commandments for the biggest Hershey's chocolate bar one could possibly imagine. I heard it mostly just listening to my grandfather's sermons. I knew God loved me and granddad's church was the main place where I experienced God's love and presence in and for my life.

But in the third grade life changed. Our family moved into town into a new home and school district. Living away from the country, in a more densely populated area, provided more and different ways to spend my time, both during school and after. The actual distance our family moved was only ten miles, but the distance it created from church and God was much greater. Our family kept attending grandfather's church, but the visits during the week became less and less frequent. As I embraced my new surroundings, I became less and less engrossed with life out at the old church.

I moved progressively further and further from the love I had known and received at the church. I lived a life less pleasing to God and my parents, getting caught up with my new crowd living more and more contrary to what parents, teachers, and other authority figures were telling me to do. By the time I entered junior high, bad decision-making escalated. Some of the choices led to close brushes with the law (with zero arrests), being grounded for at least half of junior high, and the potential for catastrophic physical injury that fortunately never materialized. It was a unique time in my life that I continue to reflect on with awe, wonder, and great gratitude that it finally came to a halt.

The further I strayed from the narrative that was most formative in my early childhood years, the less and less I knew both who I was and whose I was.

Throughout this time period that lasted from the third grade on through most of high school, I still went to church on Sunday but I experienced it only as a weekly ritual. I went through the motions of weekly church attendance, but was not open to how it could impact my life or affect the new priorities I had made for myself.

It wasn't until my freshman year of college, when I was completely caught off guard by a period of homesickness (because I attended college out of my home state), that I felt drawn to listen again to the story of God's love. I began attending church near my college campus. I went by myself every Sunday under no obligation to anyone or anything whatsoever. At this new church, a genuine Christian community warmly embraced me. The lay leaders and pastors became mentors. More importantly I heard the Gospel anew, and committed my life to Christ once again. I soon discovered God's plan for my life. When the Gospel takes a hold of our lives, we have a story that makes sense of our lives, gives us hope, renewal, and a changed life lived in the presence of God that endures through life everlasting. This discovery bridged anew my commitment to Christ in the present to the myriad ways that I will always cherish my grandfather's memory from childhood into adulthood. But there is one account, in particular, that speaks to the power and importance of hearing the old, old story, which occurred in my early years as an ordained pastor.

Like with many older people, my grandfather's dementia got the best of him in his later years evolving into full-blown Alzheimer's. The illness became most pronounced when I was in graduate school all the way across the country. But whenever home, I would go to visit my granddad at the assisted living center. The visits were frustrating and heart wrenching, because the grandfather I loved and remembered was there less and less. One of the last times I saw my grandfather, I spoke to him about the love of God, concluding with the words, "Grandpa, I love you and God loves you."

Grandpa responded, "I love you, and God loves you, too."

I then suggested, "Why don't we pray together?"

Instantaneously, Granddad closed his eyes and bowed his head. With our hands joined together, I offered a prayer.

Reflecting on this sacred moment I now recall, my grandfather could not recall his life, even his name, he couldn't pick me or anyone from my family out of a crowd, but he knew what it meant that God loved him and he always remembered how to pray. He knew the story that had held his life together; it was one his soul would never let him forget.

Interlude for Theology

The Good News that is heard and listened to in this dimension is the Word of God. The Word of God has a threefold form—preached, written, and revealed. Understanding this threefold form is important in helping us to understand how God's Word is heard. God's Word is heard when the written Word of God (Scripture) is reflected upon or proclaimed (preached) and Jesus Christ (the revealed Word of God) is present. All three forms of the Word are a unity, like Father, Son and Holy Spirit.

Characteristics of Growing in Listening

In the hearing and listening dimension people indwell the content of the Word of God presented to them in a variety of ways. They may hear the Word articulated by a friend; performed in the classical music of Handel and Bach; proclaimed at a service of worship, funeral, wedding, baptism, or confirmation service; recited in a Christmas pageant or Easter chancel drama; shown in a film. They may come to church with a friend or wander in on their own; attend a sacred music concert or pause while flipping stations to listen to any number of radio or TV evangelists. The Good News that is heard is content regarding the person of Jesus Christ.

The Christian Century magazine once invited some authors to summarize the Gospel in a maximum of seven words. Here are some of the responses:

Martin Marty: "God, through Jesus Christ, welcomes you anyhow."
Donald W. Shriver: "Divinely persistent, God really loves us."
Mary Karr: "We are the church of infinite chances."
Scott Cairns: "Christ's humanity occasions our divinity."
M. Craig Barnes: "We live by grace."[1]

The *Four Spiritual Laws* booklet of Campus Crusade for Christ encapsulates the content of the Gospel in four propositions:

1. God loves you and has a wonderful plan for your life.

2. Humanity is sinful and separated from God.

3. Jesus Christ is God's provision for our sinful human condition.

4. We must individually receive Jesus Christ as Savior and Lord.

The Ancient Apostle's Creed uses these words to capture the essence of the Gospel:
I believe in God, the Father almighty,
> creator of heaven and earth.

I believe in Jesus Christ, God's only Son, our Lord,
> who was conceived by the Holy Spirit,
> born of the Virgin Mary,
> suffered under Pontius Pilate,
> was crucified, died, and was buried;
> he descended into hell.
> On the third day he rose again;
> he ascended into heaven,
> he is seated at the right hand of the Father,
> and he will come to judge the living and the dead.

I believe in the Holy Spirit,
> the holy catholic Church,
> the communion of saints,
> the forgiveness of sins,

---

[1] David Heim. "The Gospel in Seven Words." *Christian Century*. August 23, 2012. https://www.christiancentury.org/article/2012-08/gospel-seven-words.

the resurrection of the body,
and the life everlasting. Amen.

In seven dimensions, the Gospel can be summarized:

1. (Listen): Angels herald the birth of Jesus;

2. (Follow): Who calls disciples into community;

3. (Desire): Where he teaches, preaches, and heals in accord with God's will that inspires.

4. (Humbled): Jesus then dies on a cross,

5. (Graced): Rises again,

6. (Empowered): Ascends to the right hand of God,

7. (Sent): Sends the Holy Spirit empowering believers with God's love.

This is the content of the Gospel that needs to be heard and experienced. The focus of the listening dimension is God's story of salvation told and experienced so people can respond, "I believe." The biggest stumbling block to hearing and experiencing this story with conviction is our sense of unworthiness. It gets masked in a myriad of ways including, but not limited to, living life in such an upright and honorable fashion as to cover-up our insecurity. This was the issue the Scribes and Pharisees had with Jesus.

Characteristics of Persons in the Listening Dimension

Dimension:	Persona	Focus	I Statements	Obstruction	Moving On
Listening. Hearing and experiencing the Word of God	Thinker. "I think, therefore I am."	God's story.	I believe	I don't believe God loves me. (I'm not worth lovng or I don't need God.)	Become part of a group of believers with Christ-centered leadership.

Elizabeth A. Frykberg

Seven Dimensional Maturing within the Listening Dimension
Hearing and Experiencing the Word of God

1. The primary activity of the listening dimension is exposure to the Word of God. In our culture the Word is available and may be attended to (which is what listening means) in a variety of ways: in one-on-one conversations, on radio, television, Internet, and through print media. One may hear the Good News of God's love proclaimed in sermons, songs, films, on stage, or in other art forms.

2. Beyond the Gospel message of God's love, people also need to hear and respond to the community calling them to follow Jesus Christ. A person may hear the Good News the community is proclaiming by attending worship, fellowship events, Bible studies, even going on retreats. They may do so as observers or full participants. This means hospitality is key; being welcomed as an outsider, such that one wants to become an insider. The community extends an invitation in face-to-face community, which the outsider hears.

3. Hearing of the Word also needs to create the desire to respond to what is being heard. The response at first may simply be a desire to hear more. Or it may be a desire to respond to a particular invitation heard in the midst of the Gospel being proclaimed.

4. Another aspect of growing in the listening dimension of the Jesus Fractal is hearing the call to "repent and believe." This can happen in private conversation with a believer, but happens most often during messages addressed to a larger group, where one feels individually addressed.

5. The call to "repent and believe" needs to be heard as one also hears the grace of God proclaimed. God's love is the Good News. Actually, hearing individually how this is Good News

is key. God's love is not just a great concept, it is a message addressed to individuals and needs to be heard as addressed to the person - God saying to individuals through the proclamation, "I love you."

6. To be heard as God's Word, proclamation needs to be empowered by the Spirit of God. Thus, another aspect of the hearing dimension is listening to Spirit empowered proclamation of the Good News in Word and Sacrament. This happens during worship for "where two or three are gathered in Christ's name, there he is in the midst of them." *(Matthew 18:20)* Worship is itself a manifestation of the seven dimensional Jesus Fractal:

Hear: Call to Worship
In the call to worship, God speaks through the liturgist inviting God's people to worship. Hearing the call, the people of God gather for worship. Because it is God who is doing the calling and to whom our ears are attuned, Scripture is often used when calling people to worship.

Follow in Community:
Following the call to worship, the gathered community sings praise to God. These songs sung by the community to and in the presence of the living God are also heard by the community singing. Anne Lamott describes the experience, "Somehow the singing wore down all the boundaries and distinctions that kept me so isolated. Sitting there, standing with them to sing, sometimes so shaky and sick that I felt like I might tip over, I felt bigger than myself, like I was being taken care of, tricked into coming back to life. But I had to leave before the sermon."[2]

---

2   Anne Lamott. (2000-09-05). *Traveling Mercies: Some Thoughts on Faith* (p. 48). Knopf Doubleday Publishing Group. Kindle Edition.

Desire:
In Reformed worship the commandments of God are read at this point in the service, either the Ten Commandments or the Great Commandment: "Love the Lord your God with all your heart, soul, mind, and strength and your neighbor as yourself." The desire to follow these commands is the people's grateful response to God's love. But desire to live in accord with the commands does not ensure their fulfillment. Actually, the opposite is the case in that "all have sinned and fall short of the glory of God." *(Romans 6:23)* Thus, the reading of the Law calls the community to confession.

Humbled:
The community is called to confession: "If we say we have not sinned, the truth is not in us, but if we confess our sins, God is merciful and just and will forgive us for all our unrighteousness." *(1John 1:8-9)* Humbly, the community in prayer acknowledges lack of conformity to the Law of God. The prayer of confession is corporate, it is heard by the individual as it is spoken in unison.

Grace:
The assurance of pardon immediately follows. This is the joyful declaration of God's grace, mercy, and forgiveness in Christ. God's promise of forgiveness is declared by the leader, and received by the congregation by faith in the crucified and risen Savior. "There is therefore now no condemnation for those who are in Christ Jesus." *(Romans 8:1)*

Empowerment:
Having received God's love and forgiveness, the people of God now hear the Word of God. The Word is read in the Scripture lesson, proclaimed in the sermon, and

enacted in the sacraments. This all becomes God's Word to us by the movement of the Holy Spirit in the heart and minds of those officiating and those listening. The service of the Word is a little Pentecost. As at the first Pentecost, the Holy Spirit is present in the reading and interpretation of Scripture. In the midst of the service of the Word, the giving of alms is evidence of the presence and power of the Holy Spirit at work, evidence of the people listening.

Sent:
The gathered people of God now scatter back into the world with a Song of Sending, Charge, and Benediction. Charge and benediction are pronounced.

Charge:
"Let love be genuine; hate what is evil, hold fast to what is good; love one another with mutual affection; outdo one another in showing honor. Do not lag in zeal, be ardent in spirit, serve the Lord. Rejoice in hope, be patient in suffering, persevere in prayer."
(Rom.12:9–12)

Benediction:
"May the grace of our Lord Jesus Christ, the love of God, and the communion of the Holy Spirit be and abide with you this day and forevermore."
(1 Corinthians 13:14)

What this outline reveals is that the order of reformed worship evidences and enables the people of God to hear and experience the seven different dimensions of faith relationship with Jesus Christ every time the church gathers for worship. By leaving out elements of the worship service, the experience of the seven dimensions is truncated.

7. Go: Whether through the Charge spoken at the end of the worship service or in some other way, another aspect of the listening dimension is hearing the call to go into the world for God.

To encourage and cooperate with God's desire for people to be transformed by the renewal of their minds in this way, the church must first and foremost proclaim the Good News of the Gospel. This is the church's essential listening dimension action. It means proclamation in both word and deed. All aspects of the church's ministries participate in this proclamation. Just like Jesus proclaimed the coming of the Kingdom of God with every word and action, the church also embodies a message in everything it says and does. It is in the life of the church, in its teaching, preaching, evangelism, pastoral care, and mission ministries where the Good News of the Gospel is proclaimed. A helpful corollary here is the maxim from Saint Francis of Assisi, "preach the Gospel always, and if necessary, use words" or the adage "since actions speak louder than words, mind what they proclaim."

CHAPTER FOUR
(PART TWO)
Listening Dimension
Ministry Implications

Gospel Arts

One ministry that engages people in the Listening Dimension of Hearing and Experiencing the Word of God is what at our church we call the Gospel Arts. The Gospel Arts are artistic expressions that present the Gospel. Music, drama, novels, painting, sculpture, film, photography, and dance are all potential Gospel Art forms. Because the arts with Christian content are often experienced and engaged outside of the Christian community within the general culture, they are an important means of conveying the Gospel to individual people out in the world.

The Chronicles of Narnia have been read by generation after generation, since first being published in 1950. The series has been translated into 47 different languages with more than 100 million copies in print. Disney brought the stories to the wide screen grossing over $745 million with *The Lion the Witch and the Wardrobe* and $419 million with *Prince Caspian*. Other Christian blockbuster movies include: *The Robe, White Christmas, The Ten Commandments, Ben-Hur, The Sound of Music, The Bible,* and *Lord of the Rings.* There are other successful Christian films as well: *The Passion, The Hiding Place, A Place in the Heart, The Cross and the Switchblade,* and *Les Misérables.*

Composers like Bach and Handel composed much of their music for use in church worship. Today that same music is listened to and appreciated by people who have never set foot inside a church building. Classical music played in concert halls, learned in school music classes, or heard in homes all proclaim the Gospel in secular contexts. Secular artists are also drawn into the church to help perform these major works on high Holy Days like Easter and Christmas. As such, sacred music from the classical era can introduce musicians to the Gospel.

Spirituals are another musical genre that proclaims the Gospel outside of the church. Spirituals are the religious folk songs created and first sung by African Americans during slavery. "Swing Low, Sweet Chariot"; "Joshua Fit the Battle of Jericho"; "Sometimes I Feel Like a Motherless Child"; "Go Down, Moses"; "Steal Away to Jesus"; "Didn't My Lord Deliver Daniel?"; "Wade in the Water"; are some of the best known. Americans of all ethnic backgrounds have grown up singing these distinctively American Christian songs. Another musical type widely sung and familiar to secular culture are patriotic hymns like "The Battle Hymn of the Republic" and "God Bless America."

Musicals like "Les Misérables," "Joseph and His Technicolor Dream Coat," "Godspell," "Fiddler on the Roof," "Amahl and the Night Visitors," and "Jesus Christ Super Star" also present the Gospel. I remember sitting with Christian friends watching "Les Misérables" in New York when it first came out and thinking to myself, "Wow, all of these people paying big bucks to hear the Gospel of Jesus Christ proclaimed to them!" For illustrative purposes, let's look at this one musical and how the story told on stage or in the movie theater allows people to Hear and Experience the Gospel in all seven dimensions of Jean Valjean's faith story—in a Jesus Fractal.

The Jesus Fractal in Les Misérables[3]

Listening Dimension: Hearing and Experiencing the Word of God

For Jean Valjean this first dimension of his faith journey culminates in his conversion experience. It is October 1815, Jean Valjean, a tree-trimmer from the south of France is released from prison after 19 long years. The first five years were for stealing a loaf of bread to feed his impoverished family, the next 14 for his frequent escape attempts.

After walking all day and desperately hungry, Valjean enters a town. In the town, his first stop is the mayor's office, where the law requires him to show his yellow passport identifying himself as an ex-convict. With his prison reputation instilling fear in the people of the town, innkeepers refuse to serve him or give him work. Everywhere he turns, he is rebuffed until he happens upon the Bishop's house. The Bishop isn't fearful, but cordially invites Valjean in for dinner and to spend the night free of charge. Valjean eagerly accepts, but repays the kindness by leaving in the middle of the night with the Bishop's silver.

The next day, the police stop Valjean and discover the Bishop's silver in his knapsack. When they take him back to the Bishop's home, the Bishop surprises everyone by corroborating Valjean's claim that the Bishop had given Valjean the silver. The Bishop goes on to chide Valjean for having forgotten to take the silver candlesticks as well. When the handcuffs are removed, the Bishop hands Valjean the silver candlesticks saying:

> See in this some higher plan
> You must use this precious silver
> To become an honest man
> By the witness of the martyrs

---

3 *Les Misérables* (1980, French; 1985, English) is a musical play based on the novel *Les Misérables* by Victor Hugo, with music by Claude-Michel Schönberg, original French lyrics by Alain Boubliland Jean-Marc Natel, with an English-language libretto by Herbert Kretzmer.

> By the Passion and the Blood
> God has raised you out of darkness
> I have saved your soul for God!

Later that night confronted by the reality of his malicious intention, Valjean accepts the Bishop's challenge—praying on the Bishop's doorstep saying:

> What have I done?
> Sweet Jesus, what have I done?
> Become a thief in the night,
> Become a dog on the run
> ...
> Yet why did I allow that man
> To touch my soul and teach me love?
> He treated me like any other
> He gave me his trust
> He called me brother
> My life he claims for God above
> ...
> One word from him and I'd be back
> Beneath the lash, upon the rack
> Instead he offers me my freedom,
> ...
> I'll escape now from the world
> From the world of Jean Valjean
> ...
> Another story must begin!

The story that begins with this prayer of Jean Valjean is immersion in the Following in Community Dimension of the Jesus Fractal.

Following in Community Dimension:

The Follow in Community Dimension is the pathway where people are ready and willing to commit themselves to seeking to understand and live as Christ would have them live. They follow because they have heard and experienced the difference Jesus Christ can make in a person's life. This is the junction in the road where the disciples left their nets to follow Jesus to learn daily in relationship with Jesus in community.

Following the Bishop's gracious act of giving the candlesticks, Valjean opens his heart to the redemptive power of Christ's love and compassion. He takes on the commitment to make something of himself. Living under a pseudonym, Valjean moves into the dilapidated town of Montreuil-sur-mer, where he develops a newer, cheaper method for producing black beads, the town's largest industry. As a result, the ex-con becomes a successful businessman. No one knows much about the prosperous stranger; but in time, he becomes wildly popular in the community after acting decisively to save two local children from a fire.

Desiring to Do the Will of God Dimension:

The desiring dimension embraces the "Desire" to do the will of God, to live like Christ. This becomes evident in Valjean's life in two ways, first in his philanthropy. Valjean's success in business is linked to his caring for the poor. He has taken the Bishop's graciousness and paid it forward. The second thing Valjean does is conduct his business on high moral grounds.

It is at this point that a young woman named Fantine enters Valjean's life. Fantine is a single Mom, who has been abandoned by her daughter's father while living in Paris. Thinking she would be better off in her home town, Fantine moves back to Montreuil where Valjean has become the town's mayor. Realizing that she will be unable to work if the people of the town discover she has an illegitimate daughter, Fantine leaves her daughter in the care of an innkeeper and his wife, while agreeing to send money each month.

As hoped, Fantine finds employment. She finds it in Valjean's factory. But unfortunately her secretive manner makes her coworkers suspicious. Needing to send money to the innkeepers, but being illiterate Fantine dictates her letters to a supposed confidant. The confidant, however, turns out to be a gossip, who lets the other factory workers know that Fantine is hiding an out of wedlock child. As a direct consequence, Fantine is fired from her job in Valjean's factory on charges of immorality. The unforeseen consequence of Fantine being fired (of Valjean's desire to conduct his business life with moral rectitude) confronts Valjean a little while later. When it does, Valjean is mortified and moves into the Humbled in Faith Dimension of the faith fractal.

Humbled in Faith Dimension: "I Cannot Do the Good I Will to Do."

Unemployed but still needing money to pay the innkeepers for her daughter's care, Fantine first sells her hair, then her teeth. She finally becomes a prostitute. One night, while waiting for potential clients outside a bar, a man harasses Fantine hitting her with a snowball. She snaps, attacking him back. Police Inspector Javert takes Fantine into custody threatening her with six months in jail, all the while ignoring her pleas for mercy. Hearing her pleas, Valjean now the town's mayor intervenes insisting that Fantine be set free, promising to take care of her and her daughter. This is the righteous and philanthropic Valjean, being generous to the poor and oppressed of his community.

But Fantine blames Valjean for her being fired from his factory and spits in his face. Called up short by the accusation and humiliating gesture, Valjean is forced to confront the fact that in his sincere attempt to act righteously, he remains a sinner in need of God's redemption. For the apostle Peter, this same moment of realization came when the cock crowed. It came for the apostle Paul when Jesus confronted him on the road to Damascus in a bolt of lightning. This is the humbling but necessary experience of the faith journey. Each believer individually and personally must confront the truth that their sinful condition runs deeper than their sinful acts. The experience prepares the sojourner on the faith journey to embrace the fullness of God's gracious action on their behalf. Valjean moves through and beyond the humiliation of the "spit in the face" by repeating his gracious offer to Fantine.

Seeking with one's whole heart, soul, strength and mind to do the will of God, only to discover one's inescapable failure to do the very thing one wants to do, deepens the experience of God's love. Let me explain. When the Bishop was gracious to Valjean, Valjean could rationalize stealing the silver in part because others had treated him unjustly. Such self-protective justifications limit the experience of grace. On the other hand, when people try their best and still fail, the necessity of the cross becomes apparent and the experience of God's love transformational.

Experiences of grace on the faith journey in response to sinful behavior may motivate people to try and live a life of love; but mortifying experiences of sin as human condition bring people to their knees at the foot of the cross. These kinds of experiences free individuals to love in a new way, sacrificially after the pattern of Jesus Christ, because in them people experience *agape* love, God's love that is not deserved.

Graced by God's Love Dimension: Graced by God's Love and the Giving of Self for the Sake of Another

The depth of Valjean's transformation here is soon tested. He faces an agonizing dilemma. Another man, who looks very much like Valjean has been arrested. The question is: What will the real Valjean do? Reveal his true identity freeing the innocent man or remain silent saving himself? Has Valjean matured enough in faith to love sacrificially after the pattern of Jesus Christ? This is the grace dimension of the faith journey—Love.

Valjean agonizes,

> This man could be my chance!
> Why should I save his hide?
> Why should I right this wrong
> When I have come so far
> And struggled for so long?
> If I speak, I am condemned.
> If I stay silent, I am damned!

People deceive themselves when rationalizing their self-protective actions as being for the benefit of others; the right thing to do. Valjean is no exception. Listen to his rationalization,

> I am the master of hundreds of workers.
> They all look to me.
> How can I abandon them?
> How would they live if I am not free?

In the grace dimension, love moves beyond self-serving justification. Valjean reflects on his experience of the cross. Let's hear this prayer,

> Who am I?
> Can I condemn this man to slavery
> Pretend I do not feel his agony
> This innocent who bears my face
> Who goes to judgment in my place
> ...
> My soul belongs to God, I know
> I made that bargain long ago
> He gave me hope when hope was gone
> He gave me strength to journey on

Answering his own question, Valjean appears in front of the court and confesses:

> Who am I? Who am I?
> I am Jean Valjean!

But who is this Jean Valjean? He is now the honest man, the Bishop charged him to become. The court exonerates the innocent look alike. Following the confession and in the confusion of the moment, Valjean goes back to his home, where Fantine is sick in bed. As she dies, Valjean promises to care for her daughter Cosette. He then takes time to organize his affairs giving his fortune to the poor, before leaving Montreuil to rescue Cosette.

In risking his freedom to save another, in giving up his life in Montreuil to save Cosette, Valjean fulfills his pledges to both the Bishop and Fantine. By so doing, Valjean embodies and acts out of the grace dimension of the Jesus Fractal: He loves. Not human love which is calculated and filial, but *agape* love which gives not in a self-serving or feel-good way, but sacrificially like Jesus Christ gave to humankind.

Empowered in the Spirit Dimension:

The empowered dimension becomes evident in Jean Valjean's life after Cosette has been raised and her boyfriend Marius joins the rebels of the French Revolution manning a barricade. Valjean joins the rebels to watch over Marius. In the midst of the fighting, inspector Javert, Valjean's nemesis, is captured as a spy and his execution ordered. Valjean eagerly volunteers to be the executioner, but instead sets the inspector free firing a shot in the air so the others will think the inspector dead. The experience of grace in his own life, here empowers Valjean to forgive, to love his enemy, to stop hiding behind the false persona of "upstanding citizen of Montreuil-sur-mer" to become his true self.

In this dimension, the fruit of the Spirit becomes more and more evident: love, joy, peace, patience, kindness, faithfulness, gentleness, goodness and self-control. Not as external good works or goals, but as an integral part of who the person of faith has become in Christ. A tree does not think about producing fruit. Producing fruit is just part of the tree's nature. Similarly in this dimension, the fruits of the Spirit are not an achievement of human effort, but evidence of the Holy Spirit's indwelling human spirit.

Sent into the World Dimension:
Sent to Fulfill One's Calling

Another faith movement for Valjean, as it is for each of us is to fulfill our calling. This is the Sent into the World Dimension. It was the Bishop who pronounced Valjean's calling:

> You must use this precious silver
> To become an honest man
> By the witness of the martyrs
> By the Passion and the Blood
> God has raised you out of darkness
> I have saved your soul for God

In the final scenes of the movie, musical, and book that is exactly what Valjean becomes—an honest man—confessing his true identity to the most important people in his life, Marius and Cosette. Because Valjean confesses, tells the truth about his life, his faith story is not an inch deep and a mile wide, but an epic journey of redemptive faith relationship with Jesus Christ with all its narrow twists and turns.

So why describe the seven dimensions of Jean Valjean's life as told in *Les Miserables*? To show that people negotiating any dimension of the faith journey in their own life will be exposed to all seven dimensions. The seven dimensions (Hearing, Following, Desiring, Humbled, Graced, Empowered, and Sent) can describe faith over the course of a lifetime, but also in the microcosm of each and every step of faith. This scaling of the dimensions in and over time comes about as an expression of the fractal nature of seven dimensions of faith.

CHAPTER FIVE
(PART ONE)
Community Dimension: Following Jesus Christ in Community

*Beloved, let us love one another, because love is from God;
everyone who loves is born of God and knows God.
Whoever does not love does not know God,
for God is love.
1John 4:7-8*

Another essential dimension of the Jesus Fractal is following Jesus Christ in community. It involves becoming a disciple, not just a hearer of the Word. It is following in response to the call of Jesus Christ and involves commitment to be with other followers. Peter, James, Andrew and John left their boats to follow Jesus. This brought them into everyday community with Jesus learning as individuals and as a group from the Rabbi.

Participation in face-to-face Christian learning communities is the key element of this community dimension of the Jesus faith fractal. In small groups, classes and serving experiences, people fellowship with other persons who are also taking their discipleship seriously. Following in community involves the commitment of time, energy, enthusiasm, and finances. It means taking the call to follow Christ seriously enough to get out of one's comfortable, secure boat—one's comfortable, secure way of life—stepping out in faith. As with the listening dimension, hearing and experiencing the Word of God, persons never outgrow their need for Christian community.

Following Jesus Christ in community is the only dimension of the Jesus faith fractal that people experience primarily within Christian community. As context for this dimension, the Christian community is any group of believers gathered together in the name of Jesus Christ. "For where two or three are gathered in the name of Jesus Christ, there he is in the midst of them." *(Matthew 18:20)* Thus, Christian community is not here being equated with the church, although the church could and often is the context for growth in this dimension. It should be noted in this regard that Jesus, throughout the Gospels, ate with tax collectors and sinners, welcomed children, talked with women, and healed those who were considered unclean and estranged from their faith community. Jesus practiced a ministry of hospitality.

How did you make contact with the Christian community? Did someone invite you? Did you venture in on your own? Were you warmly greeted or ignored? Throughout Christian history, hospitality—welcoming the stranger—has been a central practice of the Church. At the Council of Nicaea where the Nicene Creed was first written in AD 325, it was decreed that a house of hospitality to care for the sick, the widow, the poor, and the stranger would be established in every cathedral city. In-patient medical care, in what we today call hospitals, was a development driven by Byzantine innovation and the Christian *ministry of hospitality*. Hotels, motels, nursing care facilities, call boxes on freeways, even our 911 systems are rooted in the impulse toward hospitality as practiced by Jesus.

Hospitality Across the Seas

A young man in Cameroon, Africa writing to a group of American Christians, who have, for the last eight years, sought to be hospitable to orphans of the HIV/AIDS epidemic, enlarges and enhances provincial and parochial definitions of Christian community, even as the letter focuses on the need:

To Orphan Compassion, My Life Story After the Death of My Parents.

My father died on the 14th of February 2004 after being diagnosed with cancer of the liver. One year later my mother also died of HIV AIDS. I was in Primary 4 then. After the death of my parents I was left with my stepmother who helped me for some time, but life was really difficult.

I used to close from school at 2:00 p.m. arrive home at 3:00 p.m. change my school uniform and continue to the farm. I would work on the farm returning back home at 6:30 in the evening. Because of the difficulty with my school fees and feeding, I used to carry cocoyams on my head from Acha to Tard Market to sell, a distance of about 3 KM. When roads were bad I use to transport my stepmother's market items in a hand truck from Acha to Tard market also.

I graduated from primary school in the year 2005. Because there was no money for me to continue my education I had to stay out for a year to raise money so that I could continue my education. I did truck pushing in Tard Market carrying people's luggage from one place to the other. I did all this to raise the little funds I could so that my stepmother could add some funds to what I have worked for to enable me to go to secondary school. At last the next year that followed I was sent to GHS (government high school) Tudig to start my secondary school career.

Life too was not easy with me and my studies. This is because I had no textbooks to study. I was always sent out of class because of no textbooks to study but I kept pleading to some teachers who later understood my situation. I pleaded for textbooks from my friends to study. Doing this I was able to cope with studies and succeeded with my career in school.

God so kind helped me through His ways until I was in Form 4, when God turned my story the way He did with Joseph, David and many others in the Bible. I am very grateful for at this time God sent to me my other parents—Orphan Compassion—and change my story. My situation is now a thing of the past.

Orphan Compassion, my dear new parents, started assisting me in Form 4 until when I had my Advance Level Certificate. This situation has made me to be proud of them, because I am what I am now thanks to Orphan Compassion who sponsors me even more than my late parents could do.

Even with this great assistance given to me by Orphan Compassion, I still face some difficulties for…back in Form 5 my stepmother who used to support me in one way or another also died of a heart attack. I became confused and frustrated because to afford a daily meal was not easy for me.

I spent almost two months in an uncompleted building. The only way I could study was using the kerosene lamp to read. God so kind, again Orphan Compassion came to my rescue and provided for me free lights, water, and a better home for me to stay and study in . . . I am so grateful to Orphan Compassion for the wonderful offer given to me for my studies.

I still go home to Acha to work on farms that help me if I lack food.

I have been struggling to support myself in addition to the great support and assistance from Orphan Compassion. Using this great opportunity I would like to thank God for sending people who are not only supportive but kind enough to give me a brighter future.

May God bless you abundantly and give you more years to support us till we have some profession in life so that we can also start assisting you people by helping other orphans.

God says (in *Jeremiah 29:11-13*), "I alone know the plans I have for you, plans to bring you prosperity and not disaster, plans to bring about the future you hope for. You will call to me and pray and I will answer you."

Dear parents I promise to be a good child of Orphan

Compassion Cameroon obeying your instructions as recommended. I believe the Word of God in Jeremiah. I know that you are my parents for life.

Thank you, faithfully,

Leonard

Hospitality is the doorway that leads to the Following in Community Dimension of the Jesus Fractal. Let us see how that happens for Peter.

Peter Following Jesus Christ in Community
(Luke 5:1-11)

Question: When and how did Peter respond to the call to follow Jesus Christ as part of a community of believers?

The setting for Peter's responding to the call to follow Jesus in community is early one morning on the Sea of Galilee (which was also known as Lake Gennesaret). Jesus approaches the shore of the lake with a crowd of people trailing behind. Peter and his partners are there on the shore checking and cleaning equipment following an unsuccessful all night fishing expedition. Perhaps to protect himself from the crush of people wanting to hear his teachings concerning the Kingdom of God, Jesus boards Peter's boat requesting that he put out a little from the land. From the boat, Jesus sits to teach the people.

When the oral teaching is done, Jesus says to Simon Peter, "Put out into the deep and let down your nets for a catch." In this way, Jesus once again reaches out with care and compassion to the Galilean fisherman. Peter had been fishing all night to no avail. By making this request of Peter, Jesus in essence is saying, "Peter, will you let me into your life? Will you let me show you how to be yourself? Let me show you how to be a fisherman?" Common sense, reason, and the accumulated wisdom of Galilean fishermen everywhere counsel young Simon Peter to go home to bed. On the surface the request seems to reflect a carpenter's ignorance of the fishing trade. For one thing, Jesus tells Peter to put out into the "deep," when in the Sea of Galilee fish are found in places of moderate depth. Moreover, Jesus makes the request at noon when evening and the early morning hours are best for fishing. In light of this, one might conjecture that Peter is just humoring Jesus by putting out into the deep waters. This is not likely, however, since Peter must respond to the request within the vulnerability of a public forum, not in the anonymity of private foolishness. That is, Jesus orders Peter to put out into the deep while multitudes, some of them fishermen, line the shore. The social and cultural pressure on Peter to deny the request is enormous.

Will Peter risk obeying? Will he do something so seemingly irrational and contrary to human wisdom in front of an audience? Certainly not without making absolutely sure Jesus is serious and aware of the odds against the success of the venture. By informing Jesus that he (Peter) and his partners have toiled all night without success, Peter subtly points out to Jesus the foolish nature of his suggestion. The implication is clear. "If we failed under the best of conditions, how can you expect to succeed under the worst of conditions?" But still, Peter says, "I will put down my nets if you command." *(Luke 5:4-5)*

Obviously, Jesus is not forcing himself upon Peter. On the contrary, Peter must choose to obey Jesus. He must let Jesus into his world. He must open his life to the transforming power of divine wisdom. Peter must let down the nets of his own free will. When he does, when he dares to drop the lines, the superiority of Jesus' wisdom over that of Israel's is made manifest in a way and with such convictional force that Peter's life is decisively changed. He leaves everything to follow Jesus as a disciple in community with the other disciples.

In the hearing dimension of faith, Peter had seen and experienced revelations of Jesus' caring power—like the miraculous healing of his mother-in-law and the casting out of demons, but these other experiential revelations are not decisive in that they do not affect the transformation of Peter's cultural mindset. This experience does. How is it different? It is different, because it speaks to

Peter at the core of his being, to his identity as a fisherman. Jesus acts in the arena of Peter's own professional (ego) competence. Peter knows that it is next to impossible to catch fish in the middle of the day in deep water. To do so, one must have some special source of knowledge and power. Thus, by catching fish with Peter in the midday sun, Jesus is demonstrating in a way and in a place where Peter can see and experience it personally and convictionally that Jesus has access to extraordinary knowledge. Jesus' way of being in the world is more effective for meeting human need than the accumulated wisdom of first century Israel. Jesus not only heals the sick, he catches fish like no fisherman Israel has ever produced.

Clearly, Peter is overwhelmed by the revelation. He falls on his knees before Jesus in prayerful supplication acknowledging his own sinfulness. He pleads, "Depart from me; for I am a sinful man, O Lord." *(Luke 5:8)* Peter knows that as a sin-filled human being, he cannot exist in the presence of the Holy One - he knows that such an encounter would destroy him. Thus, in recognizing the Holiness of Jesus' action, Peter bids Jesus to depart. In turn, Jesus, recognizing the faith-filled nature of Peter's rejection, comforts Peter, "Fear not; from henceforth you shall catch people." *(Luke 5:10)*

As a function of Jesus having already chosen him, Peter becomes a disciple of Jesus Christ committing himself to follow Jesus. Disciples of Jesus Christ learn on their feet while walking with Jesus in Christian community. Jesus believes in on-the-job training. By definition, a disciple is an apprentice, a pupil attached to a teacher and dedicated to the instruction and commitments of that teacher.[4]

Peter the disciple continues to learn by watching and listening. The difference is that he now lives with Jesus and the other disciples in community. He watches Jesus heal the sick and cast out demons; listens to Jesus' teaching concerning the Kingdom of God's love. He learns in large groups like when Jesus preaches the

---

4 Paul J Achtemeier. *Harper's Bible Dictionary*. San Francisco: Harper & Row, 1985. 222.

Elizabeth A. Frykberg

Sermon on the Mount and in the small group of the twelve chosen disciples. Theological reflection also takes place in this small group of twelve like when Jesus explains the Parable of the Sower to the disciples in private. Peter is, in essence, enrolled in the School of Jesus Christ.

Deb and Annette's Stories of Engagement in the Following in Community Dimension

Let me share two very different stories of how Jesus draws people into Christian community in the 21st century.

The first time Deb Concklin came to our church, she wasn't looking for a church, she came looking for blankets to send to refugees in Ethiopia. Driving down El Camino from San Francisco, she stopped any place and every place (like schools, hospitals, and churches) where she hoped she would find people willing to help. When she got to our church she was tired and a little frustrated with the lack of response from other church communities. Because our buildings look pretty traditional and conservative, and are located in a straight-laced, upwardly mobile affluent community, she wasn't expecting a lot when she walked in asking for help for her refugees.

Office staff directed Deb to our youth pastor at the time. The pastor listened and told Deb that if she would come to church on Sunday, an appeal for blankets would be made in both services. Deb came to worship that Sunday and heard the announcement. Later in the week, when she came back to our church to collect any blankets that might have been dropped off, Deb was astounded. There were stacks of high quality new and used blankets all over Fellowship Hall. Encountering the heart of Jesus in the generosity of the community, Deb, who as I said wasn't looking for a church, found true Christian community. She has been worshiping with us ever since helping many of us to encounter the heart of Jesus.

A second story: Our chancel choir director Cort Bender has worked in various churches across the Greater Bay Area from Lafayette-Orinda to Menlo Park, all the while living in San Carlos.

Even though he led worship each week in these churches, his wife, Annette, thought it best to give their children a consistent church experience in their own neighborhood. So, for 30 years, she had been a member of an Episcopal Church in San Carlos.

When Cort started working at our church, Annette agreed to support him in his new position at our church by attending his first choir rehearsal and singing with the choir on that one Sunday. Five years later, she is still coming every Thursday and every Sunday to sing. Why? She is still coming, because in interaction with the members of the choir, she encountered the heart of Jesus. Our choir prays, cares, and loves one another. It is irresistible community.

What keeps you coming back to your church community? How have you encountered the heart of Jesus there? In Christian friendships, fellowship groups, small groups, working on a mission team, perhaps in being cared for in a time of crisis?

Interlude for Theology: *Koinonia*

Human community, as originally created by God, is community in the Trinitarian image of God. This community reflects the mystery of the Trinity, wherein identity and mutuality are simultaneously affirmed: the one God (identity) in the three persons (mutuality). The Greek word for this kind of human community is *koinonia*. In *koinonia*, the Holy Spirit works to transform our interaction with each other while creating in us corporate awareness of Jesus Christ's presence. In *koinonia*, the spiritual presence of Christ, God's Holy Spirit, indwells and constitutes the relationships among the members of the community in such a way that defensive barriers dissipate and grace, the heart of Jesus, permeates. Scripture describes this kind of community in Acts 2.

> They devoted themselves to the apostle's teaching and fellowship, to the breaking of bread and the prayers. Awe came upon everyone, because many wonders and signs were being done by the apostles. All who believed were

together and had all things in common: they would sell their possessions and goods and distribute the proceeds to all, as any had need. Day by day, as they spent much time together in the temple, they broke bread at home and ate their food with glad and generous hearts, praising God and having the goodwill of all the people. And day by day the Lord added to their number those who were being saved.

Acts 2:42-47

As such, *koinonia* is shared human participation in the very life of God. It is living with others in union with Christ, experiencing Jesus together. It is saying with the Apostle Paul, "… it is no longer I who live, but Christ who lives in me; …the life I now live in the flesh I live by faith in the Son of God, who loved me and gave himself for me." *(Gal. 2:20)*

Characteristics of People Growing in Community *(Koinonia)*

The focus of the Following in Community Dimension is relationship with the Spirit of Jesus Christ in the midst of Christian community; people experiencing God together. Relationships are highly valued. In community created by the Spirit of Jesus Christ, there is a sense of something greater, a holy something other in the praying, singing, and sharing together. That something other is God. This kind of community is *koinonia*, the fellowship creating reality of Jesus Christ. Comparing the Spirit to wind Jesus said, "The wind blows where it chooses, and you hear the sound of it, but you do not know where it comes from or where it goes." *(John 3:8)* One cannot control the experience of the Spirit of Jesus Christ in community. All one can do is be open, expectant, and responsive to it.

Valuing the experience of God in community, the conveying vehicle of the community may become idolized and overly valued in and of itself by those in the community. Being a Christian can come to mean belonging to a particular church, where things are done in a particular way, led by particular people. There is a confusion of form and content. Another temptation is to seek to control and replicate experiences of the Spirit of Jesus Christ in the midst of community. One summer the church's college group had a magnificent experience of God. When students returned to school for the fall semester, some took the materials used in the summer studies back to college with them. They were surprised and confused when the Christian groups at school didn't respond to the material with the same enthusiasm. Something, Someone is missing. Again there is the confusion of form and content. These stumbling blocks mistakenly exalt something or someone in the community as the source of the Spirit. These attitudes make an idol of community.

As opposed to these idolizing mindsets, the attitude that promotes spiritual growth is one wherein a person (having experienced Jesus Christ in community) wants the Spirit of Jesus Christ to be with them in other aspects of their life. Thus, in response to experience of God in community, longing for God grows. This is desire for the community with God that God wills to have with us.

Characteristics of Persons in the Community Dimension

Dimension:	Persona	Focus	I Statements	Obstruction	Moving On
Following Jesus Christ in community	Relational: "I am my relationships."	Living in relationship with Jesus Christ in community with others	I experience the Spirit of Christ in community (koinonia)	I am a Christian because I attend my particular church, where we have a particular leader and style	Wanting to be in a relationship with Jesus Christ in every aspect of life..

Maturing in the Following in Community Dimension

Let us look more closely at how a person grows in the Following in Community Dimension from the perspective of each of the other dimensions.

1. People will at first observe and engage the Christian community from outside the community per se. They may come to worship, attend fellowship events, Bible studies, even go on retreats, but they will do so more as observers than full participants. In many churches the event that signals movement out of this observational way of being in community is church membership. So individuals need first to hear the community calling them to follow Jesus Christ as part of a community. This means hospitality, being so welcoming that the outsider wants to become an insider. The community extends an invitation (preferably verbal face-to-face) that the outsider hears.

2. People grow in community as they become involved and invested. Following in community entails commitment, the taking on of responsibility as a participant. It means moving from casual observation to invested involvement with other believers in the presence of the Spirit of Jesus Christ. It means membership in the community, however that may be defined. Participation in a small face-to-face group within a larger community is ideal.

3. Within the community there will need to be those who are gifted to nurture and direct those whose faith is new and maturing. Willingness to be directed by a spiritual director is a third important aspect of growing in community. It involves openness to some kind of shepherding relationship where those new to the faith community are paired with compatible seasoned members. The relationship needs to be spiritual not just social.

4. A fourth aspect of following Jesus Christ in community is becoming vulnerable in community. It is removing the mask and allowing God and others to see one's true self with all of its flaws and blemishes. The first step in this is corporate (but not impersonal) confession. A trusted spiritual director may here help a person become unburdened from past and present failures. The experience of revealing one's true self is a humbling but necessary step in preparing a person to more fully receive God's love and acceptance.

5. A fifth aspect is experiencing grace, love and forgiveness in the midst of a Christian community. Having become vulnerable in community, the community now surrounds the person with love and acceptance in Jesus Christ. With this experience, people become open to the love of God in new ways.

6. A sixth aspect is the experience of being equipped and commissioned by a Christian community for service within that community. "To each is given a manifestation of the Spirit for the common good." *(1 Corinthians 12:7)* Every member of the faith community has one or more spiritual gifts to share. The gifts are listed in various places in Scripture. Romans 12:3-8 mentions the spiritual gifts of prophecy, service, teaching, exhortation, giving, leadership, and mercy. 1 Corinthians 12:7-11, 27-30 adds to these: word of wisdom, word of knowledge, faith, gifts of healing, miracles, discernment, tongues, the interpretation of tongues, apostle, helps, and administration. Ephesians 4:11,12 adds evangelist and pastor-teacher. Spiritual gifts listed in other verses include: celibacy *(1 Corinthians 7:7)*; hospitality *(1 Peter 4:9,10)*; voluntary poverty *(1 Corinthians 13:3)*; martyrdom *(1 Corinthians 13:3)*; the interpretation of dreams *(Joseph and Daniel)*; physical strength *(Judges 14:5,6)*; craftsmanship *(Exodus 35:30-36:2)*; and music *(1 Chronicles 16:41,42; 2 Chronicles 5:12,13; 34:12)*. In the midst of Christian community each brings something of value with them to share.

7. A seventh aspect of growing in community is participation with other believers in a mission experience in the world. These are important experiences of growing in Jesus Christ in community. On mission trips participants experience Christian community at greater depths and come to greater understandings of who Jesus really is. It was on a mission trip that Peter the disciple discovered for the first time that Jesus was the Messiah.

CHAPTER SIX
(PART TWO)
Community Dimension: Ministry Implications
Role Structure as *Koinonia* Stumbling Block

"Role" is another potential stumbling block for faith communities. Let me explain. A "role" is a pattern of behavior associated with a particular social position. Most roles specify the rights and duties belonging to that social position. They tell the individual what she ought to do in her role as mother, or CEO, to whom one has obligations, and upon whom one has a rightful claim. Roles are usually complementary, or reciprocal. The role of teacher is complemented by the role of the student, the role of employer by that of employee, the role of parent by that of the child. The behavior specified for each role helps to make social interaction an orderly and reliable process. Roles help us to work together toward common goals in an efficient and functional manner. They bring satisfaction and help us to survive.

But there is a tragic flaw inherent in all role-structured interaction. The tragedy is that as long as we are in our roles, we cannot be present for each other in any way that is more profound than our roles will allow. This means that we cannot engage the loss, or the emptiness of another, with our own sense of loss and emptiness.

We cannot enter with love into the suffering of someone else unless we break role. But if we break from role, the community and its goals are frustrated. So the community seeks to drive us back into our role. If we don't hear and heed the community's response, we may suffer rejection and persecution.

That is what happened to Jesus. As the Messiah, Jesus was expected to fulfill a particular role. He was to be the great military leader who would lead the people of Israel out from under Roman occupation and oppression. But Jesus broke with that role. In communion with God, Jesus gave his disciples a new law that violated first century role expectations:

> "You have heard that it was said, 'An eye for an eye and a tooth for a tooth.' But I (Jesus) say to you, 'Do not resist an evildoer. But if anyone strikes you on the right cheek, turn the other cheek also . . . and if anyone forces you to go one mile, go also the second mile . . .' You have heard it was said, 'You shall love your neighbor and hate your enemies.' But I say to you, 'Love your enemies and pray for those who persecute you.'"
>
> *Matthew 5:38-44*

The chorus of the community in response to Jesus' violation of role expectation was "Crucify Him!! Crucify Him!"

The power of the Spirit freeing persons within community to break role is well illustrated by a unique high school football game that took place between Gainesville State School and Grapevine Faith in Grapevine, Texas in November of 2008.

According to Rick Reilly, an ESPN magazine columnist, when the Gainesville State Tornadoes reached the Grapevine Faith High School football field for their game on Friday night, a strange scene greeted them. Half of the Grapevine fans were cheering for them — the rival team — instead of their home team. A 40-yard spirit line for the Tornadoes team to run through had been formed on the field by Faith High School's fans complete with a banner painted with "Go Tornadoes" at the end of the line waiting for the team to crash through. Half of Faith's cheerleaders were in the spirit line and spent the evening rooting for the opposing team. "I never in my life thought I'd hear people cheering for us to hit their kids," recalls Isaiah, Gainesville's QB and middle linebacker, "I wouldn't expect another parent to tell somebody to hit their kids. But they wanted us to!"

Even though the Tornadoes ultimately lost that game, 33-14, the Gainesville players were so happy and excited that they gave their head coach Mark Williams a sideline squirt-bottle shower like he'd just won the State Championship. Perhaps the first time a Gatorade bath was bestowed on a coach with a 0-9 record.

Gainesville is a maximum-security correctional facility 75 miles north of Dallas. Every game they play is on the road and the players are escorted to and from the field by 12 uniformed guards with handcuffs in their back pockets.

Faith's head coach, Kris Hogan, decided that he wanted to do something kind for the Gainesville team during their football matchup. Faith had never played Gainesville before but Hogan knew the odds of Gainesville winning were slim. Faith had a 7-2 winning record and Gainesville had only scored two touchdowns all year. Faith had 70 kids on the team, 11 coaches, the latest football equipment and involved parents. Gainesville's team, on the other hand, had teenagers with convictions for drugs, assault and robbery—many of whom had been disowned by their families—all wearing seven-year-old shoulder pads and outdated helmets.

So, Hogan sent a message to the Faith community. He asked that half of his fans cheer for the Tornados, half of the cheerleaders root for them, and everyone know the rival team members by name. "Here's the message I want you to send": Hogan wrote. "You are just as valuable as any other person on planet Earth."

Not everyone was initially excited about the idea. One Faith player walked into Hogan's office and asked, "Coach, why are we doing this?"

Hogan replied, "Imagine if you didn't have a home life. Imagine if everybody had pretty much given up on you. Now imagine what it would mean for hundreds of people to suddenly believe in you."

It was a strange experience for the boys from Gainesville.

"I thought maybe they were confused," Alex, a Gainesville lineman, recalled. "They started yelling 'DEE-fense!' when their team had the ball." I said, "What? Why they cheerin' for us?"

"We can tell people are a little afraid of us when we come to the games," added Gerald, another Gainesville player. "You can see it in their eyes. They're lookin' at us like we're criminals. But these people, they were yellin' for us! By our names!"

That night, the Gainesville team played the best game of their lives, scoring two touchdowns. After the game, both teams gathered in the middle of the field to pray and that's when Isaiah, Gainesville's QB, surprised everybody by asking to lead.

"We had no idea what the kid was going to say," remembers Coach Hogan.

Isaiah prayed, "Lord, I don't know how this happened, so I don't know how to say thank you, but I never would've known there was so many people in the world that cared about us."

As the Tornadoes walked back to their bus, they were each handed a bag for the ride home—a burger, some fries, a soda, some candy, a Bible, and an encouraging letter from a Grapevine Faith player.

The Gainesville coach found Hogan after the game, grabbed him by the shoulders and said, "You'll never know what your people did for these kids tonight. You'll never, ever know."

In the wake of the game, Gainesville is different.

"It's like people's hearts really have changed," Superintendent Gwan Hawthorne said.

"The boys, a lot of them, just hadn't had anybody care about them," said Styles, who has taught at the school for five years, "When they saw that, they brought that back. And then their peers heard that these people cared about them – really cared about them, not just throwing money at them or throwing a bag of stuff at them."

Both teams have since garnered national attention.

The story even caught the attention of NFL Commissioner, Roger Goodell, who was so moved that he invited Hogan and his wife to be his guests at Super Bowl XLIII.

"They showed that football is more than a game, that there are important things other than the outcome or the score," Coach Dale Meinecke of Garce Prep, another school in the area, said. "It's about people, it's about relationships."

The annual game between Grapevine Faith and Gainesville State is now known as the One Heart Bowl. Every year, fans are split between the two teams, and, as part of admission to the football game, they are encouraged to bring ankle socks and gloves for Gainesville students, who are in need of basic items.

Following the lead of Coach Hogan, the Christian community at Faith High School exercised Spirit-given freedom to break role. The point is not to abandon our roles and the role structure of society. That would be foolish. There is nothing inherently wrong with structuring social interaction. What the spiritual presence of Christ does in the midst of human community is free the individual to risk stepping out of role when prompted by the Spirit to do so. That is what Faith's coach, Kris Hogan, did. As a result, a new and larger Christian community was formed that included the kids and staff at Gainesville High School.

What does the freedom to step out of role look like in other situations? Different in different situations. For a CEO, it may mean taking a pay cut in order to give raises to employees. For a wife, it may mean forgiving her husband's adultery. For a child it may mean leading one's parents into a life of faith and compassion. For a woman of wealth and social position, it may mean reaching out in love to the downtrodden and homeless. For a homeless man, it may mean turning in a lost wallet to the police expecting nothing in return. The list is only suggestive. All of the above have happened. *Koinonia* is not found in imitating the spiritual lives of others. *Koinonia* is found and experienced as one relates to God in the midst of human community. For only as one experiences the love of God in the depth of one's being, is a person free to love and live sacrificially after the pattern of Christ, free to break role to the glory of God.[5]

---

5 Adapted from: Rick Reilly: Gainesville State high school football gets the best... http://sports.espn.go.com/espn/rickreilly/news/story?id=3789373.

CHAPTER SEVEN
(PART ONE)

Desiring Dimension:
Desiring (Willing) to Do the Will of God

> Teacher, which commandment in the law is the greatest?" He said to him, "'You shall love the Lord your God with all your heart, and with all your soul, and with all your mind.' This is the greatest and first commandment. And a second is like it: 'You shall love your neighbor as yourself.' On these two commandments hang all the law and the prophets.
> *Matthew 22:36-40*

Another dimension of the Jesus Fractal is the desire to do the will of God. It is the "doing" dimension, where gifts and talents are used. Reward comes in the form of fulfillment and satisfaction. Here, people seek to fit their lives more fully into God's design for human living. Understanding of God's will is sought and acted upon. Accordingly, the issue of vocational choice is often evaluated or reevaluated in this dimension. One may be called vocationally to give oneself to Jesus Christ as a doctor, lawyer, minister, waitress, or ditch digger. The important thing is choosing to live in accord with God's will, as Jesus did. It involves desire to do what God wants done. This dimension is engaged again and again as one "works out one's salvation in fear and trembling." *(Philippians 2:12)*

Understanding the theological relationship between grace

and works becomes critical in this dimension of the faith fractal. The two are contrasted throughout Scripture, in the Psalms, the Prophets, even in the Pauline Epistles. On the one hand, Scripture says it makes a difference whether we are good or evil, loving or selfish, honest or dishonest. It makes a real difference, an ultimate difference in the sight of God. On the other hand, Scripture also says it makes no difference. No life can ultimately justify itself in the sight of God. The evil and the good, both the more and the less good are equally in need of the mercy of God.

The Apostle Paul sums up the grace emphasis of Gospel proclamation with the words, "... all have sinned and fall short of the glory of God, and all are justified freely by his grace through the redemption that came by Christ Jesus." *(Romans 3:23-4)* But Paul also talks about works righteousness saying: "We must all appear before the judgment seat of Christ, so that each of us may receive what is due us for the things done while in the body, whether good or bad." *(1Corinthians 5:10)*

Similarly, in the Desiring to Do the Will of God Dimension of the Jesus Fractal, grace and work are both involved. In community relationship with Jesus Christ there is created within us a desire to do God's will. If that is not happening in our lives, then we may have appropriated the counterfeit grace that Dietrich Bonhoeffer calls "cheap grace."

"Cheap grace," he says, "is the grace we bestow on ourselves ... the preaching of forgiveness without requiring repentance, baptism without church discipline, Communion without confession ... Cheap grace is grace without discipleship, grace without the cross, grace without Jesus Christ, living and incarnate."

"Cheap grace ... is grace represented as the Church's inexhaustible treasury, from which she showers blessings with generous hands, without asking questions or fixing limits...."

In contrast, what Jesus proclaims and bestows, is a costly grace—grace that willingly dies on the cross for the redemption of the ungodly. Bonhoeffer says:

> Costly grace is the treasure hidden in the field; for the sake of it a person will gladly go and sell all that they have . . . Costly grace is the gospel which must be *sought* again and again, the gift which must be *asked for*, the door at which a person must *knock*.
>
> Such grace is *costly* because it calls us to follow, and it is *grace* because it calls us to follow *Jesus Christ*. It is costly because it costs us our lives, and it is grace because it gives us the only true life. It is costly because it condemns sin, and grace because it justifies the sinner. Above all, it is costly because it cost God the life of his Son: 'you were bought at a price,' and what has cost God much cannot be cheap for us.
>
> Grace is costly because it compels us to submit to the yoke of Christ and follow him; it is grace because Jesus says: 'my yoke is easy and my burden light.'[6]

In the desiring dimension there is both the desire and heartfelt trying to fulfill the Law of Christ, "Love the Lord your God with all of your heart, soul, mind and strength and your neighbor as yourself." Still in the end, the futility of human willing is what is discovered. The life of Peter sheds light on both sides of the theological issues.

Peter Desiring to Do the Will of God

Question: How did Peter first experience himself wanting to do God's will like Jesus?

Service in Discipleship

Peter is sent on a mission. Luke describes the commissioning: "Jesus called the Twelve and gave them authority and power to deal with demons and to cure diseases. He commissioned them to preach the Good News of God's kingdom and to heal the sick. He said, 'Don't load yourselves up with excess baggage. Keep it

---

6 Dietrich Bonhoeffer, *The Cost of Discipleship*. New York: Macmillan, 1959. 35-37.

simple. Get a modest place and be content to stay there until you leave. If you're not welcomed by a town, just leave. Don't make a scene. Shrug your shoulders and move on.'" *(Luke 9:1-5 The Message)*

Commissioned in this way, Peter traveled with the other disciples from town to town telling the Good News of God, curing people, and casting out demons in the name of Jesus. In other words, Peter was instructed and empowered by Jesus to "put on Christ," to go forth into the world acting *"as if"* he were Jesus himself.

I remember hearing a story about an actor who was invited to play the part of Jesus Christ. It was the actor's custom to study the character he was to play in order to feel his way into the part. As the actor prepared and then "took on" the role of Jesus, his whole life changed. The more he indwelt the character of Jesus Christ, the more he found himself looking at life through different eyes, hearing with different ears, tasting life differently. He said afterward, "It made me a new person altogether."

As Peter "put on Christ," he discovered Jesus' identity. When the disciples return from their mission trip, Jesus asks them, "Who do the crowds say I am?"

They reply, "Some say John the Baptist; others say Elijah; and still others, that one of the prophets of long ago has come back to life."

"But what about you?" he asks. "Who do you say I am?"

Peter answers for them all, "The Christ of God." *(Matthew 16:14-16)*

This insight is later confirmed on the Mount of Transfiguration in Luke 9:28-36. Taking Peter, John, and James with him, Jesus climbs the mountain to pray. While in prayer, the appearance of Jesus' face changes and his clothes become blinding white. A radiant cloud then comes and covers the top of the mountain. While wrapped in the cloud, the disciples become deeply aware of God's presence. A voice comes out of the cloud declaring: "This is My Son, the Chosen! Listen to him." *(Luke 9:35)*

When the sound of the voice dies away, they see Jesus standing there alone. They are speechless. They finally get it! Jesus the Messiah is God's Son! It stuns them into awe-filled silence. Jesus is the Messiah. God is real, not a figment of their imagination or of their pretending, but really real. Jesus is God's Son. As a committed disciple, Peter's belief in Jesus is deepened and expanded. As his faith matures, Peter continues to seek understanding in committed community.

Willing to Love Sacrificially Like Jesus
With continued experience of Jesus in community, Peter wants to love God like Jesus. He wants to do God's will. This is evidenced in Peter's response to Jesus on the night Jesus was betrayed. When the hour came [for the Passover celebration], Jesus took his place at the table with his disciples. Following supper, Jesus indicates that Satan will test Peter. More than this, he predicts Peter's threefold denial of Jesus that very night and prays for Peter's faith to not fail. Peter responds to Jesus' prediction saying indignantly, "Lord I am ready to go to prison with you and to die with you." *(Mark 14:31)*

Expanding upon Peter's thought, we can almost hear him thinking, "Lord, don't you know how much I love you? I will not falter. I understand your teachings concerning persecution at the hands of the religious authorities. I understand sacrificial service. I am ready to go to prison with you and to die with you. I am not and never will be ashamed of you or your teachings. And I do not want you to be ashamed of me when you come into your glory." Peter's spirit is willing even if his ability to follow in Jesus' footsteps is imperfect.

Louise's Story of the Desiring Dimension

I grew up in the church. My father was a pastor, my mother was the director of Christian education and taught the children and youth of our church. I accepted Jesus Christ as my Lord and Savior when I was eight years old, so I have always considered myself to be a Christian.

There is a caveat. It is the saying "God has no

grandchildren... only children!" I believe that this is true. While it was a privilege to grow up in a loving, Christian home, it was not until I started exploring and nurturing my own faith, as an adult, that I experienced a deeper growth in my relationship with Jesus Christ and a yearning to follow God's will on a daily basis.

How has my faith in Jesus Christ changed the way I live? My experience is that in addition to Sunday worship and reading the Bible each day, the more I prioritize and actively participate in the life of my church family through Bible studies, small groups, church retreats, leadership and service opportunities, the more clearly I hear Jesus speak as he guides me. My faith is enriched and my relationship to Christ has more meaning. My experience is that my faith grows proportionately to my level of involvement. This is not a one-time event, but it is ongoing. God wants to walk with me through my daily life. God is in each breath of my day.

Twenty years ago, I began to learn more about the concept of spiritual gifts and began to teach "Gifts & Call," a class about God's gifts to us and God's calling on our lives. What I have learned personally, but also observed in many who take the class is that as we use our spiritual gifts and seek to do God's will daily, we experience an uplifting, transformative movement in our character and lives. Jesus' transforming power in our minds and hearts helps us learn to love others like Jesus loved...not as a response to how we may be treated by others, but as a response to God's gift of love.

By working to discern my spiritual gifts and God's call for me, my service in the church has gotten a sharper focus that has helped my faith to grow. Each day when I pray, I ask God for wisdom that I might discern and do God's will. This discipleship, my seeking to follow Christ every moment of the day and view the world through the eyes of Jesus has resulted in paradoxical freedom: 1) Freedom from fear. We are never alone. Jesus is there to help us. 2) Freedom from self. I realize I can't change my self or my attitudes through true grit; but Jesus' gift to me of the Holy Spirit can change me. 3) Freedom from other people and what they think. My new internal question is "What would God (Jesus) have me say or do? What is God's will in this situation?"

Trying to actively follow Jesus Christ, helps me to become the person God created me to be.... and for me has brought a gratifying sense of joy and fulfillment. As the psalmist writes in Psalm 143:10:

Teach me to do your will,
For you are my God;
Your Spirit is good. Lead me...

It is a daily choice with untold benefits! The paradox, I have found, is that when I reach out to help others, I also benefit as I grow in faith and closeness to Jesus. It's a win/win situation that never ends.

Interlude for Theology

In order to understand what is involved as one matures in this dimension, an understanding of the theological term *kenosis* will be helpful. In Philippians 2:7, Paul writes that Jesus "...emptied [ἐκένωσεν (kenosen)] himself." Theologians interpret this phrase in a number of ways. The one that reflects the core of the desiring dimension is that *kenosis* involves emptying the self of one's own will and becoming entirely receptive to God's divine will. So Jesus emptied himself of his will and became obedient to God's will unto death, even death on a cross.

We see Jesus do this in the Garden of Gethsemane, "Then he withdrew from them about a stone's throw, knelt down, and prayed, "Father, if you are willing, remove this cup from me; yet, not my will but yours be done." *(Luke 22;42)* But this wasn't a stress-free decision. Luke continues, "In his anguish he prayed more earnestly, and his sweat became like great drops of blood falling down on the ground." *(Luke 22:44)* What's going on? Modern medicine tells us that there is a rare but very real medical condition called hematidrosis, wherein a person's sweat will contain blood. The condition is associated with the sympathetic nervous system and has been successfully treated medically with beta-blockers (propranolol). Accordingly, doctors believe the condition is brought on by high stress and anxiety.

So, what's going on? Jesus, knowing that he would be crucified, is stressed and sweats blood. Thus, even for Jesus, submitting to the will of God the Father is not always an easy thing to do. In the story below, a woman seeking to do the will of God is caught in the anguish.

Nancy's Story of Struggling to Know and Do God's Will

In my own life I experienced failure in a broken marriage. Divorce was not something I ever thought could happen to me. I worked hard on the issues in my marriage, going to counseling, trying to make changes, but nothing seemed to help.

Life at home had become intolerable. There was constant fighting and uncomfortable silences. I often found myself filled with anxiety; unable to relate to the man I married. The unhealthy atmosphere left me deeply concerned for our sons.

One early morning, I went into our living room and earnestly prayed for God to give me direction. "Lord, what should I do? I can't live like this any longer." In that moment of falling on my knees before God, I experienced God taking my wedding ring off and saying, "You don't have a marriage right now."

This was such a profound experience that I walked over to my friend's house in the dark and told her what had happened and she and her husband prayed for me, asking for guidance and courage to ask my husband to leave. I got home and my husband looked at me and said, "You have something to say to me." It was at that moment I asked him to move out.

The separation was very painful. I tried to keep things together for the boys but my heart was broken. My husband and I tried to talk about the future, but the battles seemed to get worse with no hope of reconciliation. I was filled with anxiety, struggling to know what God wanted me to do.

Divorce appeared as a huge mountain that loomed ahead—pulling apart from a marriage of 20 years and all we had joined together—selling our house, dividing property, wondering how I was going to support myself, and most importantly, how would this affect our sons? I scanned the pages of my Bible to know what Jesus thought about divorce. I was afraid God would stop loving me if I divorced. Divorce was letting God down.

But I finally reached the point where I could see no alternative but ending the marriage. The issues of behavior that were unchanging made divorce the only road to move down. Confronting my husband with this decision only escalated the tension. One day there was an exchange between us, words spoken that left me feeling like a knife had been stabbed into my heart. I was at the end of my road. The pain was beyond words. I cried and cried, then cried some more.

Sometimes when even our best effort fails us, all that is left is hope—the hope and prayer that the Gospel is true, that Jesus died on the cross "for us."

Characteristics of Persons Growing in Desire to Do the Will of God

In this desiring dimension, believers change their behavior. Lives become more and more conformed to the image of God in which humanity was originally created—Jesus being the original image. Sanctification is fitting our lives more fully into God's design for human living. The question becomes: Now what? What do I do? How do I live? How can I live a life centered upon the values of compassion and peace, overflowing mercy and grace, service and self-giving love? What do I do now that I believe and am a member of the Christian community? These are questions every believer asks, not once but throughout the life of faith. This is the desiring dimension of faith: desiring to live like Jesus Christ, wanting and acting in accord with the Good News one believes and follows in community.

People living primarily out of this desiring dimension are focused on doing the will of God. They feel best and most purposeful when "doing" in the name of Jesus Christ. They are achievers, who may confuse *doing* with *their being persons of value*. The danger is getting stuck. People who follow all of the rules religiously may conclude that, as a result of their effort, God is pleased with them. In their minds, their behavior has earned them God's love. To move beyond this dimension of faith, a person must experience a loss of certainty, a crisis or failure, confrontation with the limits of their human condition.

Characteristics of Persons in the Desiring Dimension

Dimension:	Persona	Focus	I Statements	Obstruction	Moving On
Desiring to do the will of God—to be like Jesus Christ.	Achiever: "I do, therefore I have value."	Doing the will of God	I am a productive and purposeful disciple "doing" in the name of Jesus Christ	God is pleased with all I do for God, because I follow all the rules.	Loss of certainty, experience of crisis, failure or limitation.

Maturing in the Desiring Dimension

There are some very concrete ways a person can grow seven dimensionally in willingness and desire to do God's will:

1. A first aspect of growing in the desiring dimension is cultivating and nurturing the longing to hear more, the wanting to listen attentively to the Word of God. This involves focus, setting aside of time, prioritizing, creating space for the Word in one's life.

2. The desire for interaction with others who are followers of Jesus Christ is another part of the willing dimension. As is the desire to be led in the life of faith by a mature Christian, openness to some kind of spiritual shepherding relationship. Spiritual direction here will center on the person and work of Jesus Christ and the expectations of the community for the life of discipleship.

3. A third aspect is actual willingness to do the will of God. Willingness will be evidenced as one seeks to live out one's deepening commitment to Jesus Christ in moral and ethical action, in the practice of spiritual disciplines, and in service within the church. "Doing" for God and the church become the focus of a person's life in faith.

4. A fourth aspect is confrontation with failure or limitation in one's willingness to do the will of God, to live out one's own ethical or spiritual commitments to Jesus Christ. This confrontation brings renewed resolve to do God's will.

5. Failure in willingness to do the will of God creates the need and longing to experience grace and forgiveness for one's failings from both the community and God.

6. Another aspect of the willing dimension is asking for Holy Spirit empowerment to do God's will. Having faced

limitation or failure in wanting what God wants, help can be sought in two ways: First is by asking God to work in conforming our will to God's will. This is asking for God to change the desires of one's heart. This gets to the root cause of the failure, seeking change from the inside out, not simply in external behavior. Second is asking for empowerment to do what God would have done. This is asking for God's partnership in doing God's will, recognizing that without God's help, one can not do the good one wants to do.

7. Another aspect is freedom to communicate with God one's heartfelt struggle with willing to do God's will. This is Jesus in the Garden, "Father, if you are willing, remove this cup from me." *(Luke 22:42)*

CHAPTER EIGHT
(PART TWO)
Desiring Dimension:
Ministry Implications:
A Bible Study Method

One of the biggest barriers we encounter to hearing God speak afresh and anew through Holy Scripture is that many of the stories are so familiar that we stop listening. "I know that one." "Mom read this story to me when I was a kid." We have heard the stories, so we don't really pay attention. We already know what the text says. Sort of like the inattentive listening we do, when a friend or relative tells us the same story for the hundredth time. Our eyes glaze over. We are, so to speak, "fused" with the text and what we think it says. The task in Bible study is to get the text to speak afresh to us. God's Word needs to come alive in this new moment and give us fresh perspective on God's will.

Transformational Bible study begins with the understanding that when we approach a text, we already think we know what it says.[7] So we start in "felt fusion."

---

[7] Note: I developed this Bible study method that involves participants in the desiring dimension of faith in dialogue with the methods of Karl Barth and Walter Wink. For a more detailed description see: Elizabeth Frykberg, "Transforming Bible Study Transformed" Religious Education: The Official Journal of the Religious Education Association, Volume 88, Issue 2, 1993.

I. Human Initiative Dominant
(Divine Initiative Implicit)

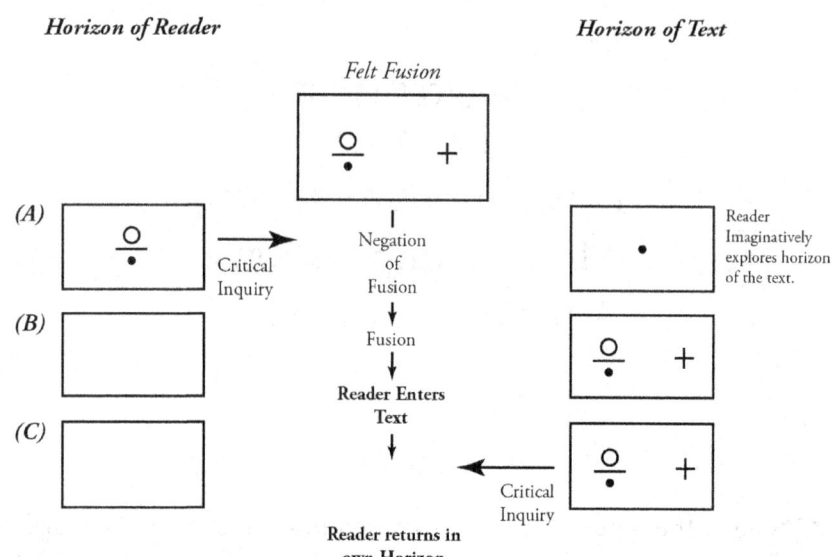

II. Human Initiative Dominant
(Divine Initiative Implicit)

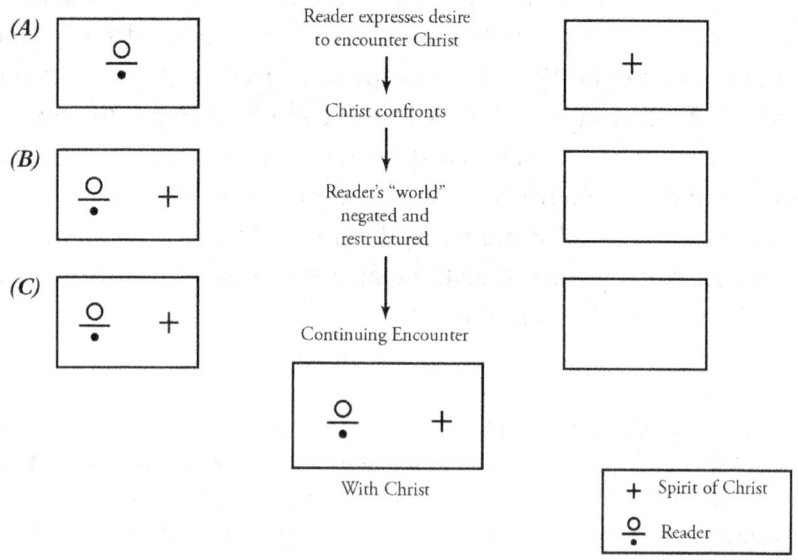

I (A) Breaking the fusion is the first step in this Bible Study method. The task is to see the text as a document, which arose out of a concrete historical situation. Readers study the text utilizing Bible study tools like commentaries, maps, and study Bibles to formulate as accurate a picture as possible of the situation, which occasioned the text and the meaning of those events for those who participated in them. As the critical tools are used the "world" of the text is removed from the reader's own "world." This breaks the fusion and creates the condition of "distance."

I(B) The second step is for the reader to enter and explore the text imaginatively. This effectively distances the reader from their own "world" as they seek to be "of" the text. By taking on imaginative roles in the world of Scripture, readers are freer to (1) recognize the presence of Jesus Christ and (2) view themselves and their "lived world" more objectively. These imaginative journeys into the text's horizon may take place through the educative power of drama, role-play, story, clowning, or an adaptation of Ignatius' exercises.

I(C) The third step is for the reader to view their "world" from the "world" of the text. Having become contemporaneous with the text and Jesus Christ, readers turn to view their "present" (which is now distant) from the "past." Here the reader's lived "world" becomes the object of inquiry. In other words, while being imaginatively with Jesus Christ in the "world" of the text, the reader engages in an act of critical self-reflection. From the distant "world" of the text, readers will be in a position to see more clearly the true nature of their human condition. Since reader defenses remain somewhat in place, rapport with God and other members of the Bible study group needs to be established for the purpose of freeing persons to more honestly evaluate the horizon of their present. Within a context of relational rapport, conflict with the self can more readily be borne.

II(A) In this fourth step the reader returns to their "world." This movement is crucial. The question becomes: Will readers who have encountered Jesus Christ in the "world" of the text and who there faced some truth about themselves return to their own "world" with a desire for more encounter with Jesus in the present? Those who return without such a desire will return needing to repair and reconstruct their lived "world." This is because they now know, having reflected upon their "world" with Jesus Christ from the "world" of the text (even if they try to repress or ignore the knowledge) that they are living in an alienated condition. Those returning who are desiring further encounter indicate by that desire their readiness to recognize the Spirit of Christ who has always been present patiently desiring encounter with them. Thus, following Bible study proper, readers need to be given the opportunity to prayerfully express any emerging desire concerning continuing encounter with Jesus Christ.

II(B) The fifth step is waiting. It is waiting in hope and faith for the Spirit of Christ to become present to the reader in the reader's lived "world." It is waiting for God to actually show up in the life of the reader.

II(C) In the sixth step, the Spirit of Christ acts. The old "fusion" with the text is gone (negated), behold the new has come, because Christ is now encountered in the text, such that the text speaks anew to the reader. This leads to Continuing Encounter with Christ in the text.

That this method can work to help even a child engage the desiring dimension of faith is illustrated by the story of Becky, a battered child. In the third grade Becky wanted to play the role of Mary in the Christmas pageant. She wanted more than anything to be the mother of the baby that was "good." In essence, she wanted to say by means of the play, "See Mom, I am good. I can make a 'good' baby."

Sensing the urgency in Becky's desire, the nuns let her play the part of Mary. It was a powerful experience for Becky as she saw her own mother from Mary's eyes. Through the experience of the Bible study that accompanied the pageant, and the role-playing that gave Becky the paradoxical experience of being the "bad" baby who is allowed to give birth to the "good" baby, Becky heard the Good News that the "good" baby was for her. She desired in her heart to be with the "good" baby. Seventeen years later, as a new mother, Becky continues to experience herself as chosen by God to bear the "good" baby; "A baby," she says, "no mother would want to hurt." Thus the sins of Becky's mother are not being visited upon the children of the third and fourth generation. That is redemption, the transformational work of the Spirit of Christ working in the life of a child in the desiring dimension of the Jesus Fractal.

CHAPTER NINE
(PART ONE)

Humbled Dimension:
Humbled in Faith

> Let the same mind be in you that was in Christ Jesus,
> who, though he was in the form of God,
> did not regard equality with God
> as something to be exploited,
> but emptied himself,
> taking the form of a slave,
> being born in human likeness.
> And being found in human form,
> he humbled himself
> and became obedient to the point of death—
> even death on a cross.
>
> *Philippians 2:5-8*

Humbled in faith is a fourth dimension of the Jesus faith fractal. It is the humility that comes as one faces one's human condition—one's inability to do the will of God, the very thing one wants, wills, desires to do. It is recognizing that Jesus died on the cross "for me." The desiring dimension leads again to this humbled in faith dimension, to humble confrontation with human limitation. The desiring dimension involves desire and willingness to do God's will, to live and love like Jesus Christ, but not the ability. This inability is the central dynamic of the humbled dimension.

Being humbled in faith is, thus, not humiliation. To the contrary, it is facing and accepting of truth regarding one's human condition. The humble are not self-deprecating. To the contrary, what the humble gain in the process of facing their true self are balanced, accurate views of themselves, and an understanding of both their personal strengths and weaknesses. Accordingly, the humble are teachable, receptive to learning, ready to serve, and self-forgetful. They are selfless in the sense of being self-giving and self-sacrificing, mindful of the interests and concerns of those around them, ready to put aside personal preferences to serve others. The "being humbled in faith" of the Humbled Dimension prepares a person to receive God's grace in the Graced by God's Love Dimension. This is not an experience in a moment in time. It is a transformational moment, where those who have been humbled in faith know they cannot do what they want to do, because they are not God.

From the outset, it needs to be understood that the humility that comes from being humbled in faith isn't self-deprecation, evaluating oneself too negatively. "Nobody loves me, everybody hates me, think I'll go eat worms," isn't humility, because it isn't the truth. Similarly, dishonest self-effacement, saying things like, "Oh I just threw this together," when in fact you have been working on the presentation for months, is also not humility. It is a lie. Both of these practices (self-deprecation and dishonest self-effacement) keep a person defensively focused on the self. The self remains hidden and protected behind the protective mask of a false persona.

So how then do people become humble? It is not something anyone does. It is better understood as the healing gift of God that is bestowed. This gift is neither sought after, nor something consciously desired. That is why this dimension is written in the passive voice "be humbled in faith." Pride, self-deprecation and dishonest self-effacement all hide the same pain. At their core, all three of these relational postures are insecure. All three are concerned that love and acceptance from others will be withdrawn

The Jesus Fractal

if one becomes truly known. That is why God is the answer to all three conditions. God knows us to our depths, and still loves us to the heights. That kind of love humbles us.

A parable Jesus didn't tell, but one that captures the spirit of humility as opposed to prideful comparison goes like this:

> One day the father of a wealthy suburban family takes his son on a trip to the country to show the boy how poor people live. They spend a couple of days and nights together on the farm of what would be considered a poor family.
>
> On their return trip, the father asks his son, "Well, what did you think?"
>
> "It was great, Dad."
>
> "Did you see how poor people live?" the father asks.
>
> "Oh yeah," says the son.
>
> "So, tell me, what did you learn from our trip?" asks the father.
>
> The son replies: "I learned that we have one dog, and they have four. We have a pool that reaches to the middle of our garden, and they have a creek that has no end. We have imported lanterns in our garden, and they have the stars at night. Our patio reaches to the front yard, and they have the whole horizon. We have a small piece of land to live on, and they have fields that go beyond our sight. We have servants who serve us, but they serve others. We buy our food, but they grow theirs. We have walls around our property to protect us; they have friends to protect them."
>
> *The boy's father is speechless.*
>
> *Then his son adds, "Thanks, Dad, for showing me how poor we are."*[8] (1)

The father is humbled!

---

8 Don C. Richter, *Mission Trips That Matter: Embodied Faith for the Sake of the World.* Upper Room Books, Nashville, TN., 2008, 28,30-32.

Elizabeth A. Frykberg

Peter Humbled in Faith:
"I Cannot Do the Good I Will to Do."

Question: When did Peter experience humbling failure as a disciple of Jesus Christ after publically giving expression to his desire to live and love like Jesus Christ?

Peter wasn't an "A+" student, even though he thought he was. For example, when walking on water, Simon Peter falters by taking his eyes off Jesus. On the Mount of Transfiguration instead of fully engaging the spiritual experience, Peter wants to start a building program. In the Garden of Gethsemane, Peter falls asleep and then lops off the ear of the high priest's servant much to Jesus' dismay.

Peter has a great time on a mission trip proclaiming the Kingdom of God, healing the sick and casting out demons. He is one of only three disciples separated out for special advanced work, experiences and teachings like those that took place on the Mount of Transfiguration. Peter is the first to identify Jesus as the Messiah of God, the Christ. Puffed up with self-importance, Peter arrogantly but mistakenly thinks he is fully capable of following in the footsteps of Jesus.

From the Mount of Transfiguration onward, Jesus moves steadily toward his Messianic destiny. He leaves Galilee traveling through Samaria, Judea, and Perea before arriving in the city of Jerusalem. Every day in Jerusalem, Jesus goes to the Temple where crowds gather to hear him proclaim the coming Kingdom of God. The Jewish people are enthralled; the religious authorities are angered. Eventually, the angered authorities devise a plot to put Jesus to death. Aware of the plot, Jesus, on the night of his betrayal, teaches his disciples one last time concerning the events that are about to take place:

> At the Passover celebration that night, Jesus took the bread, gave thanks to God, broke it, and gave it to his disciples saying, "This is my body, which is given for

you. Do this in memory of me." In the same way, he gave them the cup after supper, saying, "This cup is God's new covenant sealed with my blood, which is poured out for you."

Luke 22:19-20

Peter had studied hard and learned his lessons well. He understood the symbolism of the broken bread and the poured cup. He knew they stood for the body and blood of Jesus. But there was more to learn. Peter understands that Jesus is going to suffer and die, but he does not yet fully comprehend the meaning of the Messiah's death being "for him." He does not understand because he does not yet appreciate the seriousness and depth of his own sinful condition. Peter could not imagine himself abandoning Jesus.

Following supper, Jesus indicates that Peter will turn away. Peter protests that he will not turn or run away from Jesus. Despite the protest, Jesus persists, "Before the rooster crows tonight, you will deny me three times."

Jesus does not here pray to eliminate Peter's humiliation; rather Jesus predicts the humbling experience, while praying for Peter to experience God's grace. Peter must understand his human predicament before he can comprehend the redemptive significance of the Messiah's action of dying on the cross "for him."

Thus, in a very real but paradoxical sense, Peter's denial of Jesus is a step of faith. For in denying Jesus, Peter denies his over-identification with Christ. Peter is not the Messiah, but a sinner for whom Christ must die. His sin-filled human condition is revealed to Peter convictionally as he actualizes the prediction.

Following Jesus' arrest in the Garden of Gethsemane most of the disciples flee. Only Peter and one other disciple (probably John) follow their arrested leader. The soldiers take Jesus into the house of the High Priest.

> Joining a group of people sitting around a fire, Peter waits outside in the courtyard. Eventually, one of the servant

girls at the fire looks straight at Peter and says, "This man too was with Jesus!"

Peter in response denies the identification, "Woman, I don't even know him."

After a little while, a man notices Peter and says, "You are one of them, too."

Again Peter denies it, "Man, I am not!"

About an hour later another insists strongly, "There isn't any doubt that this man was with Jesus, because he also is a Galilean!"

Peter answers, "Man, I don't know what you are talking about!" At that very moment, a rooster crows, Jesus turns and looks straight at Peter. Peter remembering the prediction goes out from the courtyard and weeps bitterly.

(Luke 22:55-62 Good News Translation)

Peter weeps because in that moment he comes face-to-face with his personal involvement and responsibility for Jesus' death upon a cross. As he later says to the people of Jerusalem, "You, I, we killed Jesus by letting sinful people crucify him."

Acts 2:23b

The Humbled in Faith Dimension climaxes with the humbling experience of confronting one's sinful condition. Apart from the grace and empowerment of God, we cannot do the good we will to do. Here, a person's understanding of sin deepens from action to being. It is not that Peter committed the sin of denying Jesus three times; it is that Peter the sinner cannot do the good he wills to do, because he is in need of transformation at the core of his being, in need of Jesus dying "for him." This is the hard lesson Peter learns in failing Jesus. It is the hard lesson each of us must learn. It is the humbled dimension of faith.

A Cop Story: Humbled in Faith

The year was 1973. My young wife and I had begun worshipping weekly at First Presbyterian Church of Berkeley where the pastor, Earl Palmer, had become a great friend. I was committed—I wanted to make my life count for Christ the Lord. At that point in my life, I worked each day from 4:00 p.m. to midnight as a cop on the streets of Berkeley; I had secured my dream beat—beat nine. On beat nine, virtually all of the people lived under the poverty line, just trying to make it through life. So, I watched out for them. They had a lot people preying on them. I could help protect them from a ton of bad actors.

Pretty much every night I made at least one felony arrest, the beat being something of a magnet for criminals trying their hand at crime. One evening it was a car thief that I arrested off the street. I got him into the Hall of Justice and a holding cell, where I took off his handcuffs. I turned to leave to go write up my report of the crime for the district attorney to review in the morning. The suspect was young, still of high school age; the enormity of what he had done, the extensive, irrevocable trouble he had gotten into overwhelmed him and he began to cry.

With tears streaming down his face, he asked me, begged me if I would please pray with him.

I refused, and turned away.

I'm not proud to confess this to you; I'm not at all pleased to have this memory of this night in my police work. But it is true. Here I was trying to serve God by being a good cop, and a kid asks me to pray for him, and I turned my back. It brings tears to my eyes just to tell you now—this is a shameful thing.

Paul, the man who tells this story, is a man of prayer and compassion—a man who would not refuse to pray with anyone, anywhere, anytime. Yet, he did the very thing he would not do. Like Peter, Paul needs Jesus Christ to die "for him."

A Biblical Theological Interlude

God's remedy for our human situation is Jesus Christ acting in history, Jesus Christ descending the staircase from divine to human form, not climbing the ladder. Soren Kierkegaard in his parable, The King and the Maiden, reveals why God must be humbled in the incarnation:

> Suppose there was a king who loved a humble maiden. The king was like no other king. Every statesman trembled before his power. No one dared breathe a word against him, for he had the strength to crush all opponents.
>
> And yet this mighty king was melted by love for a humble maiden who lived in a poor village in his kingdom. How could he declare his love for her? In an odd sort of way, his kingliness tied his hands. If he brought her to the palace and crowned her head with jewels and clothed her body in royal robes, she would surely not resist—no one dared resist him. But would she love him?
>
> She would say she loved him, of course, but would she truly? Or would she live with him in fear, nursing a private grief for the life she had left behind? Would she be happy at his side? How could he know for sure? If he rode to her forest cottage in his royal carriage, with an armed escort waving bright banners, that too would overwhelm her. He did not want a cringing subject. He wanted a lover, an equal. He wanted her to forget that he was a king and she a humble maiden and to let shared love cross the gulf between them. For it is only in love that the unequal can be made equal.
>
> The king, convinced he could not elevate the maiden without crushing her freedom, resolved to descend to her. Clothed as a beggar, he approached her cottage with a worn cloak fluttering loose about him. This was not just a disguise—the king took on a totally new identity—he had renounced his throne to declare his love and to win hers.[9]

---

9 Soren Kierkegaard. *Philosophical Fragments.* Princeton University Press, Princeton New Jersey, 1962, 32-37.

The big theological word for what the king did is *kenosis*. In Chapter Seven (Part One of Desiring to Do the Will of God), we looked at *kenosis* as the 'emptying of self' of one's own will and becoming entirely receptive to God's will. This is what Peter could not do. This is the very thing Jesus Christ did do. He humbled himself becoming obedient unto death, even death on a cross (Philippians 2:5-11) (For a more in depth look at how Jesus Christ's self-emptying is another expression of the seven dimensional Jesus Fractal, see Appendix H.)

Characteristics of People Growing in Humility

The focus of this Humbled in Faith Dimension is mortification in the face of Jesus Christ's willingness to die "for" the person. It is confronting human limitation, one's essential need of God's grace. People become aware here that they are unable to do the things they will to do for God. The redemptive twist is that they also become aware of God's loving presence even as they experience themselves as incapable and unworthy.

The temptation of this dimension is denial, "It wasn't my fault"; and/or self-depreciation and shame, "I am unforgivable." People continue to grow in and through being humbled in faith when they risk opening themselves up to God's love and acceptance even in the midst of failure, when their dark side is exposed. It is in this sense that, like Peter's, their faith does not fail them.

Characteristics of Persons in the Humbled Dimension

Dimension:	Persona	Focus	I Statements	Obstruction	Moving On
Humbled in faith	Failure: "I am incapable and unworth."	Facing human limitations and need of redemption in Jesus Christ	I am a sinner, who is unable to do the will of God that I desire to do.	Denial: "It wasn't my fault"; and shame, "I am unforgivable."	Failure is exposed as one's dark side is revealed to God, self and other Christians

Growing in Humility

1. A hearing aspect of growing in the dimension of being humbled in faith is hearing the call to "repent and believe." This can happen in private conversation with a believer, but happens most often during proclamation of the Word addressed to a larger group, where one feels individually addressed. It is important that the context of the call is God's grace—Gospel, Law, Gospel.

2. Another aspect of growing in the Humbled Dimension is becoming vulnerable with others with whom one is in community. A trusted spiritual director, priest, or pastor may here help a person become unburdened from past and present failures. Small group ministry may also become important in this regard. In covenant groups, where trust is high, members can become real with one another and experience the response of love and acceptance from the community in the presence of God. This is relational confession. It is taking off the self-protective mask of posturing for the crowd. The experience of revealing one's actual identity is a humbling but necessary step in preparing a person to receive God's love and acceptance more fully.

3. A third aspect of being humbled in faith is confronting failure of will—of being unable to will what God wills. This is Peter being told that he would deny Jesus. Confronting failure of will may bring renewed resolve (desire) to seek to do God's will. This new resolve is seen in Peter saying to Jesus, "All of the others may fall away, but I won't."*(Mark 14:29)*

4. Failing to do God's will is the central aspect of being humbled in faith. This is the person not doing what they will to do—God's will. For Peter this was denying Jesus three times. This is not confronting failure in the eyes of others; it is confronting spiritual inability to do what one feels called to do for Jesus Christ.

5. This failure opens a person up to the grace of God in a new way. This is the truth producing error of Peter denying Jesus the third time and then making immediate eye contact with Jesus. In that moment Peter becomes open to understanding Jesus in love going to the cross "for him" not just for others. This is recognition of Jesus being on the cross "for you." Once a person understands Jesus' death on the cross as being "for" them, deeper understanding of sin as human condition (not mere behavior) results.

6. Recognition of human powerless over one's sinful condition opens one up to empowerment. Even Jesus as a human needs spiritual empowerment to go to the cross. Jesus is empowered to go to the cross by an angel in the Garden.

7. Acknowledging one's limitations while choosing to surrender to God's will is another aspect. This is Jesus in the Garden of Gethsemane confessing desire for this cup to pass from him, but still choosing to do God's will.

CHAPTER TEN
(PART TWO)
Humbled Dimension:
Ministry Implications
Transformational Process[10]

According to Arthur Koestler, humor depends upon bisociation, the bringing together of two otherwise unrelated frames of reference in a surprising way. Bisociation is also the mechanism responsible for creative insight. Because of the similarity in the dynamics of humor and insight, geniuses like Christopher Columbus, the Wright Brothers, or Steve Jobs are oftentimes laughed at before their ideas are accepted. "You're going to fall off the earth if you keep sailing west!" "You can't fly, you don't have wings!" "Who would want or use a personal computer?" In order to learn something new, something that transforms instead of just adding to our understanding, we need to experience insight and risk being laughed at. As we confront the reality of our human condition, new insight that transforms us must emerge where ego-willing solutions have been found wanting. There is a seven step

---

10 Although adapted from a five step to a seven step process, the understanding of creativity and transformation presented in this section is indebted to the mentoring of Dr. James E. Loder during both my Master of Theology and Ph.D. programs at Princeton Theological Seminary. The paradigm was learned under his tutelage and continues to undergird my understanding of how God seeks and works to encounter us in the world today. Loder, James E. The Transforming Moment. Colorado Springs: Helmers & Howard, 1989. Print.

patterned process by which this and all transformational discovery takes place. Each of the seven steps parallel a dimension of the faith fractal:

The seven steps are:

1. **Hearing and Experiencing:** Presentation and preparation for engaging a *conflict, problem or question* in a context of rapport stimulating curiosity
2. **Following:** *Scanning* for resolution using established (community) wisdom
3. **Desire:** Significant *investment of caring energy* while seeking solution
4. **Humbled:** *Pause* in the process of seeking resolution, due to failure of best efforts to find resolution (but out of consciousness is not, however, out of mind)
5. **Graced:** *Insight* felt with intuitive force
6. **Empowered:** *Tension Release* as energy is no longer needed in seeking resolution
7. **Sent into the World:** *Interpretation* of the insight into resolution of conflict to make public

This is the transformational learning process Jesus employed throughout his ministry as he explored the faith fractal with his disciples. The post-resurrection story of Jesus encountering the disciples on the Emmaus road will help us see the process:

> Now on that same day two of them were going to a village called Emmaus, about seven miles from Jerusalem, and talking with each other about all these things that had happened. While they were talking and discussing, Jesus himself came near and went with them, but their eyes were kept from recognizing him.
> And he said to them, "What are you discussing with each other while you walk along?"

They stood still, looking sad. Then one of them, whose name was Cleopas, answered him, "Are you the only stranger in Jerusalem who does not know the things that have taken place there in these days?"

He asked them, "What things?"

They replied, "The things about Jesus of Nazareth, who was a prophet mighty in deed and word before God and all the people, and how our chief priests and leaders handed him over to be condemned to death and crucified him. But we had hoped that he was the one to redeem Israel. Yes, and besides all this, it is now the third day since these things took place. Moreover, some women of our group astounded us. They were at the tomb early this morning, and when they did not find his body there, they came back and told us that they had indeed seen a vision of angels who said that he was alive. Some of those who were with us went to the tomb and found it just as the women had said; but they did not see him."

Then he said to them, "Oh, how foolish you are, and how slow of heart to believe all that the prophets have declared! Was it not necessary that the Messiah should suffer these things and then enter into his glory?" Then beginning with Moses and all the prophets, he interpreted to them the things about himself in all the scriptures.

As they came near the village to which they were going, he walked ahead as if he were going on. But they urged him strongly, saying, "Stay with us, because it is almost evening and the day is now nearly over." So he went in to stay with them.

When he was at the table with them, he took bread, blessed and broke it, and gave it to them. Then their eyes were opened, and they recognized him; and he vanished from their sight. They said to each other, "Were not our hearts burning within us while he was talking to us on the road, while he was opening the scriptures to us?"

That same hour they got up and returned to Jerusalem;

and they found the eleven and their companions gathered together. They were saying, "The Lord has risen indeed, and he has appeared to Simon!" Then they told what had happened on the road, and how he had been made known to them in the breaking of the bread.

Luke 24:13-35

With this story in mind, let us examine the process by which the eyes of the disciples were opened to recognize Jesus. It is the same process the Holy Spirit still uses to open our eyes to Jesus and spiritual truth.

1. Problem, Crisis, or Conflict is Encountered and Engaged (Disruption of the Lived World of the Knower):

All transformation begins with a problem, crisis, a disruption of the lived world of the knower. What exactly is the problem facing the disciples? Well it is huge. The nation of Israel was in danger—threatened from within by internal corruption from the priests; threatened from the outside by the oppressive rule of Roman occupation. It was expected that the Messiah would save Israel from this corruption. But Jesus died before saving them. So their world is falling apart, their world is being given over to corruption and oppression. Understandably, the disciples are depressed and confused.

2. Scanning for a Solution:

Looking to reconstruct their world following the devastating experience of Jesus' death upon the cross, the disciples take a walk to get some air, clear their heads, in search of a fresh perspective on things. This is the scanning step of the discovery process, where they search for a solution utilizing all of the tools and knowledge at their disposal.

3. Investment of Caring Energy:

It is in this context that the visible but unidentified stranger shows up. He helps the disciples search for prototypes in the history of

Israel. With Jesus' help, they look into Scripture for something that will put their world back together for them. Scripture by the way is a great resource in times of trouble or when confused—a great place to meet the Holy Spirit.

Later reflecting on this roadside study of the Torah, the disciples say, "Were not our hearts burning within us while he was talking to us on the road, while he was opening the Scriptures to us?" They were "getting hot." Like in the children's game, they are getting close to something hidden. They are beginning to get it. Everything is about to fall into place.

Desire: At this point, it looks like Jesus is going to continue down the road. The disciples must act to invite Jesus to come and stay the night with them.

Spiritual insight is not something that God forces upon us. It is something we must truly desire. Scripture says, "seek and you will find; knock and the door will be opened unto you." *(Matthew 7:7)* God isn't going to throw pearls before swine. God waits patiently to be invited into our lives—Divine accommodation. Desire is a critical spiritual attribute.

4. Pause:

The disciples reach Emmaus and stop. It is time for dinner. They have found lodging for the night.

5. Insight:

Jesus comes inside with the disciples, breaks the bread and hands it to them. The broken bread is a charged symbol. It symbolizes Jesus' brokenness taking into itself their brokenness held out in resurrected hands. In the breaking of the bread they see and experience who Jesus really is for the first time.

The disciples are humbled and convicted more deeply than they were before. Why do I say humbled and convicted? Because these two, who were close disciples of Jesus, didn't even know who he was. Blinded by enculturation into first century Israel, the world as it appeared to be, they didn't know what was going on. The pain of conviction and humiliation is driven deep within them. The conflict is worse than they thought. The conflict that needs resolution isn't just out there in Israel. It is in them.

What's the effect of this? The effect is that their eyes are opened! They finally recognize him! But as soon as they recognize him, he vanishes. Why? Why when their eyes are opened do they suddenly see less? For the same reason that Jesus tells Mary not to hold on to him when she recognizes him at the tomb. Jesus protects Mary and the disciples from the temptation of finding a place for Jesus to be in their world. Here is the figure-ground shift that shakes the world. Jesus has to vanish! As soon as we see who Jesus really is, Jesus has to disappear in order for us to be recreated in God's world. If we hold onto Jesus and continue to see Jesus, we will recreate him as an object in our world. But that would undo the transformation. What must happen instead spiritually is for Jesus to become the lens through which we see everything. Jesus cannot be an object out there in the little worlds we create. Instead, we need to become objects in what God is doing through Jesus in our hearts, and out there, in God's cosmic reign.

6. Tension Release:

Once the two disciples figure out that they have seen the crucified Jesus alive, they are so excited they go running out into the dark, seven miles back to Jerusalem. Running around in the dark isn't too smart, unless of course you are not afraid of the dark anymore. What's there to be afraid of? These disciples are now tied in with the Creator of the whole world, light or dark are both the same to them. With the release of tension comes a new capacity to be thrust into the world without fears, boundaries, or restrictions.

7. Interpretation:

With the excitement of their new discovery, the two disciples arrive back in Jerusalem and go in to where the other disciples are, but before they can say anything, the other disciples say to them, "Jesus has risen and appeared to Peter." "But wait," they say, "that is our story too! Jesus has risen and appeared to us."

What is this all about? What is going on here? What have we got? We've got the church, the body of Christ, the communion creating reality of Jesus Christ—this is the church, which has been proclaiming Jesus' life, death, and resurrection from that day until this. Because where two or three are gathered in his name there he is in the midst of them according to Matthew 18:20.

In the center of this transformational process is felt failure, the humbling experience of recognizing that what one has been thinking, believing, counting on is somehow ineffective, wrong and misguided. No one enjoys these moments of defeat, but to grow spiritually, they need to be embraced, not hidden. Not only felt failure in the middle of the process but disrupting life experiences may also throw us into the void of the humble dimension. Some examples of these humbling experiences are: moving to a new community, retirement, changing jobs, getting a divorce, dealing with an affair, a suicide, the death of a loved one, an injury or serious illness. Growth in faith requires embracing, not avoiding, minimizing, or denying the reality of human brokenness.

CHAPTER ELEVEN
(PART ONE)
Grace Dimension:
Graced by God's Love

For God so loved the world that he gave his only Son, so that everyone who believes in him may not perish but may have eternal life.
John 3:16)

Philip Yancey in his book, *What's So Amazing About Grace?*, tells the story of how during a British conference on comparative religions, experts from around the world debated what belief, if any, was unique to the Christian faith. They began eliminating various possibilities. Incarnation? No. Other religions have their different versions of gods appearing in human form. Resurrection? No. Other religions have accounts of persons returning from the dead. While the debate waged on, C. S. Lewis wandered into the room.

"What's all the rumpus about?" he asked. When he heard that his colleagues were discussing Christianity's unique contribution among world religions. Lewis responded almost instantaneously, "Oh, that's easy. It's Grace."[11]

That's right. It is the experience of grace in the Graced by God's Love Dimension that makes Christianity unique. Hindu *karma*,

---
11 Phillip Yancy. *What's SO Amazing About Grace?* Zondervan; Unabridged edition, September 9, 2008, p. 45.

New Age meditation, the Buddha's eightfold path, Jewish *tzedakah* (righteousness), and Islam's Five Pillars, each offer a way to earn approval. Only Christianity dares to proclaim God's unconditional love for each and every person, forgiveness for all offences.

Grace is so counter intuitive and such a difficult concept to grasp that some have gone to extremes to teach the concept. One of those teaching moments was so creative and on point it is worth sharing an eyewitness account:

> In the spring of 2002, I left work early so I could have some uninterrupted study time before my final exam in the Youth Ministry class at Hannibal-LaGrange College in Missouri. When I got to class, everybody was doing their last-minute studying. The teacher came in and said he would review with us before the test. Most of his review came right from the study guide, but there were some things he was reviewing that I had never heard. When questioned about it, he said they were in the book and we were responsible for everything in the book. We couldn't argue with that.
>
> Finally, it was time to take the test. "Leave them face down on the desk until everyone has one, and I'll tell you to start," our professor, Dr. Tom Hufty, instructed.
>
> When we turned them over, to my astonishment every answer on the test was filled in. My name was even written on the exam in red ink. The bottom of the last page said: "This is the end of the exam. All the answers on your test are correct. You will receive an A on the final exam. The reason you passed the test is because the creator of the test took it for you. All the work you did in preparation for this test did not help you get the A. You have just experienced grace."
>
> Dr. Hufty then went around the room and asked each student individually, "What is your grade? Do you deserve the grade you are receiving? How much did all your studying for this exam help you achieve your final grade?"

Then he said, "Some things you learn from lectures, some things you learn from research, but some things you can only learn from experience. You've just experienced grace. One hundred years from now, if you know Jesus Christ as your personal Savior, your name will be written down in a book, and you will have had nothing to do with writing it there. That will be the ultimate grace experience."[12]

Peter Graced by God's Love (John 21:1-19)

Question: How did Peter experience God's grace, God loving and caring for him in spite of and in the midst of his failure to love God with his heart, soul, and mind and his neighbor as himself?

Jesus checks in with Peter following the events of Holy Week, as the central concern of the resurrection appearance by the Sea of Galilee as recorded in John 21 is Peter's denial of Jesus on the night Jesus was betrayed.

After fishing and eating their catch for breakfast together, Jesus says to Peter, "Simon son of John, do you love me more than these?" "Do you love me more than these other disciples love me?" In other words, "Peter, are you still full of yourself?"

In responding, Peter professes love for Jesus, but this time he does so without elevating or comparing his love for Jesus to the love and devotion of the other disciples. Peter declares simply without referencing the others, "Lord, you know I love you." No bravado, no ego. Jesus commissions Peter saying, "Feed my lambs." Take care of my flock of disciples.

Jesus then asks a second question, similar to the first, but a little

---

[12] In 2002, Dr. Tom Hufty while a Professor at Hannibal-LaGrange College gave the "Grace Test" to his Youth Education class to reinforce the semester-long debate between law and grace. An article about the unusual final exam was written by HLGU Alumna Denise Banderman and submitted to *Youth Specialties*, an organization designed to train and equip youth ministers, and from there was printed in *Leadership* magazine, used as an illustration in Chuck Swindoll's book *Job: A Man of Heroic Endurance* and shared on his nationwide and global radio broadcast.)

different. In this second question, Jesus leaves out the comparative clause "more than these" asking the straight forward question, "Simon son of John, do you love me?"

Peter answers, "Yes, Lord; you know that I love you." In the Greek language different words are used to describe different kinds of love. Four of these are *phileo, storge, eros, and agape*. *Phileo* is the love of friendship. *Storge* is family love, *eros* is sensual, sexual love, and *agape* is pure unconditional love.

That there are these four different words in Greek that all translate as the same English word "love," helps us to understand that Jesus is not asking Peter the same question three times. The nuances of the Greek have Jesus in this second question effectively asking, "Simon son of John, do you love me sacrificially, the way I have loved you. Is your love unconditional? Is it *agape* love?"

Peter answers using a different word for love, *phileo,* "Lord, you know that my love for you is the love of friendship, the love of one human being for another. I *phileo* you."

In this second question-answer couplet, Peter's reply exhibits genuine humility not ego bravado or overstatement. Following the events of Holy week and his three denials of Jesus, Peter does not profess to love Jesus sacrificially, as he had earlier. He has become aware of his humanity, of his human limitations. Jesus commissions him again saying, "Tend my sheep."

The third time Jesus asks the question, he asks the question Peter has been answering all along. Jesus says to Peter the third time, "Simon son of John, do you love me as a friend? Do you *phileo* me?"

Peter feels hurt when Jesus asks this third question in this way. By Jesus descending to Peter's love level, Peter once again must confront his failure. He is not hurt by Jesus or by the question per se, but by his own inability to love sacrificially, his inability to do the very thing he wants to do. It is hard to be human and not divine, to have limitations that cause us to fail.

Peter responds, "Lord, you know everything; you know that I love you only as a friend. I am incapable of loving you sacrificially and unconditionally. You know that I denied you three times."

Jesus responds by commissioning Peter a third time saying, "Feed my sheep."

Then Jesus says, "Very truly, I tell you, when you were younger, you used to fasten your own belt and to go wherever you wished. But when you grow old, you will stretch out your hands, and someone else will fasten a belt around you and take you where you do not wish to go." (He said this to indicate the kind of death by which Peter would glorify God.) After this Jesus said to him, "Follow me!" *(John 21:18-19)*

In asking the love question three times, in three different ways, and calling upon Peter to follow him, Jesus is asking Peter if he will now do the very thing he cannot do. "Peter will you be my disciple and will you follow me no matter what the cost?" Jesus alludes to the cost of discipleship both in the word "love" and in the use of the shepherding metaphor.

The minute Peter fully acknowledges his inability to love sacrificially after the pattern of Christ, Jesus calls Peter to follow him to the cross, to love and glorify God sacrificially, to do the very thing he cannot do. Why would Jesus do that? Jesus can ask the impossible of Peter, because this calling of Peter is grounded in God's grace, not in Peter's human qualities or character. There is a paradoxical, spiritual truth of incredible significance imbedded within this turn of events. Once you know you can't love, God can empower you to love. Peter had an ego. That ego needed transformation before it could love. That is the double bounded condition of all human egos.

The crushing of Peter's ego by his own unfaithfulness, his denial of Jesus three times, paradoxically frees Peter to experience the self-confirming face of God, the face of Jesus—the face that even death cannot destroy. Grace in the midst of human failure transforms human lives, because it transforms human egos and frees the person to give and receive love. This experience of God's grace in Jesus Christ in the face of being confronted and aware of one's inability to be the person one wills to be is the graced by God's love dimension of faith.

Susan's Contemporary Story: Graced by God's Love

Acknowledging and actually living in the unconditional love of God is something that I'm still growing into, and I certainly don't feel that confidant about talking about it. This is partly because I'm from New England—New Englanders work hard and they're self-reliant.

Oh, I know I am loved by God. I've read about it, heard sermons on it, gone to retreats about it. The problem is that I know this in my head. And the journey from the head to the heart is the longest journey known to humankind.

Most of the breakthroughs I have had on this journey have not been when I've experienced a failure—though heaven knows I've had a number of those. They have happened when I have come to the end of myself—when it has become obvious that my own inner resources, knowledge, and skills are not enough to do a job I am called to do or deal with a situation that I am called to deal with.

It is then that I have turned to God and cried "Help!," which a priest I know says is God's favorite prayer. This can actually happen to me on a daily basis, if I'm really paying attention to what is going on in my life. The last time it happened in a big way was when we moved from San Diego to San Francisco five years ago.

My husband Vince lost his job in June of 2008 in a very nasty, hurtful, and unfair way. Six months later, he had an opportunity that was the perfect job for him here in San Francisco. It called upon all the knowledge and skills he had gained in his life so far, and it was for a bank with a mission that was more than just making money. He was thrilled, and I was thrilled for him.

For myself, I was not thrilled. I would be leaving a wonderful network of friends that I had developed over a period of 26 years; I would be leaving my work in a nonprofit that teaches contemplative prayer and a small spiritual direction practice, both of which I loved. I would also be selling a beautiful home that we had built ourselves, which looked through a grove of Torrey pines down to the ocean.

Come September, I would be dropping off our youngest son at college and moving to San Francisco where I would have a very empty nest indeed.

I was sad, mad, and scared.

How could I possibly do this?

My journey to a better place mentally and spiritually took place in two major steps. The first step occurred during a time of prayer. I suddenly remembered Exodus 33:12-16, where Moses says he won't lead these people unless God goes with him.

God responds, "My presence will go with you and I will give you rest."

I dropped to my knees and sobbed. I begged God to go with me, and let me know that he was there.

Second step, several weeks later: One morning, out of the blue, lying in bed, I prayed, "God, I'm going to trust that you love me as much as you love Vince, and that this move will be as good for me as it will be for him. I do not see that right now, but I am going to trust that this is so." I did not decide to say that to God. It was prayed through me.

I still had to go to counseling to sort out the swirling caldron of feelings that lay in my heart. But on that day, the "sting" went out of those feelings, and they didn't have as deep a hold on me as they had before, and by the time I got to San Francisco by God's grace and my cooperation, I had a good attitude about it.

I also found that once we got to our new home, I felt surrounded by God's love. I was so tired that for 6 months I didn't care that I didn't know many people. I rested in a little cocoon, surrounded by God's love.

I am still learning, day-by-day, to live in awareness of God's unconditional love and I expect that I'll be doing that until the day I see Jesus face to face.

Interlude for Theology:

It is impossible for me as a student of theology and the history of the church to write about being graced by God's love without thinking immediately of the Protestant Reformation and Protestant Reformer Martin Luther—*sola gratia—grace alone*. Through Luther's study of Romans and his experience of grace in his own life, the Reformation was born. In Appendix I, Martin Luther's life and how his faith story dramatically climaxes in the experience of God's grace in this dimension is described.

Characteristics of Persons Growing in God's Love

The focus of the grace dimension is the experience of God's grace, forgiveness, and love. All are God's free gifts to humankind. People living primarily out of this dimension will say things like, "I love God and God loves me." "I am God's beloved." According to Blaise Pascal, there is a love void in each of us that only the love of God can fill. Experiencing God's grace filling this heart shaped void, persons feel themselves to be God's "beloved."

It is possible to become entrenched or stuck in this dimension when the experience and sharing of God's love becomes confined or isolated within a community or focused on a limited number of people to the exclusion of others. "I love the people in my church so much and they love me." One hopes, of course, that people will feel this way about their church community. The problem arises when the sentiment is accompanied by a sense of self-satisfaction that, "I have arrived." This is opposed to living and loving from God's love in all aspects of one's life, God's love being the source of all shared love.

Characteristics of Persons Graced by God's Love

Dimension:	Persona	Focus	I Statements	Obstruction	Moving On
Graced by God's love.	Beloved: "I am loved and I love."	Experiences of grace, forgiveness and love.	"I am God's beloved child."	I love people in my church so much and they love me; I have arrived.	Living in and from God's love in every aspect of one's life.

The power of the Graced by God's Love Dimension has already been seen in the Biblical story of Peter being encountered by the resurrected Jesus in John 21; as well as, in the Protestant Reformation that results from Luther's understanding and proclaiming God's free gift of grace.

Maturing in the Graced by God's Love Dimension

Grace, the love of God is a free gift, as we have said, but it is also something that we grow into as we encounter all seven dimensions in the life of faith. The experience of love is not a single event or isolated experience.

1. One thing that helps us grow in our experience of the grace of God is hearing the grace of God proclaimed by other people. This happens in worship with the Assurance of Pardon each week, but also during times of testimony or in stories told during sermons. It can be heard in the reading and interpretation of Scripture.

2. A person may experience love and forgiveness in the midst of Christian community—God loving them through other people. This often happens before or in conjunction with a more direct spiritual experience of God's love. The Christian community, as the body of Jesus Christ, loves people for Jesus Christ. This may prepare people for the spiritual experience of God's love in that it alerts a person who is experiencing the love void in their soul that there is love for them in the world.

3. The desire to love like Jesus Christ in response to God reaching out in love is another aspect of growing in grace. When we are loved, we are freed to love. When we are loved, we have love to give.

4. Another aspect of growing in the grace of God is in experiencing the "for me" of the cross. Humbled by one's inability to love like Jesus or one's failure to do the will of God, people

come to experience and recognize Jesus dying on the cross specifically "for" them. This is the gracious gift contained in the realization that one cannot do the very thing one wants to do – the will of God.

5. The foremost experience of being graced by God's love in response to one's failure to love sacrificially, of not being "for others" like Jesus Christ is, is the experience of being loved by the one who stands outside of you and says, "I love you." It is a spiritual experience of God loving and addressing the individual spiritually.

6. Once experienced, the grace of God empowers a person to forgive both one's self and others. It is the experience we have been taught to pray for: "Forgive us our trespasses (sin), as we forgive those who trespass (sin) against us." Being gracious to others is another aspect of growing in grace.

7. Living and loving daily in gracious interaction with God, self and others is the ultimate experience of God's grace. In this aspect of grace, a person grows in being indiscriminately gracious in interaction with believers and non-believers alike.

CHAPTER TWELVE
(PART TWO)
Grace Dimension:
Ministry Implications

The Uniqueness of God's Love

God's love, given to us in the Graced by God's Love Dimension, is not only unique amongst religions, it is also unique and different from human love as our interpretation of the story below will indicate:

> The story is told of a fourteen-year-old boy, who shot and killed an innocent teenager just to prove himself to his gang. At the trial of the juvenile offender, the victim's mother sat impassively silent until the end of the trial. Once the guilty verdict was announced, she stood up slowly and stared directly at her son's murderer and said, "I'm going to kill you." The youth was then taken away to serve several years in a juvenile facility.
>
> After the first half year the mother of the slain child went to visit her son's killer, who had been living on the streets before the killing. She was the only person to visit him in jail. They talked for a time, then when she left she gave him some money for cigarettes. As time passed, she started visiting him more regularly, bringing food and small gifts. Near the end of his three-year sentence, she asked him

what he would be doing when he got out. He didn't really know. He was confused and very uncertain, so she offered to help set him up with a job at a friend's company. Then she inquired about where he would live. Since he had no family to return to, she offered him temporary use of the spare room in her home. For eight months he lived there, ate her food, and worked at the job. Then one evening she called him into the living room to talk. She sat down opposite him and waited.

Then she said, "Do you remember in the courtroom when I said I was going to kill you?"

"I sure do," he replied. "I'll never forget that moment."

"Well, I did it," she went on. "I did not want the boy who could kill my son for no reason to remain alive on this earth. I wanted him to die. That's why I started to visit you and bring you things. That is why I got you the job and let you live here in my house. That's how I set about changing you. And that old boy, he's gone. So now I want to ask you, since my son is gone, and that killer is gone, if you'll stay here. I've got room and I'd like to adopt you if you let me."

And she became the mother he never had.[13]

This powerful story follows the classic structure of transformational narrative common in all religions and cultures. The mother negates the negation of her son's death, by killing the killer with her love, then acting to recreate him as a function of that love. Jesus Christ's life, death and resurrection follow this same transformational pattern, but with one crucial difference. The difference can be discerned in these words from Scripture:

> God so loved the world that he gave his only Son, so that everyone who believes in him may not perish but may have eternal life. Indeed, God did not send the Son into

---

13 George E. Vaillant, *Spiritual Evolution: A Scientific Defense of Faith*. New York: Broadway Books, 2009. 2-3.

The Jesus Fractal

the world to condemn the world, but in order that the world might be saved through him.

John 3:16-17

God's love was revealed among us in this way: God sent his only Son into the world so that we might live through him. In this is love, not that we loved God but that he loved us and sent his Son to be the atoning sacrifice for our sins.

1John 4:9-10)

You did not receive a spirit of slavery to fall back into fear, but you have received a spirit of adoption. When we cry, "Abba! Father!" it is that very Spirit bearing witness with our spirit that we are children of God, and if children, then heirs.

Romans 8:15-17a

What then are we to say about these things? If God is for us, who is against us? He who did not withhold his own Son, but gave him up for all of us, will he not with him also give us everything else?

Romans 8:31-32)

Did you see the differences? The mother RESPONDS in love and compassion to the killer of her son with life transforming results for both herself in her grief and for the young murderer. He gained a mother, she an adopted son. It is a story of death and resurrection, the killer's death and resurrection, a son's death and resurrection.

By contrast in the Gospel narratives, God *GIVES* God's Son in love and compassion to redeem the Son's killers. Moreover, the one who dies in the Gospel narratives is innocent, not guilty. The Son of God voluntarily goes to the cross so that his murderers might live after God the Father set the whole plan in motion.

It would be extraordinary, but imaginable that a person could actually be as loving and gracious as the mother in the story. Her response to her son's murder speaks to the best of humankind. What is harder to conceive is for her or any other loving parent sending their child to die in order to rescue a killer. I could perhaps conceive of dying myself to rescue a killer (not likely mind you, but I can conceive and hold in my brain the possibility of that much sacrificial love). But send my son to die for the redemption of his killer! No way! I can't even hold that thought in my mind for an instant. I just wouldn't do it, couldn't do it, couldn't bear the pain, but that is exactly what God did. That speaks volumes regarding how much God loves us. God loves us far beyond our human understanding.

Laying Down One's Life for Another

Another way of looking at the issue of the uniqueness of Jesus Christ's sacrificial love is to consider this question: What is the difference between Jesus Christ and firefighters, police officers, and military personal? One answer is that professional heroes, people who go to work anticipating that they will be called upon to help people in distress (firefighters, police officers, and military personal), accept the possibility that they may die; but they do not EXPECT to lose their lives when they go to work each day, because they are hopeful and self-confident in their abilities. Their actions are often heroic and potentially sacrificial, but not necessarily so. In other words, they RISK their lives, but they do not GIVE them. Now you may think I am splitting hairs here, but I think the distinction is critical in understanding the extent of Jesus Christ's love for us. Jesus Christ GAVE his life for our redemption. He KNEW he was going to die.

Another important distinction is that firefighters, police officers and soldiers RISK their lives not for their own families and friends, but usually for complete strangers. They run into burning buildings, without doing background checks to see if the people inside "deserve" to be saved! Firefighters, police officers and military personal RISK their lives heroically in selfless acts on behalf of others without judgment, because it is their job, their sworn duty to do so. But here again what Jesus Christ did was quite different. Jesus *GAVE* his life knowingly and willingly with complete judgment. According to Romans 5, "... rarely will anyone die for a righteous person—though perhaps for a good person someone might actually dare to die. But God proves God's love for us in that while we still were sinners Christ died for us." Jesus Christ KNEW about our sinful condition, the evil that grows out of the human heart, still Jesus CHOSE to "GIVE" his life for us; to die in our place.

Now I don't know about you, but the one person in the world I am pretty sure I would GIVE my life for would be my son. Even though my son is not perfect, I love him more than life itself; therefore, I think I would GIVE my life for him. Who would you GIVE your life for? Who do you love more than life itself? The love that you have for that person is the kind of love that God has for us. Love like a devoted parent, lover, sibling, or friend . . . Love that would GIVE its own life to save the loved one.

It is that kind of amazing love that God commands us to have for one another. Wow! For my son, Yes!! For my sister, Marie, probably. But beyond them I wish I could say I would love enough, but I am not sure. Impulsively, without thinking, I could see myself reaching out to save someone else all the while thinking we would both live. In other words, I could see myself RISKING my life for another, but GIVING my life knowing that I would die an agonizing death in the place of someone else, especially a someone else who deserved to die, I don't know if I would do that. Why? Because I don't love enough. That is why I need a Savior to die for me. Do you need a Savior to die for you, too?

CHAPTER THIRTEEN
Empowered Dimension:
Empowerment in the Spirit

> But you will receive power when the Holy Spirit has come upon you; and you will be my witnesses in Jerusalem, in all Judea and Samaria, and to the ends of the earth.
> *Acts 1:8*

> Repent, and be baptized every one of you in the name of Jesus Christ so that your sins may be forgiven; and you will receive the gift of the Holy Spirit. For the promise is for you, for your children, and for all who are far away, everyone whom the Lord our God calls to him.
> *Acts 2:38-39*

The Empowered in the Spirit Dimension is focused on fulfillment of the promise made by Jesus to his disciples at his ascension: "You will receive power when the Holy Spirit has come upon you." Holy Spirit empowerment given at Pentecost is still available today, but must be accessed. It is the power of prayer and communion with God in worship, not prayer and worship as ritual, but as intimate relationship with God through the ministry of the Holy Spirit. It is the empowerment sought in the prayer hymn:

> Spirit of the living God, fall fresh on me.
> Melt me, mold me, fill me, use me.
> Spirit of the living God, fall fresh on me.

Spiritual empowerment requires human participation and cooperation. As Saint Augustine suggested, we need to "pray as if everything depends on God, then work as if everything depends on us."

In the empowerment dimension of the Jesus Fractal, the Holy Spirit empowers people to make a difference, to share their faith with the joy and love of Jesus Christ, to serve after the pattern of Jesus Christ. Stephen Curry, a Christian, who also plays an amazing game of basketball, wrote in 2014, a year when the Golden State Warriors didn't win the NBA Finals or even get close, losing in the first round of the playoffs:

> The Holy Spirit is moving through our locker room in a way I've never experienced before. It's allowing us to reach a lot of people, and personally I am just trying to use this stage to share how God has been a blessing to my life and how He can be the same in everyone else's.
>
> God's given me talents to play basketball for a living, but I still have to work hard to improve every day. I know that in the grand scheme of things, this is just a game that can be taken from me at any moment. But I love that basketball gives me the opportunities to do good things for people and to point them towards the Man who died for our sins on the cross. I know I have a place in Heaven waiting for me because of Him, and that's something no earthly prize or trophy could ever top.
>
> There's more to me than just this jersey I wear, and that's Christ living inside of me.

The Christ inside of Stephen, the Christ inside of you and me, is the Holy Spirit. The Holy Spirit, who empowers, enables believers to do the thing humans cannot do on our own, the will of God. It is the victory won at the cross, confirmed at the resurrection, fueled by the love of God that is way bigger than any form of human success.[14]

Peter Empowered in the Spirit *(Acts 1-5)*

Question: How did Peter first experience the Spirit in intimate relationship?

During his resurrection appearances, Jesus tells his disciples that they will be empowered by their baptism in the Holy Spirit to witness to the world regarding their experience of Jesus Christ.

> "Do not leave Jerusalem," he says, "but wait for the gift I told you about, the gift my Father promised. John baptized with water, but in a few days you will be baptized with the Holy Spirit.... When the Holy Spirit comes upon you, you will be witnesses for me in Jerusalem, in all Judea and Samaria, and to the ends of the earth."
>
> *Acts 1:4b-5; 8*

After making these statements, Jesus is taken up into heaven.

Following Jesus' death and resurrection appearances, Peter emerges as the group's new leader. Jesus' prayer is answered. Peter's faith does not fail him. It is Peter who directs the disciples in the process of selecting Matthias to replace Judas Iscariot. Then at Pentecost, when . . . the believers . . . are all filled with the Holy Spirit for the first time, Peter, empowered by the Holy Spirit, preaches so powerfully that 3,000 people repent and believe. Baptism in the Spirit is the climax of Peter's journey to inwardly strong faith. Baptism in the Holy Spirit is the sign and the seal of God having transformed the Galilean fisherman's ego. Transformed from within, Peter becomes Spirit empowered to

---

14 Stephen Curry, *"The Holy Spirit Is Moving Through Our Locker Room" Says NBA MVP Stephen Curry*. N.p., 19 May 2015. Web. 26 May 2015. <http://www.breakingchristiannews.com/articles/display_art.html?ID=15990>.)

follow and stand up for Jesus in the way he wanted to on the night Jesus was betrayed.

Over the next few years, Peter proves himself to be a courageous witness for Christ *(Acts 2:14; 4:31; 5:29)*; continues to effectively proclaim the Gospel so that large numbers of people come to believe *(Acts 2:41, 47; 4:4)*; performs mighty works *(Acts 2:43; 5:12)*; rejoices in suffering persecution for the sake of the Kingdom of God *(Acts 5:41)*; and finds himself united in one Spirit with the other disciples instead of in competition with them *(Acts 2:44)*. Twice, Peter is arraigned before the Sanhedrin and directly defies its orders *(Acts 4:7–22; Acts 5:18–42)*. What a change from the Peter who envisions and identifies with Jesus' Messianic mission in terms of earthly power; the Peter who argues with the other disciples concerning their relative greatness; the Peter who humanly wills to follow Jesus into prison even unto death, yet denies the Lord Jesus three times on the night of his betrayal. This is the dimension of empowerment in the Spirit.

My Father's Story: Empowerment in the Spirit

My Father was a successful achievement-orientated businessman, who loved his family. For members of the family, Dad would do anything, but for those outside the bloodline, charity was meager. Spirit empowered encounter with Jesus Christ changed all of that.

It was June of 1987 when doctors told us that he had brain cancer. For me, the learned inhibitions of a lifetime, which made it safer and easier to allow conversations with my father to remain focused on mundane issues, dissolved. More than anything I wanted to share my faith with him.

Having prayed with friends before leaving Princeton, New Jersey, I arrived at San Francisco International Airport concerned, but joyful—at peace—maybe even a little excited, because I was assured in both, my heart and head, that God was at work. I went right from the airport to the hospital even though it was one o'clock in the morning. Dad was clearly not himself. He couldn't concentrate, stand without assistance, or communicate his desires to his own body. Also, he was obviously disorientated for, no matter how many times I told him that he was in the hospital, he insisted that we were at home in our family room. Underneath the facade of listlessness, I could sense his fear.

Off and on throughout the night I tried to get some sleep without much success. At about six o'clock, I finally gave up. Rummaging through the dresser draws, I found a *Good News Bible*. Picking up the book, I asked Dad if he would like me to read him some Scripture.

You have to understand. I had never read Scripture with my father before. And so, when he responded, "Sure," I was both delighted and relieved. "Is there any particular passage you would like me to read?" I asked.

"How about the one, 'There is a time to die'," he replied.

Even though my heart was now in my throat, I opened the Bible to the 3rd chapter of Ecclesiastes and read the first few verses out loud.

I then asked if there was a particular New Testament passage he would like read.

Dad responded, "How about the 'Feeding of the 5000.'"

Since I already knew how he would interpret that Scripture, I said, "No, I'm going to read something else. You want me to read that story so you can explain away the miracle. Here, try this one. How do you explain what happened in this story?"

As we were talking, I had turned to the story of the healing of the epileptic boy in Luke 9:37-43. When I finished reading it, I asked Dad to tell me how the boy got healed?

"The father had faith," he responded.

"Yeah. Anything else?"

"The three disciples had faith."

"Yeah. Anything else?"

"Jesus had faith."

"Yeah," I said with a smile, "And Jesus in faith commanded the evil spirit to get out of the little boy."

"Hum. Hum." Dad nodded.

"Would you like me to do that for you, right now?" I asked.

"Yes," Dad responded without hesitation.

So, we held hands and prayed. In the name of Jesus Christ, I commanded the spirit of dis-ease to depart from my father's head. I prayed for the swelling to lessen—for the cancer cells to stop multiplying.

When we finished praying, I sang a song. While I sang, Dad was smiling and crying all at once. Hoping that he would pray with me, I closed with the Lord's Prayer.

When I opened my eyes again, Dad in one sentence concisely proclaimed from his own silent experience in prayer what Jesus Christ taught concerning the efficacy of prayer. Gesturing with folded hands, he said tearfully, "Hands folded in prayer are much more powerful than hands grasping in strength."

That afternoon, our lawyer came with some legal papers. Before signing, Dad read the documents and even asked for the meaning of some legal phrasing to be clarified. There was no question; he understood their content. Later that evening after everyone else had left; Dad got out of bed, walked into the bathroom, and took a shower.

The following morning (I slept on the couch at the hospital), I again picked up the Bible. In response, Dad said, "Oh good."

This time I read I Corinthians 13. Dad seemed distracted, so I decide not to push for interpretation. But he was listening, for later that afternoon he asked me to mark the passage. He wanted to read it with his wife. (My mother died in 1971.)

The third morning as I was about to leave for Sunday services, Dad silently took my hands and "folded them in prayer." We prayed. I began by thanking God for Dad's healing and ended with the 23rd Psalm. Then, together we prayed the Lord's Prayer. Following the "Amen," my father thanked God in his own words for all his blessings and asked God to be with our family and with all the people in the world who were hurting. With tears in my eyes, I left for worship.

Several months later on our way to church (now a regular event), Dad said, "You know those transforming experiences you write about?"

"Yeah."

"Well, I've had one."

"I know."

"I have a whole new way of viewing the world. My myopic vision has been healed. I pray a hundred times a day. I am filled with so much joy. If I could, I wouldn't not have had this brain tumor."

Prior to being hospitalized, when my dad would on occasion go to church (usually only because I was preaching), he would place a twenty-dollar bill in the offering plate, no more and no less. After this experience, participation in this aspect of the worship service evidenced transformation. For on the way to church each Sunday, he would insist that we stop first at the office to write a check. The checks we wrote ranged in value from 500 to 2500 dollars. The Spirit of Christ had opened not only his heart, but his pocketbook as well.

After a gracious year of continued fellowship with the Lord, my father died on Holy Saturday in 1988. If death can be perfect, such was his. For my father passed away on the one day in the church calendar when we celebrate Christ's presence with us in death. My sister, his wife, and I were all there. We sang, prayed, and expressed our love. Finally, I was moved to raise my hand to say the benediction:

"May the grace of our Lord Jesus Christ, the love of God, and the communion of the Holy Spirit be and abide with you this day and forever more."

When I finished, Dad took one more breath as if to say "Amen." Then he was gone. It was a glorious, glorious moment for:

> When the perishable puts on the imperishable, and the mortal puts on immortality, then shall come to pass the saying that is written:
> "Death is swallowed up in victory."
> "O death, where is thy victory?"
> "O death, where is thy sting?"
> The sting of death is sin, and the power of sin is the

> law. But thanks be to God, who gives us the victory through our Lord Jesus Christ.
>
> 1 Cor. 15:54-57

My father's physical healing which was temporal passed away. His spiritual healing abides still.

Faith is more than a simple exchange of invitation and acceptance, no matter how dramatic. It is in fact a complex, multidimensional, psycho-historical process requiring the complete reworking of one's understanding of self and others in interaction with the Spirit of Christ—a complete reworking of the story of one's life—the story constructed in childhood, and rehearsed in adulthood. Thus in my father's case, it is probably not without significance that he read an early version of my dissertation on spiritual transformation, worshiped with a joy filled black congregation, and visited his only brother's grave for the first time only months prior to his hospitalization. In other words, the Spirit of Christ was at work in his life long before June of 1987.

An Interlude for Theology and The Butterfly Effect

In 1963 Edward Lorenz, a meteorologist at MIT, presented a startling hypothesis to the New York Academy of Science. He told the assembly that a butterfly could flap its wings and set molecules of air in motion. Those molecules of air in turn moving other molecules of air could eventually result in a hurricane being experienced on the other side of the planet. Lorenz was reporting on one of those important accidental discoveries that change the way the world thinks.

Two years earlier in 1961, Edward Lorenz had been running weather simulations on one of the earliest computers available to researchers at universities. He was using a set of three equations describing the dynamic relationships between pressure, temperature, and wind speed. At one point, he wanted to recreate a particularly interesting run. So, he re-entered the set of starting conditions from the printout of the earlier run. He then started the weather simulation program a second time. To his surprise, the second run almost immediately began to diverge from the first, and after a short time, became completely different.

After closely examining and comparing the two sets of data, Lorenz discovered that the only difference between the two runs was that when entering the initial conditions for the second run, he had rounded down the number 0.506127 to 0.506. It was a small difference. Seemingly, inconsequential, yet the small difference had led to enormous changes in the system.

What Lorenz witnessed and later reported on has come to be known as "the butterfly effect." A butterfly flapping its wings in the Andes might set into motion a cascading chain of events that could cause flooding in Bangladesh or a tornado in Minnesota.

Eventually, scientists accorded Lorenz's "butterfly effect" the status of a "law"—the Law of Sensitive Dependence Upon Initial Conditions. The principle has been found to be operative not just in weather systems, but also in a wide variety of other non-linear systems such as the stock market, biology, microbiology, economics, finance, philosophy, physics, politics, population dynamics, psychology, and robotics. I would like to suggest that "the butterfly effect" is also operative in theology; especially in the empowerment dimension of faith relationship with Jesus Christ.

Jesus said, "The kingdom of heaven is like a mustard seed that someone took and sowed in his field; it is the smallest of all the seeds, but when it has grown it is the greatest of shrubs. . . If you have faith the size of a mustard seed, you will say to this mountain, 'move' and it will move." *(Mark 4:31-32; Matthew 17:20)*

Have you ever wondered whether your prayers matter? If they change or effect anything? The "butterfly effect" suggests that prayer may actually be just as effective and significant in bringing about desired outcomes, as the Bible says it is.

Each of the past four years, I have been on a medical mission trip to Guatemala for our church with a group called *Faith in Practice*. One year while setting up on Sunday for Monday's surgeries, the team discovered that an expensive piece of equipment that we had brought down the year before and was needed again this year by the Urology surgeon was missing. Another team had used it, but now it couldn't be found. The nurses and hospital staff looked everywhere, but to no avail. Made aware of the problem and the anxiety it was producing, I set team members praying both that night and early the next morning at our 6:15 a.m. devotions. Later that same morning when I arrived at the hospital, concern had turned to praise as team member after team member joyfully reported that the lost machine had been found.

If so much of reality rests like a pencil balancing on its tip with only a hairsbreadth difference needed to change the course of history, then prayer may really be as effective as Jesus suggested. "Ask and it shall be given to you, seek and you will find." *(Luke 11:9)* All prayer need do is alter a situation, ever so slightly, and exponential change can result!

At our first team meeting the day before we discovered the machine missing, I had suggested to this amazing group of doctors and nurses that the effect of the work they would be doing during the week could not be measured or predicted. Now don't misunderstand, I know we preformed 109 surgical procedures on 83 different patients. That is a lot of surgery, but still just a drop in the bucket of the health needs among Guatemala's poor. From a faith perspective, the most important thing about these surgeries is that they constitute the very drop in the bucket that God willed for us to place there. However, how this work figures into God's larger plan is something the team will probably never know. Rather in faith, the ultimate impact and meaning of the work is left in God's hands. "I planted, Apollos watered, but God gave the growth," says the Apostle Paul.

We often credit and honor one person when a great discovery or event takes place. But the truth is, there are so many small and faithful actions that need to be in place that it is really difficult to determine who is ultimately responsible.

For instance, on Friday April 2, 2004, ABC News honored a man who, at the time, was 91 years old. They honored him on their regular segment called, "Person of the Week." Each week on this segment, the honoree's accomplishments are listed first. Usually, viewers can guess the honoree's identity before that week's recipient is actually announced. But this week, the buildup left many viewers puzzled.

Finally, ABC anchor Peter Jennings made the announcement, "Our person of the week is Norman Borlaug." Who? Who is Norman Borlaug? Do you know who Norman Borlaug is? According to Peter Jennings, Norman Borlaug was personally responsible for drastically and dramatically changing the world by saving the lives of two billion people.

Novelist Andy Andrews quarrels with the claim.[15] Applying the "butterfly effect" he thinks perhaps others could and should have been honored, because without them Norman Borlaug's work may never have been accomplished.

By the way, what Norman Borlaug did in the early 1940s was develop "hybridized high yield, disease resistant corn and wheat for arid climates. From the dust bowl of Western Africa to the deserts of the Southwestern United States . . . from South and Central America to the plains of Siberia . . . across Europe and Asia . . . Borlaug's seeds flourished and regenerated where no seed had ever thrived before." Super Seeds!

Andrews suggests that perhaps the person really responsible for saving those two billion lives by means of those hybrid seeds was a man named Henry Wallace. Do you know who Henry Wallace is? Henry Wallace was one of the three Vice Presidents who served under Franklin D. Roosevelt. Before assuming that prestigious office, Wallace had been Secretary of the Agriculture, a position for which he was gifted and passionate. One of the things Wallace did, while Vice President, was use the power of his new position to create an agricultural research station in New Mexico whose sole purpose was to hybridize corn and wheat for arid climates. Wallace also hired a young man named Norman Borlaug to run the research station.

So Norman Borlaug won the Nobel Prize and was awarded the Presidential Medal of Freedom, but considering the connection,

---

15 Andy Andrews, *The Butterfly Effect: How Your Life Matters*. Naperville, IL: Simple Truths, 2009. Print.

Elizabeth A. Frykberg

Andy Andrews thinks it actually could be argued that it was really Henry Wallace who saved the two billion people by establishing the station and hiring Borlaug in the first place.

Or was it really George Washington Carver, who saved the two billion people? You remember learning about George Washington Carver in elementary school. Right? He was the African American agricultural inventor born into slavery, who developed crop rotation methods and a myriad of new uses for the peanut. When George Washington Carver was 19 years old and a student at Iowa State University, he would take his dairy professor's six-year-old son on "botanical expeditions." That boy's name was Henry Wallace. So it was George Washington Carver, who instilled in Henry Wallace a love for plants and a vision for what plants could do for humanity. It was Carver, who pointed six-year-old Wallace's life in the direction of agriculture long before he became the Vice President of the United States. So maybe it is really George Washington Carver who is responsible for saving the lives of more than two billion people. Perhaps Carver should have been named Person of the Week.

Or maybe it should have been the farmer from Diamond, Missouri named Moses Carver. Carver lived in a slave state, but didn't believe in slavery. This made him a target for Quantrill's Raiders who terrorized the area burning property and killing abolitionists. One cold January night, Quantrill's Raiders rode through Moses' farm. They burned the barn, shot several people and abducted from the farm a woman named Mary Washington who refused to let go of her infant son, George.

Mary Washington was a friend of Moses' wife Susan. Distraught over the kidnapping, Susan set to work writing messages and contacting nearby farms in search of George and Mary. Eventually, through neighbors she arranged for her husband to meet with the Raiders. The meeting took place several hours to the north in Kansas. There, at the appointed time, in the middle of the night, Moses met up with four of the Raiders. They were on horseback, carrying torches, flour sacks tied over their heads with holes cut out for their eyes. Moses traded the horse he was riding for a dirty burlap bag.

The Jesus Fractal

As the Raiders thundered off on their horses ponying Moses' horse with them, Moses fell to his knees and pulled from the bag a cold and naked, almost dead baby boy. Quickly, he opened his coat, then his shirt placing the child next to his skin. Covering the baby back up with his own clothes, Moses used the warmth of his own body to warm the child; he then turned and walked toward home. Moses walked through the night and into the next morning to get the child safely to Susan. When he got home, Moses and Susan committed themselves to raising the baby promising to provide an education for the child to honor his mother, Mary, who they already knew was dead. They gave the baby their own name. That is how Moses and Susan Carver came to raise George Washington Carver.

So when you think about it, it may have been Moses, the farmer from Diamond, Missouri who saved the two billion people. Or was it his wife who was responsible. Certainly, it was Susan Carver, who organized the effort and demanded immediate action. Unless it was really . . . . Okay, I will stop there. You get the point! It is an unending story?

The things we do today, this week—our actions, decision, choices—will ripple out with consequences foreseen and unforeseen, for good or for ill, for the health or damage of the world. The question isn't whether, but what...what will we do this week to make a difference in the world. Some of our actions may be big, bold, and courageous; others small, and hardly noticeable. Yet they all have potential to ripple out, affecting countless lives. We have no idea what effect our actions will have on future generations. How far forward would we have to go to discover the difference we make?

The butterfly effect of Jesus Christ's life is powerfully articulated in the classic essay by Francis Allen entitled, *One Solitary Life*:

> He was born in an obscure village, the child of a peasant woman. He grew up in still another village, where He worked in a carpenter shop until He was 30. Then for three years He was an itinerant preacher. He never wrote a book.

He never held an office. He never had a family or owned a house. He didn't go to college. He never traveled more than 200 miles from the place He was born. He did none of the things one usually associates with greatness. He had no credentials but Himself.

He was only 33 when public opinion turned against Him. His friends deserted Him. He was turned over to His enemies and went through the mockery of a trial. He was nailed to a cross between two thieves. When He was dying, His executioners gambled for His clothing, the only property He had...on earth. When He was dead, He was laid in a borrowed grave through the pity of a friend.

Nineteen centuries have come and gone, and today He is the central figure of the human race, the leader of mankind's progress.

All the armies that ever marched, all the navies that ever sailed, all the parliaments that ever sat, all the kings that ever reigned, put together, have not affected the life of man on earth as much as that One Solitary Life.[16]

In the surgeries that the doctors and nurses perform on a *Faith in Practice* medical mission trip to Guatemala each year, I can see the difference they are making. Seventy-two-year-old Mr. Cuts needed to be circumcised because of a severe infection. The first three sentences he said to his nurse upon waking were, "Thank you. I want whiskey. I'm a sexy man." Baby Kimberly and five-year-old David Lopez both had "minor" surgeries to clip a tongue tie, but their lives have been changed immeasurably as they will now be able to speak properly.

Hernia repairs, gallbladders removed, prolapsed uteruses raised, hysterectomies performed… cleft lips and cleft palette restructured, dilated and expanded urethras for 11-year-old boys. Clearly, life will be better for all of these individuals, but the ripple effect is still unknown. The year before, 14-year-old Joselyn had

---

16 James Allan Francis. "Arise Sir Knight!" *The Real Jesus: And Other Sermons.* Philadelphia: Judson, 1926. 123-24. Print.

come to our team believing she was ugly and that nothing could help. The next year she came back for follow-up surgery believing in miracles.

Behind the big events that change the world for good, there are always a series of small faithful actions. Our lives may not be honored with Nobel Prizes or Presidential Medals of Freedom. We may never be named the Person of the Week on ABC or anywhere else, but that doesn't mean our lives are not significant. Our lives have eternal significance as they are lived out in faith, empowered by the Holy Spirit, contributing our little part to what God is doing in the world.

Characteristics of Persons Growing in Spiritual Empowerment

The focus of the empowerment dimension is intimate relationship with the Spirit of God who empowers us from the inside out. In this dimension people become aware of God's powerful, loving presence working and residing in them and in every aspect of their lives. Life is contemplative in that people experience themselves as human spirit in dialogue with the Spirit of God. This dialogue is contemplative too, because the Spirit resides in them and can be accessed by centering one's self on God.

The temptation of this dimension is spiritual self-righteousness: "I have arrived. I am righteous. The Spirit of God lives in me. The Spirit speaks to me. To be right with God, others need to be like me." There is a confusion of authority. A person becomes authoritarian on the basis of the Spirit residing inside. There is an assumption of absolute human authority. This is a dangerous spiritual condition, especially for people in leadership positions.

People continue to grow in and through this dimension as they are empowered by the Spirit. In humble dialogue with the Spirit, they seek to do the will of God, the very thing they could not do. The difference is that in the Spirit, they can now do "all things through Christ who strengthens them." This is spiritual empowerment grounded in humble recognition of one's human sinful condition, in one's inability to do the will of God without Jesus Christ having died on the cross.

Characteristics of Persons Empowered in the Spirit

Dimension:	Persona	Focus	I Statements	Obstruction	Moving On
Empowered by the Holy Spirit	Contemplative: "I am spirit and the Spirit of God lives in me."	Intimate relationship with the Spirit of God, who empowers.	I am aware of God's powerful, loving presence strengthening me.	I have the Spirit. I am spiritually empowered. I know what is best, so follow me.	Seeking to do the will of God in humble dialogue with the Spirit.

Maturing in the Empowerment in the Spirit Dimension

We grow in our experience of being empowered by the Spirit of God as we encounter all seven dimensions. God's Spirit grows and matures in us over time.

1. One aspect of maturing in the Spirit is hearing Spirit empowered proclamation of the Good News of the Gospel in Word and Sacrament. It is hearing the Word proclaimed and enacted in the presence of the Holy Spirit that equips and empowers the believer to go back out into the world.

   What the seven dimensions help us to see more clearly is the complexity and vitality of the threefold Word—written, proclaimed, and revealed in the person of Jesus Christ. Encounter with Jesus Christ, who is the Living Word, is the focus of worship, as the Word is read, proclaimed and enacted. Thus the *Service of the Word* and the *Response to the Word (Service of the Table)* are both designed to promote and facilitate encounter with the living Word, the Spirit of Jesus Christ. They are not ends in themselves. In other words, Word and Sacrament are not engaged for their own sakes, but for the purpose of facilitating encounter with Jesus Christ the Living Word.

Seeker-friendly services, revivals, and crusades designed to evangelize are worship services conducted with the *hearing dimension* as primary goal, not *empowerment*. The model for worship as empowerment is Pentecost with the disciples gathered together in the Upper Room. The model for seeker-friendly worship is Jesus on the hillside proclaiming the Kingdom of God to the multitudes in the listening dimension.

2. Maturing in the sixth dimension involves empowerment as the Holy Spirit is encountered within a community of believers. As mentioned in Chapter Five, this kind of community is known by the Greek name *koinonia*. In *koinonia*, the Holy Spirit works to transform our interaction with each other while building up in us a corporate awareness of Christ's presence. In *koinonia*, the spiritual presence of Christ, God's Holy Spirit, indwells and constitutes the relationships among the members of the community in such a way that defensive barriers dissipate and grace, the heart of Jesus, permeates. Also the Holy Spirit equips each member of the community with spiritual gifts to share. (See the Maturing section in Chapter Five for a list.)

3. Another aspect of empowerment can be seen most clearly in Jesus' prayer in the Garden of Gethsemane, when he prays, "Father, if you are willing, remove this cup from me; yet, not my will but yours be done." Without the Spirit empowering the believer, the courage, confidence, even the will to do God's will is not available in us. In the Spirit all things are possible. The Spirit empowers Jesus in the Garden. It is even possible to do the will of God that one desires to do, but finds impossible to do. "Then an angel from heaven appeared to him and gave him strength." *(Luke 22:43)*

4. There is also an aspect of the empowerment dimension embedded in the humbling experience of God's grace.

Joshua Bennet, a young African American poet, illustrates this power in a poem he wrote for his sister Tamara and performed for President Obama at a poetry slam at the White House in 2011:

Tamara's Opus[17]

Tamara has never listened
to hip-hop
Never danced
to the rhythm of raindrops
or fallen asleep to a chorus of chirping crickets
she has been Deaf
for as long as I have been alive
and ever since the day that I turned five
My father has said:
"Joshua. Nothing is wrong with Tamara.
God just makes
some people different."
And at that moment
those nine letters felt like hammers
swung gracefully by unholy hands
to shatter my stained-glass innocence
into shards that could never be pieced back together
or do anything more
than sever the ties between my sister and I.

I waited
was patient numberless years
anticipating the second
her ears would open like lotuses
and allow my sunlight sentences to seep
into her insides

---

[17] Joshua Bennett. "Tamara's Opus." Disability Studies Quarterly. Vol. 32, No. 3, July 2012. http://dsq-sds.org/article/view/3273/3106

make her remember all those conversations
we must have had in Heaven
back when God hand-picked us
to be sibling souls centuries ago

I still remember her 20th birthday
readily recall my awestruck eleven-year old eyes
as I watched Deaf men and women of all ages
dance in unison to the vibrations
of speakers booming so loud
that I imagined angels chastising us
for disturbing their worship
with such beautiful blasphemy
until you have seen
a Deaf girl dance
you know nothing of passion.
There was a barricade between us
that I never took the time to destroy
never for even a moment
thought to pick up a book and look up
the signs for *sister*
for *family*
for *goodbye, I will see you again some day*
remember the face of your little brother.
It is only now I see
that I was never willing
to put in the extra effort to love her properly
So as the only person in my family
who is not fluent in sign language
I have decided to take this time
to apologize
Tamara, *I am sorry*
for my silence.

But true love knows no frequency
So I will use these hands

> to speak volumes
> that could never be contained
> within the boundaries of sound waves
> I will shout at the top of my fingertips
> until digits dance and relay these messages
> directly to your soul
> I know
> that there is no poem
> that can make up for all the time that we have lost
> but please, if you can
> *just listen*
> as I play you a symphony
> on the strings of my heart
> made for no other ears on this Earth
> but yours.

When asked about Tamara's response to seeing him perform the poem with sign language, Joshua says, "Tamara loved the piece, and was really excited the first time she saw it, which was at my sister Latoya's house, where we watched it on a big, pull-down, movie screen. Afterwards, I did a slightly condensed version of my live show for my family. From the beginning, my Dad signed the poems as I performed for Tamara, but she eventually asked him to stop. She said she could actually feel the words. It was truly a miraculous moment, and a testament to God's power, and willingness to do above and beyond what we can ask or think."

With regard to his performance at the first White House "poetry slam," Joshua says, "Easily one of the coolest days ever. I received the phone call during the spring of my junior year, and was quite shocked. It's quite the humbling request, you know? To have someone call and ask you to perform for the President. I was sitting on my bed, in my dorm room, reading, when I got the call. I was just some college kid from New York, with some poems about his life, who was blessed with the opportunity of a lifetime. To God be the glory for His favor."

Asked what is the best part of being a performing poet? Joshua responded, "At the end of a show, feeling that God was glorified, and that lives where transformed in some way. If people remain unchanged, then what I'm doing really doesn't matter. If God's love isn't communicated, in some form, then it's just words."

Joshua is humbly empowered making himself vulnerable through his poetry; while giving God the glory.[18]

5. Still another aspect of the empowerment dimension is the freedom to bestow grace on self and others, because of experiencing one's self as loved and forgiven. This is the prayer Jesus taught his disciples to pray saying: "Forgive us our sins, as we forgive those who have sinned against us." It is also the lesson Jesus taught Peter in the parable of the Unforgiving Servant in Matthew 18:21-35. God's grace empowers graciousness.

Then Peter came and said to him, "Lord, if another member of the church sins against me, how often should I forgive? As many as seven times?" Jesus said to him, "Not seven times, but, I tell you, seventy-seven times."

"For this reason the kingdom of heaven may be compared to a king who wished to settle accounts with his slaves. When he began the reckoning, one who owed him ten thousand talents was brought to him; and, as he could not pay, his lord ordered him to be sold, together with his wife and children and all his possessions, and payment to be made. So the slave fell on his knees before him, saying, 'Have patience with me, and I will pay you everything.' And out of pity for him, the lord of that slave released him and forgave him the debt. But

---

18 Nzinga, "People You Should Know: Joshua Bennett." *Jucy Africa.* WordPress, 10 Mar. 2011. Web. 04 Aug. 2014. <http://www.jucyafrica.com/people-you-should-know-joshua-bennett>

> *that same slave, as he went out, came upon one of his fellow slaves who owed him a hundred denarii; and seizing him by the throat, he said, 'Pay what you owe.' Then his fellow slave fell down and pleaded with him, 'Have patience with me, and I will pay you.' But he refused; then he went and threw him into prison until he would pay the debt. When his fellow slaves saw what had happened, they were greatly distressed, and they went and reported to their lord all that had taken place. Then his lord summoned him and said to him, 'You wicked slave! I forgave you all that debt because you pleaded with me. Should you not have had mercy on your fellow slave, as I had mercy on you?' And in anger his lord handed him over to be tortured until he would pay his entire debt. So my heavenly Father will also do to every one of you, if you do not forgive your brother or sister from your heart."*

The Apostle Paul discovered and grew in this aspect of the empowerment dimension when he experienced a "thorn in his flesh." Paul writes,

> *Three times I appealed to the Lord about this, that it would leave me, but he said to me, "My grace is sufficient for you, for power is made perfect in weakness." So, I will boast all the more gladly of my weaknesses, so that the power of Christ may dwell in me. Therefore, I am content with weaknesses, insults, hardships, persecutions, and calamities for the sake of Christ; for whenever I am weak, then I am strong.*
>
> 2 Corinthians 12:8-10

6. The central aspect of the empowerment dimension is the experience of the Holy Spirit. This is an experience we await and anticipate, but not one that can be controlled or manufactured. Receptivity and response are our only bywords.

7. A seventh aspect of empowerment is Holy Spirit empowerment to do God's work in the world. Jesus is very clear with his disciples that they needed to wait in Jerusalem until the

power of the Holy Spirit came upon them. We move into the world—to Jerusalem, all Judea, Samaria, and to the ends of the earth—empowered by the Holy Spirit. The great missionary of the church in the first century, the Apostle Paul put it this way, "I can do all things through him who strengthens me." *(Philippians 4:13)*

Ministry Implications of the Empowered Dimension

At the time of the Protestant Reformation, there were two kinds of people in the church: the clergy and the laity, and they had two different kinds of work. The work of the priesthood was sacred. The work of the laity was secular. It was just that simple. But then the Reformers started asking questions:

- What if Christianity isn't one aspect of life, but life itself?

- What if Christianity isn't merely what priests do during the week and Christians do on Sunday, but what everybody does every day of their lives?

- What if Christianity includes not only what happens between the Call to Worship and the Benediction, but also everything that takes place between the Benediction this Sunday and the Call to Worship next Sunday?

- What if Christianity is life—life lived before God?

Reading the Scriptures for themselves, the Reformers discovered that from a Biblical perspective, this is precisely what Christianity is. They traced the etymological root of the word "laity" back to its source in the Greek word *"laos,"* the term used in Scripture to designate the people of God. They read in 1 Peter 2:4-10 that this *"laos* of God," the laity is to become a kingdom of priests—a royal priesthood: "You are a chosen people, a royal priesthood...a people belonging to God...you are the people *(laos)* of God..."

This discovery shook the foundation of the church's structure.

The result was not the destruction of the priesthood, but its extension out to include each and every believer. The result was not the elimination of the sacred, but its extension to include every facet of human existence.

Every believer in Jesus Christ became a priest before God, and all of life sacred as it was lived before God. That is why Martin Luther could claim in all seriousness that the scullery maid on her knees in the kitchen rendered more effective service to God than the priest on his knees in the cloister.

A Biblical understanding of the laity requires the elevation and empowerment of every member of the congregation to minister. Biblically, there is no justification for the split-level distinction between "ordinary believer" and "clergy"; between "novice" and "professional" Christian. One doesn't have to be smart, specially trained, or super holy to be a minister for Jesus Christ. One simply needs to be a believer empowered by the Holy Spirit.

CHAPTER FOURTEEN
(PART ONE)
Sending Dimension: Sent into the World

*Then I heard the voice of the Lord saying,
"Whom shall I send, and who will go for us?"
And I said, "Here am I. Send me!"*
Isaiah 6:8

The final dimension is "Sent Into the World." It is summed up in Jesus saying to his disciples, "Go therefore and make disciples of all nations, baptizing them in the name of the Father and of the Son and of the Holy Spirit, teaching them to obey everything that I have commanded you. And remember, I am with you always, to the end of the age." *(Matthew 28:19-20)* Disciples have a story to tell. It is our God-given responsibility to tell it.

The sending dimension concerns being sent by God back into the world to interact with peoples of all nations and ethnicities. As the missional dimension, it involves the sharing of the Good News in both word and deed in interaction with people just as Jesus proclaimed the Kingdom of God, while at the same time healing the sick, feeding the hungry, and stilling the storm. Going out into the world for Jesus Christ is thus a multifaceted dimension.

Elizabeth A. Frykberg

Peter Sent to Fulfill Calling *(Acts 10:1-48)*

Question: To what ministries was Peter called and commissioned to serve? How did this come about?

It is ten years after Jesus gave this final command to "go and make disciples of all nations," to be his "witnesses in Jerusalem, and in all Judea and Samaria, and to the ends of the earth." *(Matthew 28:19; Acts 1:8)* Ten years since Peter's baptism in the Spirit. During those ten years the Gospel had been preached in Jerusalem (Acts 2), Judea, and Samaria *(Acts 8:1, 4, 5, 25)* But it had not yet been preached to the nations. The Gentile mission had not yet begun. It had not begun, because Jewish Law prescribed the separation of Jew from Gentile. As a New Testament scholar, F.F. Bruce writes, "Association with Gentiles was not categorically forbidden; but it did render a Jew ceremonially unclean, as did even the entering of Gentile buildings or the handling of articles belonging to Gentiles. The most ordinary kinds of food, such as bread, milk or olive oil, coming from Gentiles, could not be eaten by strict Jews…to accept Gentile hospitality and sit at table with them was the most intolerable."[19]

Given these cultural restrictions, Jews did not and could NOT conceive of Jesus' command to "disciple the nations" as meaning "disciple the Gentiles." For them, "Go into all the world baptizing in the name of the Father, Son and Holy Spirit" meant preaching to the Jews living outside of Israel, not preaching to the Gentiles who lived there. To disciple Gentiles went against the precepts of Jewish culture and tradition. Not yet fully understanding the full scope of the Gospel or its intended audience, the Christian church originally drew its membership exclusively from the Jewish community.

Like the rest of the early church, Peter's missionary vision was also eclipsed by culture and tradition. On his own, he could not break free from its shackles. Yet, there is evidence that the Gospel of grace was beginning to change Peter's attitude. For example, when Peter was in Joppa, he stayed at the house of Simon the tanner.

---

19 F.F. Bruce, *The Acts of the Apostles*, William B. Eerdman's Publishing, Grand Rapids Michigan, 1990.

The tanning trade was considered unclean, because tanners killed unclean animals, worked in blood, and were in constant contact with different things that might make them unclean. Most orthodox Jews wouldn't stay in such a place. Yet Peter did.

One day, Peter is standing on the roof of Simon the tanner's house waiting for food to be prepared. All around him are reminders of the uncleanness of the place: the smell and squeals of animals being slaughtered, skins hanging in the sun to dry, the blood-stained hands of those working on the tanning process. Still, Simon the tanner is Jewish. It is a Jewish home that Peter is in. At least the food would be kosher.

What happens next is described in Acts 11:1-18. While standing on the roof prior to lunch, Peter has a vision—a vision of a cloth coming out of the sky filled with all kinds of creatures—all kinds of unclean animals. A voice from heaven says, "Get up, Peter. Kill and eat." *(vs. 13)* Since Peter knows to not eat that which was unclean, he replies, "Surely not, Lord! I have never eaten anything impure or unclean." *(vs. 14)*

Peter then hears a heavenly voice saying: "Do not call anything impure that God has made clean." *(vs. 15)* This happens three times, before the sheet is taken back up into heaven. *(vs. 16)* The vision leaves Peter thinking and wondering about its meaning.

What happens next reads like the sequel to the story of the disciples' baptism on Pentecost. Many of the details are exactly the same. The new twist is that this time the community being baptized in the Holy Spirit is Gentile, not Jewish.

While Peter is still thinking about the vision, the Spirit says to him, "Look, three men are searching for you. Now get up, go down, and go with them without hesitation; for I have sent them."

The day before Peter's vision of the sheet coming down out of heaven, an angel of the Lord appears to a man named Cornelius, a Roman centurion, who lives 30 miles away in Caesarea. He is a devout man who fears God with his whole household. He gives alms generously to the people and prays constantly to God. The angel says to Cornelius, "Your prayers and your alms have ascended as a memorial before God. Now send men to Joppa for a certain Simon who is called Peter; he is lodging with Simon, a tanner, whose house is by the seaside." So Cornelius calls two of his slaves and a devout soldier from the ranks of those who serve him, and sends them to Joppa. When they arrive, Peter, encouraged by the Spirit, breaks Jewish tradition by agreeing to go with these men to the home of Cornelius, a Gentile.

When Peter gets to Caesarea, Cornelius explains that he has sent for Peter because a heavenly voice instructed him to do so. Having had a couple of days to think about his own strange vision, Peter hears and interprets the events saying, "I truly understand that God shows no partiality, but in every nation anyone who fears God and does what is right is acceptable to God." What an insight for a first century Jew! "Any person in any nation who reverences God and works righteousness may belong to God."

This new fuller understanding of God's graciousness prompts Peter to introduce Cornelius and his household to the Lord Jesus — preaching the Good News of Jesus Christ to a Gentile audience for the first time. While Peter is speaking, the Holy Spirit falls upon Cornelius and all those listening in Cornelius' home. The Jewish Christians who have accompanied Peter from Joppa to Caesarea are amazed, because God has poured out the Holy Spirit upon Gentiles! Peter in response asks the Jewish Christians with him, "Can anyone withhold the water of baptism from these people who have already received the Holy Spirit just as we have?" It is a rhetorical question. So Peter orders Cornelius and his household to be baptized in the name of Jesus Christ.

What happens in this series of events is that the transformed Peter becomes outwardly focused; he and the church are sent fully into the world, the sent dimension of faith. Fulfillment of Peter's calling by Jesus is realized, "I will make you fishers of people." (*Matthew 4:19*)

Peter's Seven-Dimensional Faith

With the baptism of Cornelius and the opening up of the Gospel to the whole world, Peter has fully engaged all seven dimensions of faith. He now lives out of the seven dimensions, continually reengaging them. Peter proclaims the Good News of Jesus Christ (Listening Dimension); lives in community with the other disciples forming the early church (Community Dimension); wills and does the will of God, boldly preaching the Gospel in the face of opposition without fear (Desiring Dimension); humbly leads the church, not from ego strength but in the Spirit for the sake of Jesus Christ (Humbled Dimension); Peter bestows grace, forgiving the unforgivable as seen in his acceptance of the Apostle Paul (Grace Dimension); teaches, preaches, heals, and leads the church empowered by the Holy Spirit (Empowered Dimension); leads the church into preaching the Gospel to the whole world, Jew and Greek, slave and free. (Sent Dimension)

Once the seven dimensions of the Jesus faith fractal are transformationally experienced, they continue to be engaged and re-engaged. A disciple of Jesus Christ needs to continually:

1. Hear the Word

2. Live in Christian Community

3. Desire to Do the Will of God

4. Humbly Acknowledge Ones Human Limitations

5. Experience Grace and Forgiveness

6. Stay in Communion with God in the Holy Spirit

7. Go into the World

Elizabeth A. Frykberg

Two Contemporary Stories: Sent into the World Chantielle's Katrina Story

On August 29, 2005, Hurricane Katrina made landfall on the Gulf Coast causing catastrophic damage. That evening I fell asleep to images of unimaginable desperation, while unabashedly begging God to use me, send me. Without knowing how fully and wildly God would grant my request, I drifted off without turning off the television. God answered before dawn. I woke up at 2 a.m. to a man on the screen holding up his baby to the camera saying, "I don't care what you have to do to get here, just come"

"Done! Hold on, I'm on my way!"

I impatiently waited until a reasonable hour to start making phone calls. Friends answered, said they were all in, as I outlined a plan, which was really no plan at all just framework. But I knew this: I was going and I was taking supplies for babies. By noon, I had spent next month's house payment to rent a 25-foot moving truck and had a team of people willing to help. By sunset we had made contact with the Houston Food Bank, had a parking spot in front of a major retailer and were collecting diapers, wipes and formula. That's it.

Word quickly got out. Another church across town set up a truck for the same thing and added all their donations to ours. Three days later we had received what was estimated to be $60,000 worth of supplies. In addition, there was enough money donated to cover the cost of gas, the truck rental, and eventually a plane ticket. In those three days, we met hundreds of generous people. People who gave the last of the change out of their ashtray; people who came with their cars packed with supplies, because they had to go all over town to find anything left. The manager of the retailer we were parked at came out and told us the shelves were empty. Empty! In fact, all the baby supply

The Jesus Fractal

shelves in all the local stores were empty. It was all inside our truck. Everything we needed, everything was provided. There was not one thing God left out no matter how small.

Two other people joined me on the drive to Texas for safety, for company, and (for my main motivation) to be able to drive continuously until we arrived. My husband, who championed the effort all along, stayed at home with our children. The three of us left at dark on the third day. It wasn't until we reached the freeway that I realized I didn't have a map. I had no idea how to get to Texas from our hometown of Vancouver, Washington. Head south just wasn't going to cut it. Laughing, we pulled over, got a map and were on our way.

It took us three and a half long, air conditioning free days to get there. While driving 2300 miles, there was a lot of opportunity to stare out across the plains. I split my time, as both passenger and driver, calculating time and distances all while in disbelief as to what had taken place over the week. Somewhere in that quiet time, only for a split second, I wished I was going to be home in time for our son's fifth birthday. The math just didn't add up. There was just no way to get the truck back home in time.

We arrived at the Houston Food Bank, the non-profit I had originally contacted, but soon drove away from their facility with all of the baby supplies still loaded in the truck. It was explained to us that items donated there were going to be distributed to everyone in Houston not just the victims of Katrina. I knew immediately, it was time to go. This wasn't the plan! Right. Going to the food bank was my plan, not God's. That was the problem. We left the food bank asking for directions to the Astrodome.

Found it! We pulled up to the guard shack amongst thousands of displaced traumatized people. We were there without any contact inside. We didn't have formal paperwork. We were, on paper and in every other way completely unauthorized, untrained and unqualified to enter into the Houston Astrodome that day, except that God unquestionably sent us here. The guard looked at me as if I was supposed to respond with a secret password. I said nothing. He waited.

I said, "We were sent here with a truck load of diapers, wipes and formula for the people."

He paused, and sent us in saying, "Drive around to the loading bays. They will help you from there."

We were in. I backed the truck up into loading bay Number 3 and was greeted immediately. The man took one look at us and couldn't help but ask this road weary trio where we were from. In disbelief, he unloaded the truck for us in minutes.

Now what? Do we turn around and go home? This was enough for sure, but do they need us here? What can we do while we are here? Again, we say, "Use us."

They did. We were taken to the Salvation Army lead coordinator, put on the Houston Pastoral Care Team, given name badge identifications that read "Chaplain," before being sent into the dome. We spent the rest of that day meeting people, hearing their stories of being rescued by helicopter from the floodwaters. We watched the reunion of a family, who had been fearfully waiting for news of their family member's safety. I offered prayer for a woman. When she began to speak, she didn't wail for her losses; she praised God she was alive.

Around sundown, I received a phone call from my husband. My family at home had been in a very minor car accident. It was a bump, a tap, but they needed me to know nonetheless. That was the moment every detail of the last week caught up with me. Exhausted, overwhelmed, I bawled. I really bawled. My companions hugged me; there in that insufferable Texas heat and said, "You've done what you were called to do. It's time for you to go home."

They drove me to the airport and dropped me off before starting to drive the empty truck north. The airlines were offering next to free tickets for relief workers. The

Chaplain's identification badge was the only thing I had to show evidence of my eligibility to fly out that night. I was on the next plane home. It was the night before our son's fifth birthday. I arrived at 2:30 a.m. home by 3:30 a.m. and woke up to the sound of my son yelling, "It's my birthday! It's my birthday!! Mom!! You're home!"

"Yes, I am."

Man J. Kim

While contemplating what example to use to illustrate this sending dimension, I received an email from a member of our congregation suggesting that I go pick up the *San Mateo Daily Journal* and read the article on the front page about a new restaurant opening on B Street. When I read the article, I said, "Wow! That is the refiner's fire at work in the life of an individual, recreating them in the image of God to "go" into the world right here in our community."

This is what I read:

> New life will soon be breathed into the long-standing ornate site of the former Ristorante Capellini in downtown San Mateo...
>
> After the historic building on the corner of Baldwin Avenue and B Street sat vacant for more than a year, (the) owner of several well-known San Francisco restaurants, turned a longing eye toward the 10,000-square-foot, three-story property that once served as a high-end Italian eatery for more than 26 years.
>
> Although his wife thinks his plans are bold if not crazy, (this restaurateur) envisions two concepts at one site—tentatively named Lori and Capellini.
>
> Unlike the former Capellini, (the new owner) said he wants to open as an American-style diner for breakfast and lunch before heeding to the site's roots as an Italian restaurant during the evening.
>
> Another unique aspect, the Korean-born Hillsborough

resident said is that he plans to donate 20 percent of the restaurant's net profit to local charities.

"We're going to make sure that our local charities are going to get some support from small business people, so I hope this kind of movement can spread. I don't have to put money in the coffin, I have to help other people who need help."

The self-made businessman grew up poor before moving to the United States in 1972 to attend college in San Francisco. Starting out as a cab driver, (he) forged a successful career with this new San Mateo endeavor marking his ninth restaurant.

"Business people are so infatuated with making money. I am a Christian at the Burlingame Presbyterian Church, we learned we have to help each other and help the poor. I believe this is something our business people have to learn and practice…. While I only have about 20 years of my life left, I want to make a small difference in our community. So that's been my dream."

Man J. Kim said his daughter, who recently graduated from Columbia University and studied nonprofit management, inspired him to commit to benefiting local charities, particularly those that promote education and job training for youth.

Man, who is in church every Sunday, went on to say, "We are not perfect restaurant operators. But we try our best. As much as we can, our first priority is the customer. We never dispute or disobey their request. And always try our very best so they can have a good memory and experience, that's our philosophy. And another philosophy of running our business is accuracy, honesty and transparency. So we're always hungry for an IRS auditor," Kim said. "I'm so happy to have this location and to explore possibly having the business be useful and beneficial for our community."[20]

---

20 Samantha Weigel. "New Life for an Old Site: San Francisco Restaurant Owner Man J. Kim Takes over Former Capellini." *The Daily Journal* [San Mateo] 3 June 2015: 1. Print.

I was humbled and moved, as I read this article. The man who comes as a team member on our medical mission trips to Honduras to run the children's ministry and do magic tricks doesn't need to get on an airplane to "go" into the world. He does so everyday.

That is what the sending dimension looks like in the life of Man J. Kim and his family.

Interlude for Theological Reflection:

God is love. God in love sends Jesus Christ the Son of God into the world, because God the Love Fractal (see Introduction) wants a Love Fractal replica of God's Self in humankind. Jesus Christ is sent to restore the Love Fractal by means of the Jesus Fractal, to enable and empower humankind to reflect and embody the life of the Trinity—and to build new community that reflects the quality of life shared by Father, Son and Holy Spirit. This is also our motivation for going into the world.

Characteristics of Persons Growing in the Sending Dimension

People living out of this sending dimension live in the world focused on living out of the Good News of God's love made manifest in Jesus Christ's life, death, and resurrection. This living out of God's love is not a program or an isolated event; rather it is life empowered by the Holy Spirit. There is a sense of "I serve with God in the world in my daily life. I am a conduit of God's love, empowered and sent by the Spirit to do the will of God in the world." Living in union with Jesus Christ in the sending dimension, people live out their calling and purpose as ordained by God, even when they are called to serve sacrificially after the pattern of Jesus Christ. They live as humble servants of God loving sacrificially, when called to do so.

People who fail to grow through this dimension are those who do Christian good works, self-directed and self-empowered, not as humble servants sent by the Father. They don't live empowered by the Spirit. The ego is still singular, not in dialectical relationship with the Spirit who lives in them.

Characteristics of Persons Sent into the World

Dimension:	Persona	Focus	I Statements	Obstruction	Moving On
Sent into the world.	Missionary: "I am an empowered servant of the Triune God."	Living the Good News of Jesus Christ.	I am a conduit of God's love, empowered and sent by the Triune God.	I send myself into the world to do the good works, because that is who I will to be.	Union with Christ; living ones calling.

Maturing in the Sending Dimension

We grow in serving God in the world as we encounter all seven dimensions on our faith journey. The missional mind of Jesus Christ grows and matures in us over time. There are many aspects to growing into seven dimensional living.

1. An initial aspect of maturing in the sending dimension of the Jesus Fractal is hearing and acknowledging the call of God to go. This involves the discovery of God's purpose for one's life.

2. A second aspect of living the seventh dimension is actual participation with other believers in a mission experience in the world. It could be as part of a service worship experience going into one's local community for a day or a short-term mission trip to serve a hurting or needful people further away. What this involves is the experience of being in the world for Jesus Christ with the support of the community of faith. It is a precursor to living as a Christian in the world on one's own. Here, the support of a small covenant group on the mission where one can reflect, share and explore how one is

living for Christ in one's daily life is also important. Through these kinds of mission experiences participants experience Christian community at a greater depth and come to greater understanding of who Jesus Christ really is. It was during a short-term mission trip, when the disciples discovered that Jesus was the Messiah.

3. A third aspect of growing in the missional dimension of faith is to seek congruence of purpose with God's will. This requires the courage and the freedom to communicate with God exactly where one is in one's thought process. This is Jesus in the Garden, "Father, if you are willing, remove this cup from me." *(Luke 22:42)*

4. A fourth aspect of the sending dimension is humbly confessing one's inability to do what God wants done, yet still choosing to surrender to God's will.

5. A fifth aspect of being sent into the world is living and loving sacrificially after the pattern of Jesus Christ in daily and gracious interaction with God, self and others. One does not just love friends, family and those who agree with us, but also our enemies.

6. A sixth aspect is living out of one's dialectic identity with Jesus Christ, living out of Jesus Christ's death and resurrection. As the Apostle Paul wrote, "I have been crucified with Christ; and it is no longer I who live, but it is Christ who lives in me." *(Galatians 2:19-20)* This means allowing God to work God's wonders through the person.

7. A final aspect of the sent dimension is ascension with Jesus Christ to the Father at death.

> As was the man of dust, so are those who are of the dust; and as is the man of heaven, so are those who are of heaven. Just as we have borne the image of the man of dust, we will also bear the image of the man of heaven. ...

> For this perishable body must put on imperishability, and this mortal body must put on immortality. When this perishable body puts on imperishability, and this mortal body puts on immortality, then the saying that is written will be fulfilled: "Death has been swallowed up in victory." "Where, O death, is your victory? Where, O death, is your sting?" The sting of death is sin, and the power of sin is the law. But thanks be to God, who gives us the victory through our Lord Jesus Christ."
>
> *1 Corinthians 15:48-49; 53-57*

CHAPTER FIFTEEN
(PART TWO)
Sending Dimension:
Ministry Implication: Flowing Fountain of the Seventh Dimension

Our being sent into the world has been helpfully visualized as a fountain.[21] In a classic tiered fountain, water is carried upward through a central column before cascading back down into the tiers below. Like water in a tiered fountain, the Holy Spirit brings God's love afresh to us each day; God's love then flows into and through our lives. Experiences of God's love and grace are awesome, but they are not primarily given for, nor can they be contained in, individual spiritual experience, no matter how moving or profound. Accordingly, the apostle Paul describes the movement outward saying, "May the God of hope fill you with all joy and peace as you trust in him, so that you may overflow with hope by the power of the Holy Spirit." *(Romans 1:15)*

Where are we to overflow?

---

21 *Outflow* by Steve Sjogren and Dave Ping, 2007 Group Publishing

Jesus commissioned his disciples saying, "You will receive power when the Holy Spirit has come upon you; and you will be my witnesses in Jerusalem, in all Judea and Samaria, and to the ends of the earth." *(Acts 1:8)* So the first tier of the fountain of the sending or going out dimension is *Jerusalem*; *Judea* the second; *Samaria* the third; and *the ends of the earth* the fourth tier. If we think about this verse and the fountain metaphorically, as ever widening ripples of relational engagement. *Jerusalem* is about our personal relationship with God within the church community; *Judea* concerns engagement with friends and family; *Samaria* our relationships with the larger community; and *the ends of the earth* is reaching out to encounter the poor and marginalized peoples of the world.

Jerusalem, the first tier, catches and then distributes the love made manifest to and in us through the Holy Spirit. This first tier is about our personal and corporate relationship with God. Jerusalem is where God's temple, God's dwelling place, is located. Today, Jerusalem is still a place of pilgrimage where Jews, Christians and Muslims alike go to feel close to God. This first tier of the sending dimension is about our being sent into the world from worship. We move into the world from our worship of Jesus Christ. Ever wonder why on mission trips, devotions are not optional? Well this is why! Worship and our experience of God's love in worship is where the energy and passion (empowerment) for Christian mission originates. It is an energy and passion that must be shared. Trying to contain God's love, treating it as one's own personal and private possession is like continuing to blow air into a balloon until it pops. When we treat God's love as our possession we become overinflated. God's love cannot be contained.

The most natural place for the love of God to overflow is into our relationships with friends and family, this is *Judea*, the place we call home. So the second tier of the fountain represents our relationships with friends and family. It is to the peril of the Christian community that we ignore or minimize this tier, because Christianity is, as the maxim says, "Just one generation from extinction."

When I was a youth pastor in Pasadena, California, I opened

up my home to kids who were alienated from their parents for a variety of reasons. At one point I had 11 young people under my care, all with the consent and appreciation of their parents. I was only 27 at the time, still I was affectionately known as "the old woman who lived in the shoe." You remember the Mother Goose rhyme:

> There was an old woman who lived in a shoe.
> She had so many children, she didn't know what to do;
> She gave them some broth without any bread;
> Then whipped them all soundly and put them to bed

I believe the Spirit of Christ worked in the midst of our home on Atchison Street transforming the old rhyme to read:

> There was a young woman who lived in a shoe,
> With teenage children, who needed love too.
> She thanked the Lord Jesus, for sending them bread.
> Hugged each one gladly then sent them to bed.

Family is not limited to blood relations, but includes any and all whom we would invite into our homes to share a meal, a conversation, or hospitality in any form.

God's love spilled out from our home in Pasadena into the larger community.

Samaria is the third tier of our metaphorical fountain. It represents the sending dimension. One day, Ralph Story, a popular Los Angeles newscaster, came with a camera crew to interview us—me and the teenagers in my home. He did this soon after the Jonestown massacre. The filming took place in our home and then over at the church. We were the feature story on ABC's evening news one night. Mr. Story wanted the people of Los Angeles to understand that the Reverend Jim Jones was an anomaly and not at all representative of the vast majority of ministers or Christian ministries. Ralph Story and ABC News came knocking on our door, because people in the community were talking about us. Word about our home was out on the street. God's love experienced in the home overflowed into *Samaria,* the community. (By the way, the young people who lived in my home all eventually professed Jesus Christ as Lord and Savior and as far as I know continue in adulthood to live in faith relationship with our Lord raising their own children to know Jesus.)

How ever it happens, moving out into the community is the third tier of the sending dimension of our being sent into the world. So from relationships with friends and family, the loving Spirit of God flows outward spilling over into our relationships with the larger community. This is the *Samaria* tier. *Samaria* is right next door to Judea but very different. While traveling from Galilee in the north to Judea in the south, many Jews would avoid Samaria. Like Samaria to the Jews, witnessing to God's love in the larger community may seem scary. That is why some people block or ignore the flowing waters of the Spirit of this tier—rejection, embarrassment, mockery, and public humiliation are the hells we fear. The service-worship movement is the worshiping community moving out into *Samaria.* My friend, the Reverend Dr. Kim Engelmann, tells the story of Service-Worship in her West Valley Presbyterian Church this way:

> Five years ago the leadership of West Valley Presbyterian Church met to discuss next steps for the health of the church. We all agreed that we had a problem.
>
> Doing the same thing over and over on a Sunday morning was only appealing to the same set of people again and again. The mission of the church to do outreach coined in our statement of purpose "to know Christ and make Him known" was not being fulfilled on a regular basis beyond our walls.
>
> That is when we decided to cancel our regular Sunday morning worship service once a quarter and, in place of the traditional service, worship by serving others. That is how the phrase "Service-Worship Sunday" came into being. We

remembered Jesus' statement, "Whatever you do to the least of these my children, you do it unto me." (Matthew 25:40) We recognized that by showing compassion and mercy to those around us, we were glorifying God and worshipping in a whole new way. Helping others in tangible ways was something un-churched people could understand. Again and again, as we engaged in community service on Sunday mornings we heard observers tell us, "This is so wonderful. This is what the church should be doing."

Of course, there were many unknowns as we got started. We weren't sure how the congregation would react, and we had no idea how we were going to find enough community service projects for everyone to engage in on a Sunday morning. Still we were confident that it was the direction that the Holy Spirit was leading us. For the most part, people in the church responded with cautious optimism. It was worth "giving it a try." Five years later we are still going strong. We also discovered a host of opportunities available to us on Sundays—from feeding over 150 homeless people at CityTeam, to stocking and cleaning the food bank at the local community service center. We've cleaned up yards for senior citizens, knitted caps for cancer patients, helped Habitat for Humanity build a home, assisted a local school with a garden for children, and provided a worship service for a nursing home. The list goes on and on. On any given Service-Worship Sunday we have about 15 projects where our congregation can serve.

Not only has Service-Worship benefited the larger Cupertino/San Jose community but, as we had hoped, it has benefited us as a faith community as well. We have grown in our relationships with one another as we have served together with a common purpose. No longer are we reaching the same people over and over again. New people have joined our church because of the Service-Worship program. There is a growing awareness of the wide range of services we provide and non-profits are calling us now to see if we might be available for various needs.

The best part? Everything we do, we do in the name of Jesus Christ for his glory and honor. We think people can understand God's love for them a little bit better when we stop talking about God in our churches, and start putting his love into action in our communities.

The fourth and largest tier the Spirit works to fill with God's love is the "ends of the earth." God calls on us to reach out to the poor and marginalized people of the world in ever widening circles of love. At our church, we have identified and are seeking to fulfill the needs of poor and marginalized people locally through our food bank, the homeless shelter we host in our Fellowship Hall six weeks a year, in our involvement with Habitat for Humanity, Service-Worship, our Spirit Care's seniors ministry, and the Hillcrest Chaplaincy up at our local juvenile detention center. We reach out regionally through programs like the Center for Students Missions. We serve the poor nationally on mission trips with Amor Ministries to the Apache Reservation in San Carlos, Arizona, and when teaming with Presbyterian Disaster Assistance. We reach out internationally through our Orphan Compassion Ministry to 214 vulnerable children in Cameroon like Leonard whose story is in Chapter Four, bringing medical and dental care to rural villages in Honduras, building homes with Amor in Mexico, and in our surgical mission trip to serve Guatemala's poor with Faith in Practice.

Through these kinds of mission opportunities, churches bear witness to Christ through their actions and proclaim the Good News when telling people why they are there. So why does the church go there? They have been sent by Jesus to love in the manner of Jesus. The mission programs of churches are also reflective of Jesus' commissioning of his disciples in Acts 1:8, "You will receive power when the Holy Spirit comes on you; and you will be my witnesses in *Jerusalem (locally)*, and in all *Judea (regionally)* and *Samaria (nationally)*, and to *the ends of the earth (internationally)*."

All of us are called to be missionaries. We are not sent into the world to "go forth and live comfortable, complacent lives." We are sent into the world to bring glory to God witnessing to Jesus Christ in word and deed. Our faith is not to be compartmentalized or walled into our church buildings. No part of our lives is off limits to God. When deeply touched by the Good News of Jesus Christ, God's love can't help but overflow into every aspect of our lives.

The sending dimension is not limited to church programs. This dimension is lived out in the life of each and every believer wherever they are in the world. It is in this way that God's love can most effectively reach the world.

PART THREE:

So What?

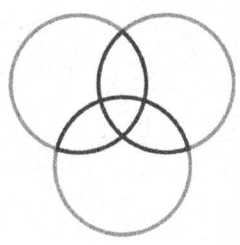

CHAPTER SIXTEEN
(PART ONE)
Spiritual Practices for Each Dimension

Dallas Willard defines a discipline as an "activity within our power—something we can do—which brings us to a point where we can do what we, at present, cannot do by direct effort." In other words, the spiritual disciplines enable us to participate and cooperate with the transformation God wills and works in our lives through the ministry of the Holy Spirit. The disciplines prepare us for God's redemptive activity. They do not in and of themselves accomplish the task of maturing us spiritually. That is the work of Holy Spirit.

In this chapter, we will outline seven spiritual disciplines that function within each of the seven dimensions and seven different practices within each discipline, as they function within each dimension. The seven disciplines that parallel the seven dimensions, and then refract as spiritual practices are:

1. **Scripture:** The Word of God given to us in the Old and New Testaments.

2. **Prayer:** Communication with God spoken, thought, enacted, and visceral.

3. **Silence/Solitude:** Removing distractions of sound to focus on God and God's will for one's life.

4. **Confession:** Facing one's fallen human condition honestly and in the context of God's grace.

5. **Grace/Rhythm:** Opening the self to receive the gift of God's grace.

6. **Celebration/Worship:** Praising and connecting to God who empowers the individual and the community to do God's will.

7. **Service:** Serving God in the world.

These seven disciplines parallel with the dimensions in the following fashion.

Dimension	Discipline
Listening	Scripture
Following in Community	Prayer
Desire to Do God's Will	Silence/Solitude
Humbled in Faith	Confession
Graced by God's Love	Grace/Rhythm
Empowered by the Spirit	Celebration/Worship
Sent	Service

The following chart depicts the relationship of a particular practice to a discipline and a dimension.

Spiritual Practices of Seven Spiritual Disciplines Reflecting the Seven Dimensions

	Listen	Follow in Community	Desiring God's Will	Humbled	Graced by God's Love	Empowered by the Spirit	Sent
Scripture	Listen to the Word of God	Fellowship/ Small group Bible Study	Read, study, and memorize Scripture by repeated reading (God's will in general can be found in Scripture)	Self-reflective/ journaling response to how Scripture interacts with your life (convicting you)	Transforming Bible Study Transformed/ Ignatian exercises	Lectio Divina (Reading in the Spirit)	Testify to the effect of the Word of God in your life
Prayer	Listen to the concerns of your heart; talk to God about them.	Conversational prayer with prayer partner/ prayer group	Prayer for guidance meditation/ silence	Private/personal Confession to God	Centering prayer—doorway to contemplative (wordless) prayer.	Prayerfully explore and discern your spiritual gifts	Intercessory Prayer
Silence/ Solitude	Listen to creation on a walk in nature.	Corporate silence	Lonely place: seeking guidance in solitude/ Silence	Self examination using The Examen	Receive love letter from God/ Write love letter to God	Write your Seven Dimensional Faith Story (or about an encounter you had with the Holy)	Neighborhood Prayer Walk

Confession	Respond to hearing the Good News of God's love, explore any resistance to God's love	Corporate confession; Confession to God in small accountability group setting	Seek guidance in Spiritual Direction	Engaging in Spiritual Direction on an ongoing basis; confessing to God when appropriate—"A long look at the real"	Confess your weakness asking to experience the sufficiency and power of God's grace	Practice Abstinence Simplicity Frugality Letting Go to God	Confess to others what God has done for you; tell your Seven Dimensional Faith Story
Grace/rhythm	Listen for the deepest desire of your heart; the rhythms of your body and soul.	Create margin in your day, slow down, to find more time for God and others.	Body Rhythm Fast Celibacy Body stewardship	Secret good works, open confession of failure and misdeeds	Take a weekly Sabbath rest	Wait for grace filled spiritual empowerment	Develop and live your own Seven Dimensional rule (rhythm)
Celebration/Worship	Listen to God speak in Word centered Worship	Corporate Worship on an ongoing basis with your faith community	Ordination/ Commissioning Dedication/ Marker event celebration	Confessional, repentant, themed worship like: World Peace, Unity, Hunger	Contemplative Worship	Praise Centered/ Spirit lead Worship	Live the two greatest commandments
Service	Experience the Gospel in your doing	Service to faith community using spiritual gifts	Service in daily life in every moment	Sacrificial, self-giving service	Compassionate Service	Use spiritual gifts in larger community	In the Spirit, live God's calling, God's will for your life

There are 49 different practices listed in this Spiritual Disciplines vs. Spiritual Dimensions Chart. These are not the only practices that intersect the disciplines and dimensions at those specific points. You may know and engage in comparable practices at some of the intersections. Thus, the chart is suggestive, not prescriptive. The hope is for you to find it helpful, while realizing that it is neither all-inclusive nor set in stone. God is way too dynamic and creative a communicator for that to be the case. Most of the practices suggested are structures without specific content. For instance, specific Scriptures to read are left up to you to populate. Enjoy the adventure of drawing closer to God, as you engage with God in seven dimensional spiritual practices. To get you orientated, we will first describe each of the seven practices for each of the seven dimensions in more detail in this chapter before explaining how to use the chart in the next.[22]

Listening Dimension Practices

The *Shema* is the first prayer of the Jewish prayer book and usually the first prayer a Jewish child learns. The prayer commands Israel to "hear"—to "listen."

> Hear, O Israel: The LORD is our God, the LORD alone. You shall love the LORD your God with all your heart, and with all your soul, and with all your might. Keep these words that I am commanding you today in your

---

[22] Note: There are other lists of disciplines organized in different ways. Dallas Willard in *The Spirit of the Disciplines* talks about the disciplines in terms of "Disciplines of Abstinence" and "Disciplines of Engagement." Richard Foster in *Celebration of Disciplines* breaks the disciplines into Inward, Outward, and Corporate Disciplines. These organizational schemes have been incredibly useful to many. Their work and that of others has been groundbreaking in helping those outside the Orthodox and Roman Catholic traditions to intentionally participate in growing in intimacy with God. This book's different way of organizing seeks to build on their work in light of the seven dimensions. The practices described here are therefore not new, just utilized and viewed in light of the seven dimensions.

> heart. Recite them to your children and talk about them when you are at home and when you are away, when you lie down and when you rise. Bind them as a sign on your hand, fix them as an emblem on your forehead, and write them on the doorposts of your house and on your gates.
>
> *Deuteronomy 6:4-9 NRSV)*

Devout Jews recite the prayer when they awake, when they go to bed, and when they instruct their children. *Shema* means "hear." Listening has from the beginning, then, been a foundational spiritual dimension in the Judeo-Christian tradition. Listening to the voice of God coming from outside of the self is not something that is done once. It is a practice for morning and night, part of one's daily life, passed on from generation to generation.

Below are seven spiritual practices (one for each of the seven disciplines) that can help us to listen to God, who speaks in a myriad of ways if we will just listen:

Scripture: Listen to Scripture read aloud. Pay attention; attend to the words, the meaning. Let the words in Scripture speak to you as if for the first time. Set aside your prior understanding and your memory of what you believe the passage says; instead listen anew.

Prayer: Moving through your day, hear the prayers of your heart, the concerns you have for yourself, your family, and friends, but also for circumstances and people as you encounter them in the moment. Lift your concerns to God as you experience them. These are known as arrow prayers. Set aside a specific time to talk to God about what is on your heart.

Solitude/Silence: Walk in nature in silent meditation and listen with all of your senses to nature, the world God spoke into existence. What do you hear God saying to you through creation?

Confession: While hearing some form of presentation about how much God loves you, be open, honest, spontaneous and unguarded with God as to how you are feeling and hearing that message of love. Confess any doubt, insecurity, resistance, or guilt you experience standing in the way of you embracing God's love for you.

Grace/Rhythm: In 1670, Blaise Pascal in *Pensées*, a defense of Christianity, wrote,

> What else does this craving, and this helplessness, proclaim but that there was once in man a true happiness, of which all that now remains is the empty print and trace? This he tries in vain to fill with everything around him, seeking in things that are not there the help he cannot find in those that are, though none can help, since this infinite abyss can be filled only with an infinite and immutable object; in other words by God himself.[23]

This thought has been reworked into the concept: "There is a God-shaped hole in the human heart." In this practice, seeking this place of internal void, a person listens to the deepest desires of their heart to discover their deep longing for God that nothing else can satisfy. Another listening practice that takes place, as a person turns inward self-reflectively, is discovering the rhythm of the body and soul. This means getting in touch with and respecting one's personal and God-given circadian rhythm. Both of these introspective exercises help a person get in touch with their heart, mind, strength and soul.

Worship/Celebration: Listening for God to speak through the Word of God heard in worship with a community of believers is another essential Christian practice. In Reformed tradition in particular, worship is designed to attend to the Word of God in its threefold form: read, proclaimed, and enacted in the sacraments in the presence of Jesus Christ. Listening for a personal word enlivens the worship experience. This hearing also leads to the next practice of "acting on what one has heard."

---

23 Blaise Pascal, *Pensées*, a defense of Christianity, Penguin.148/428

Service: Having listened and heard the Word of God, the culminating listening practice is to act on what one has heard. Jesus said:

> Why do you call me "Lord, Lord", and do not do what I tell you? I will show you what someone is like who comes to me, hears my words, and acts on them. That one is like a man building a house, who dug deeply and laid the foundation on rock; when a flood arose, the river burst against that house but could not shake it, because it had been well built. But the one who hears and does not act is like a man who built a house on the ground without a foundation. When the river burst against it, immediately it fell, and great was the ruin of that house.
>
> *Luke 6:46-49*

Responding to the Word is what it means to really listen and hear.

Following in Community Practices

> "They devoted themselves to the apostles' teaching and to the fellowship, to the breaking of bread and to prayer."
>
> *Acts 2:42*

Central to following Jesus Christ in community is the experience of fellowship (*koinonia*). This is not just drinking coffee or enjoying a glass of wine together. Fellowship happens as people engage in community activities with other believers in the presence of the Spirit of Jesus Christ. These communal activities will often be spiritual practices, such as Bible study, prayer, worship, celebration, and service, but may also involve activities of table fellowship like sharing a meal. In either case, the spiritual gift of hospitality in these community settings is key. Hospitality involves the selfless practice of opening one's life, home, church groups, and hearts to others to the glory of God and for Christ's sake. It is inviting the stranger, the lonely, the new, even the outcast into your community in the hope that the making of room for the outsider results in their becoming insiders.

With this as background, some possible spiritual practices (one for each of the seven disciplines) that can help people follow and experience Jesus Christ in community are:

Scripture: One significant and multidimensional practice is small group Bible Study. Like worship services, small group Bible studies may in and of themselves touch all seven dimensions. That is not a requirement of small group ministry, just the potential. In small group Bible studies members can pray for one another. Prayers shared with a small group can provide insight into a person's heart in ways discussion may not. Creating a context of rapport, where each member of the group feels safe, is crucial, and requires mutual trust and shared commitment to confidentiality. When these are experienced, people will risk becoming more vulnerable. Everyone wants to be known and loved, warts and all, without fear of judgment and condemnation. The small group mediates God's love and care. As Dietrich Bonheoffer writes in *Life Together*, "A Christian fellowship lives and exists by the intercession of its members for one another, or it collapses."[24]

Prayer: Prayer as conversation with God in the presence of other believers is another spiritual practice that involves following in community. Talking to God with others overhearing the conversation raises the stakes. It is amazing how many perfectly articulate people can become tongue-tied trying to talk to God with others in the room. In the beginning, people may want to simply bring their prayer concerns to the group and have others pray; but hopefully in time with practice, they will feel free to speak conversationally with God by voicing their own and the concerns of others.

Silence/Solitude: Corporate silence as a spiritual practice allows us to be alone with God in the presence of others. At first the practice is difficult and a minute or two seems like an eternity; but once our

---

24 Dietrich Bonheoffer, *Life Together*, Harper and Row, New York, 1954.

uneasiness with silence in the presence of others dissolves, being alone with one's own thoughts in community may create the sacred space necessary for a powerful encounter with the Holy. It may also bring direction, insight, and new perspective on an old issue.

Confession: Corporate confession at first may be unison reading of printed prayers in a worship bulletin. This helps to teach what confession is and how one can confess before God. Assurances of pardon following confession in worship help us to better understand God's forgiveness. They help free people to bring their personal and private confession before God. Thus, the movement in corporate confession is from general to personal confession. Without confessional booths to enter, Protestants have found accountability groups to be safe venues for public confession. Ground rules need to be established in these groups to build trust, familiarity, confidentiality, commitment, truth-telling, and non-judgmental rapport.

Grace/Rhythm: In lives that are jammed with activity from morning until the lights go out at night, following in community can be difficult because we are too busy to take the time necessary to relate to God, self and others. With technology keeping us always connected and overloaded, creating margin for God and space for significant experiences in Christian community is a gracious gift from God that we need to be intentional about receiving. The practice of slowing down and making this space for God in the presence of others will bring blessing. We can begin this intentional practice with the simple act of turning off our electronic devices as we engage in face-to-face community and spend quality time with God. This can begin in the home as we relate with family members and expand from there out into our other communities.

Worship/Celebration: Corporate worship isn't always the best show in town. But regular attendance in worship with one's faith community is an important spiritual practice. Worship is designed to bring us into the presence of God, creating space for personal encounter with the God who is there. Christ's presence is promised in community for "where two or three gather in his name there he is in the midst of them." *(Matthew 18:20)*

Service: Another spiritual practice that helps people following Jesus Christ in community is the exercising of their spiritual gifts in service to the community. This is service within the community, not to the world. Spiritual gift(s) are given for the edification of the community not to feed the ego needs of believer's. *(1 Corinthians 12-14 and Romans 12)* These gifts are given primarily for building up the community of faith, not for outreach.

Desiring to Do the Will of God Practices

The person whose life is becoming more conformed to the image of God, will want to be doing the will of God. But what God's will is in a particular circumstance is not always easy to discern. God's original or intentional will can be found in Scripture.[25] God's ultimate will is sure and certain, having been secured for us in Jesus Christ. But exactly what God wants us to do in the moment in the midst of our life circumstance, where there is evil and sin with which we must contend, is not always transparently clear.

Below are seven spiritual practices (one for each of the seven disciplines) that can help people grow in their discernment of and desire to do God's will:

Scripture: In the desiring to do the will of God dimension, Scripture needs to be studied, not just read. Scripture is full of commands and admonitions that are pleasing to God. One can learn a great deal concerning what God would have us do by simply studying the Word of God as a spiritual practice. Scripture can be read, prayed, and meditated upon by those seeking to do God's will. The Sermon on the Mount is a particularly good passage in this regard. Memorizing Scripture is also a helpful practice. Scripture committed to memory is available in the moment, when decisions

---

25 Concept comes from Leslie D. Weatherhead's book *The God's Will*.

and action need to be taken. Memorized Scripture is a resource God can use in the moment.

Prayer: Prayer as a spiritual discipline is important in discerning God's will in the midst one's daily life. Doing the will of God is not something that has a beginning, middle, and an end. It is a lifestyle "a way of fashioning the energy of one's life." Prayer is essential in seeking guidance and in asking for God to be present in the midst of one's daily service. Guidance is listening to God and living in response to God's leading. By cultivating the discipline of guidance people are helped to hear and discern where, how, and when God would have them move.

Solitude/Silence: The spiritual practice of retreating to a lonely place to seek guidance in silence, prayer, solitude, and meditation helps us prepare to receive guidance from the Holy Spirit. In the lonely place, we create space to listen to God. This was Jesus' practice. Before all the big turning points in his ministry, he went to a lonely place. Before choosing his disciples and before his arrest, trial, and crucifixion, he retreated to lonely places. In a lonely place, God has an opportunity to speak to us without our being distracted.

Confession: A confessional practice in the dimension of Desiring to Do the Will of God is the seeking out of guidance through spiritual direction. This is like Peter and Jesus in conversation about Peter's denying Jesus three times on the night of his betrayal. Peter disagreed with Jesus' assessment of what Peter would do. But because the conversation took place, Peter's faith did not fail him. Making sure that we rightly discern what the Holy Spirit seeks to communicate is an important aspect of guidance. Accordingly, seeking consultation with a spiritual director is an important practice when desiring to do God's will. In consultation with a spiritual director, "we engage the experience of those in our fellowship who are qualified to direct our efforts in growth and who then add the weight of their wise authority on the side of our willing spirit to help us do the things we would like to do and refrain from the things we don't want to do," says Dallas Willard.[26] But spiritual directors are not God; their authority and knowledge are limited. This spiritual practice can lead to spiritual abuse, if the person seeking direction relinquishes too much power to the director or if the director relishes the power.

Grace/Rhythm: Paying attention to our body rhythms is another spiritual practice that may help us to discern the will of God. Fasting from fulfilling the desires of our body can help people grow in their desire to do the will of God. Fasting is the practice of abstaining from food or food and drink for a designated amount of time. Fasting is a spiritual practice according to Dallas Willard because, "Fasting confirms our utter dependence upon God by finding in him a source of sustenance beyond food."[27] Fasting can teach us what it means and what it takes to desire to do God's will, as we experience our body's desire for food. Jesus fasted for 40 days before beginning his earthly ministry. Two other body rhythm practices are celibacy and body stewardship. Celibacy is abstaining from sexual relations for a period of time while exclusively resting in God's love. Those who are married are admonished by the Apostle Paul not to withhold oneself from one's partner for long. *(1 Corinthians 7:3-5)* Body stewardship, as opposed to body idolatry, is caring for the body as the temple of God's Holy Spirit. It is exercising, eating right, getting enough sleep and doing what needs to be done to keep the body healthy. It is taking care of the body as a good gift from God, not obsessing over the body for ego gratification.

Worship/Celebration: Once a person has discerned the will of God, ordination or commissioning, as spiritual practice, works to inaugurate the new direction and highlight its importance. As does the celebration of marker events, which bring closure to the old as a new course is undertaken in accord with God's will. Dedication of

---

26 Dallas Willard, *The Spirit of The Disciplines* (San Francisco: Harper & Row Publishers, 1988), 190.
27 Dallas Willard, *The Spirit of The Disciplines* (San Francisco: Harper & Row Publishers, 1988), 166.

Christians to their vocations (in the context of where God is calling them into service) helps to increase the breadth and depth of where people will seek to do God's will.

Service: The practice of serving God in one's daily life is where Desiring to Do the Will of God takes on concrete value and meaning. Desiring God's will is not only about the big moments in our lives. It is also about the little decisions and actions we take everyday. The practice of serving God in every decision, in every action, in every word spoken is ultimately the life of faith that we are all called to live. We will not succeed without missteps, bumps and lumps. But we are even blessed here in that these have the grace of opening the humble dimension up to us in a new way.

Humbled in Faith Practices

In confession we acknowledge our weaknesses and failures before God and other believers. Confession can be practiced in solitude, in direct prayer to God, in conversation with another trusted believer, in a large group in corporate confession or in the midst of a small accountability group.

Neither confession nor self-examination is in and of itself the goal. We enter into confession seeking forgiveness, the grace of God. This grace may be experienced directly from God or mediated by others. As Richard Foster says, "It is God who does the forgiving, but often He chooses human beings as the channel of His forgiving grace."[28] Because of the vulnerability experienced in the act of confessing, it is important for confession to be practiced in a safe hospitable atmosphere flowing with grace, not judgment or condemnation.

Below are seven spiritual practices (one for each of the seven disciplines) that can help us experience the Humbled in Faith Dimension:

---

28 Richard J. Foster, *Richard J. Foster's Study Guide For Celebration of Discipline* (San Francisco: Harper & Row, Publishers, 1983), 59.)

Scripture: In the humbling dimension of faith, self-reflective journaling in response to Scripture read and studied is a helpful practice. Reading passages like the Sermon of the Mount or studying the parables, allowing Jesus' stories to be heard with parabolic force in one's life, is humbling. Journaling while in the process of reading and studying provides food for thought in prayer. With a record of what God seems to be saying, those insights in the context of one's life can later be looked at and tested, either by further study, the passing of time, or in consultation with another mature believer. Journaling does not need to be arduous or burdensome. Simply write what comes to mind, as you listen self-reflectively to the Word of God.

Prayer: One helpful practice in unburdening the soul is writing out what one feels remorseful or sorry about in a prayerful letter to God. This is personal and private prayer between the individual and God. This practice can, however, be done in a community setting if for instance confessions are written on flash paper and go up in smoke with the assurance of pardon. Of course, one can also just confess verbally to God, but for some seeing the confession written down on paper and destroyed is especially helpful.

Solitude/Silence: In the humbling dimension, the use of the *Examen* (the spiritual self-review exercise developed by Saint Ignatius of Loyola) done in solitude and silence at the end of the day is an impactful, insightful practice. The steps of the *Examen* are as follows:

1. Prepare: Take some time to prepare your heart to be open and receptive. Read something in Scripture to remind you of God's love for you. This is to context self-examination in God's love.

2. Invite: Ask God to go with you as you review your day or week, to show you where and how God was present with you.

3. Review: Now list the events of your day or week looking for times and ways in which God was present; be reminded of

God's love for you. Give thanks for the ways you honored God with your actions or grew in Christlikeness.

4. Confess: Pray Psalm 139:23-24 asking God to show you where in your day or week you fell short in attitudes, actions, or character. As you recall these moments, reflect on how you could have acted differently or contributed to the situation more positively.

5. Forgiveness: Ask if there are ways to right any wrongs, determine what you could do differently next time, and then ask for forgiveness.

Confession: As a follow up, in conjunction with, or independent from the practice of the *Examen* above, talk with a spiritual director about the self-knowledge you are gaining. When appropriate, a spiritual director may helpfully become one's confessor. As a spiritual direction relationship matures over time, it helps a person risk confrontation with the self at deeper and deeper levels. I remember a time, when after journaling a confession of some depth and significance, I took the journal to my spiritual director to read. I did so with some trepidation because I was confessing actions my director had cautioned me not to take. However, as he read the journal, the room filled with a loving presence. It no longer mattered what my director said, I knew I was loved and forgiven.

Grace/Rhythm: The spiritual practice of secrecy may be powerfully exercised as a humble rhythm, a grace within the Christian community.

> "But when you pray, go into your room, close the door and pray to your Father, who is unseen. Then your Father, who sees what is done in secret, will reward you."
>
> *Matthew 6:6)*

Secrecy, as a spiritual practice, is giving of ourselves in ministry in such a way that others do not know what we are doing. Dallas

Willard remarks: "As we practice this discipline, we learn to love to be unknown and even to accept misunderstanding without the loss of our peace, joy, or purpose."[29] As secrecy is practiced within the community, one potential benefit is becoming less enamored and solicitous of the approval of others. A second is that it grows our desire to please God, not ourselves or other people. Secrecy combined with humble confession works to filter the living waters of the soul. The good inside stays secretly hidden; what is removed and disposed of is that which pollutes. Using this rhythm, when what is hidden comes to mind, we smile instead of cringe in fear of revelation.

Worship/Celebration: The humble dimension is touched in the practice of participation in worship that acknowledges and seeks forgiveness for the systemic sin of individuals, community, nation, and world. Examples would be, repentant-themed worship for world peace, global unity, hunger, or God's creation; prayer services for oppressed populations; services of repentance and mourning in the face of disturbing events like the shootings at Sandy Hook Elementary School, Ferguson, or the Emanuel Church in Charleston. As a spiritual practice, these services involve acknowledgment of non-volitional participation in systematic evil.

Service: The kind of service practice that is directly related to being humbled in faith is service that requires the giving of self for the sake of another. This is service that requires one to go the extra mile. It is sacrificial giving, not giving from excessive abundance. It is the giving of time, when we have none to give; the giving of resources, when there is not enough; and/or participation in an event for the love of another, when the energy banks are empty.

Graced by God's Love Practices

In the Graced by God's Love Dimension, God's grace is received. The spiritual task is to cooperate with God's desire to grace us with

---

29 Dallas Willard, *The Spirit of The Disciplines* (San Francisco: Harper & Row Publishers, 1988), 172.)

God's love in the form of God's intimate loving presence. In this dimension, spiritual practices seek to create space for God. There is nothing that can actually be done to bring these graces about. They are, as Saint Teresa of Avila said "mystical." At the same time, they are the transforming experiences that let us know that the Good News is "for us."

Below are seven spiritual practices (one for each of the seven disciplines) that can help us experience the Graced by God's Love Dimension:

Scripture: Read Scripture using the Transformational Bible Study Transformed method described earlier, which opens people up to God's grace. This is an adaptation of the imaginative contemplation exercises of Saint Ignatius of Loyola. The events of Jesus' life from the Gospels are studied, visualized, and entered imaginatively in the hope of facilitating encounter with the living God by means of a deeper encounter with the written Word of God.

Prayer: Saint Gregory the Great described contemplative prayer as knowledge of God impregnated with love. This is the prayer of people living out of the Graced by God's Love Dimension. The mind, heart, and soul do not seek God, as much as they find themselves "resting in God." It is an intimate prayer of presence initiated by God to which we consent. Centering prayer practices are a doorway to this contemplative prayer experience. Select a sacred word or short phrase as symbol of your intention to consent to God's presence and action within you such as, "Lord, Jesus Christ, Son of God, have mercy on me, a sinner." Now sit quietly and comfortably with eyes closed repeating the word or phrase (this is you consenting to God's presence). If distracting thoughts, sounds, or images enter your mind, gently return to the word or phrase. At the end of your prayer time remain silent then slowly open your eyes when ready. God may or may not grant the grace of contemplative prayer. The practice is designed to simply open a door and prepare you for God to make God's presence felt.

Silence/Solitude: Read a compilation of Scripture concerning God's love, such as *Father's Love Letter: An Intimate Message From God To You*.[30] Sit in silence, feel the depth of God's love addressing you personally, then when ready, write in response your own love letter to God.

Confession: Practice seeing the gift of God's grace revealed in your experience of limitation. Confess your weaknesses to God while waiting God's gracious response in God's time and in God's way. The Apostle Paul writes, "...a thorn was given me in the flesh, a messenger of Satan to torment me...Three times I appealed to the Lord about this, that it would leave me, but he said to me, 'My grace is sufficient for you, for power is made perfect in weakness.' So, I will boast all the more gladly of my weaknesses, so that the power of Christ may dwell in me. Therefore, I am content with weaknesses, insults, hardships, persecutions, and calamities for the sake of Christ; for whenever I am weak, then I am strong." *(2 Corinthians 12:7-10)*

Grace/Rhythm: Practice the Sabbath. Take one day a week to rest, worship, and delight in God. "The point of the Sabbath is to honor our need for a sane rhythm of work and rest. It is to honor the body's need for rest, the spirit's need for replenishment and the soul's need to delight itself in God for God's own sake. It begins with a willingness to acknowledge the limits of our humanness and take steps to live more graciously within the order of things."[31]

Worship/Celebration: Contemplative worship, for example worship of the Taizé type, is worship that creates space for God to graciously fill our cup to overflowing with God's loving presence. Founded in 1940, the Taizé community is an ecumenical monastic order in France visited by 100,000 people making spiritual

---

30 See poem at end of chapter
31 Ruth Haley Barton, (2009-12-14). *Sacred Rhythms: Arranging Our Lives for Spiritual Transformation (The Transforming Center Set)* (p. 138). InterVarsity Press. Kindle Edition.

pilgrimages each year. These services make use of silence and repetition in ways that foster communion with God. "Short chants, repeated again and again, give it a meditative character," the brothers explain in a brief introduction printed in their paperback songbook. "Using just a few words, (the chants) express a basic reality of faith, quickly grasped by the mind. As the words are sung over many times, this reality gradually penetrates the whole being." [32]

Service: We are called to compassionate service, loving as we have been loved. Christians seeing a need, hurt, pain, or wound, respond out of the grace they have received. "Christ has no body now but yours. No hands, no feet on earth but yours. Yours are the eyes through which he looks with compassion on this world. Yours are the feet with which he walks to do good. Yours are the hands through which he blesses all the world. Yours are the hands, yours are the feet, yours are the eyes, you are his body. Christ has no body now on earth but yours."[33]

Empowered in the Spirit Practices

At Pentecost the Holy Spirit descended and empowered the church to go out into the world to proclaim the Good News of Jesus Christ. Before the coming of the Spirit, the disciples huddled together in fear, praying, hoping that what Jesus said was true, even though not fully understanding its meaning. Jesus' last words to them were, "But you will receive power when the Holy Spirit has come upon you; and you will be my witnesses in Jerusalem, in all Judea and Samaria, and to the ends of the earth." *(Acts 1:8)*

Their waiting ended when suddenly, like the rush of a mighty wind and with tongues of fire, the Spirit descended upon them. Peter stood up and explained to the crowd of onlookers what had just happened. Empowered by the Spirit, he told the crowd the seven dimensional story of Jesus Christ's life, death, and

---

32 From the Introduction of the Taize Community Songbook.
33 Saint Teresa of Avila.

resurrection. He challenged them to repent, be baptized, and receive the Holy Spirit. That day 3000 believers were added to the followers of Jesus Christ. That is the power of the Spirit, who is still alive and working in our midst today.

Below are seven spiritual practices (one for each of the seven disciplines) to help people live into and out of experiences of empowerment in the Spirit:

Scripture: A spiritual practice that helps a person enter a text imaginatively in the Spirit to receive a Word from God is the ancient practice of *Lectio Divina*. The *Lectio Divina* consists of four movements or rhythms:

1. *Lectio* (Listen/Read): The passage is attentively, reverently, slowly read out loud. *Lectio* is reading that listens, that seeks to hear the Word of God (Jesus). The reader becomes drawn into the passage. As the Scripture is heard multiple times, attention may (and hopefully will) become focused on a particular word or phrase. The reader then stays focused on that word or phrase as the passage is read again and again. The reading is not rushed. There is a gentle lingering on the Word.

2. *Meditatio* (Meditate/Reflect): Having heard the Word, readers ponder it, savoring and meditating on what they have received. It involves opening oneself up allowing God the opportunity to touch the heart. Meditation involves entering the text in thought, imagination, emotion and desire. The question becomes: What does this text mean for my life?

3. *Oratio* (Pray/Respond): The next movement is prayer from the heart in response to the experience of God in the passage. The prayer is the reader's prayer - personal, honest and heartfelt.

4. *Contemplatio* (Contemplate/Rest): The final movement is awaiting God's response. Contemplation is beyond human control.

It is not something human effort can create. Contemplation is the gift God gives. The reader contributes by remaining still, waiting in anticipatory silence, simply listening.

Prayer: The Spirit comes bearing gifts. In response and anticipation of the Spirit's gift giving, in this practice, the spiritual gifts a person has been given and/or would like to be given are discerned. The nature of these gifts and God's purpose for giving them at this time is also explored. The question is: Why and for what community has/will God give me these spiritual gifts?

Silence/Solitude: Recall times of encounter with the Holy, God's Holy Spirit. Remembering and re-imagining these Holy moments from the past brings them into the present where they can be relived in the imagination. This helps with the writing of seven dimensional faith stories, as these moments are central in those stories. With memory of these Holy moments refreshed, utilize the questions from the worksheet "Telling Your Initial Faith Story" to write your faith story.

Confession: Following Pentecost and the coming of the Holy Spirit, the Spirit became manifest as "all who believed were together and had all things in common; they would sell their possessions and goods and distribute the proceeds to all, as any had need." *(Acts 2:44-45)* Thus, the Spirit created a community marked by the two spiritual practices of abstinence: simplicity and frugality. These practices can still work to help people live more humble, Spirit-empowered lives.

By means of the discipline of simplicity (the removal of unnecessary clutter) life becomes more focused, purposeful and prioritized. *"In frugality,"* says Dallas Willard, *"We abstain from using money or goods at our disposal in ways that merely gratify our desires or our hunger for status, glamour, or luxury. Practicing frugality means we stay within the bounds of what general good judgment would designate as necessary for the kind of life to which God has led us."*[34]

---

[34] Dallas Willard, *The Spirit of The Disciplines* (San Francisco: Harper & Row Publishers, 1988), 168.

Another practice that empowers people in the Spirit is "letting go to God." This is relinquishing tight fisted control, to the wisdom and agency of God and God's timing. Letting go starts with acknowledgment of one's desire to control; followed by recognition and confession that our desires for the situation may not be God's desire; leading to a giving back over of control to God. Imagine the situation held in your hands, then lift your hands upward, giving the situation over to God.

Grace/Rhythm: Waiting is not a spiritual practice we normally schedule into our day. Still, waiting is a spiritual practice that comes to us as a gracious gift of God's timing. It is a gift often rejected, ignored, or destroyed by our impatience. The disciples were waiting in Jerusalem for the Spirit to come. If they had not waited, if they had ventured out without the Spirit, what would have happened? In preparation for waiting on God, we can practice waiting. Get in the longest check out line; let impatient people push ahead; drive in the slow lane, never passing a slower driver. See what God shows you as you slow down and wait. Whenever you are waiting, wait actively, look into the faces of the people around you, the people God loves. Let God teach you in the created margin.

Worship/Celebration: Worship, centering on thanksgiving and praise for what God has done for us in Jesus Christ, is the particular focus of worship in the dimension of empowered by the Spirit. This is lively, uplifting music-filled worship that glorifies God and allows the congregation to participate. Easter services in most traditions capture the essence of this kind of celebratory, praise-centered worship. It is charismatic worship in the original sense. It is singing with passion Handel's *Hallelujah Chorus* or *In Christ Alone* depending on your music preference.

Service: The Spirit empowers and produces the fruit of the Spirit as we live our lives in community with others. Even though these fruits are the empowering work of the Spirit, we can intentionally cultivate them by practicing them as character virtues in our life and service. The fruits of the Spirit are love, joy, peace, patience, kindness, goodness, gentleness, faithfulness, and self-control. So we reach out in love, live at peace, and control our tempers, asking God to empower us to do all the good we will to do.

Sent into the World Practices

The sending dimension is where the faith community and its individual members interface with the world empowered by the Spirit. In this dimension, the Good News of Jesus Christ and the Kingdom of God is brought to the world and proclaimed in word and deed. Members of the faith community fulfill their calling in the world, loving the world for God, being the Good News of the Gospel.

Below are seven spiritual practices (one for each of the seven disciplines) that help us to do this:

Scripture: Testify to the redemptive effect of the Good News of the Gospel in your life. This can be done as a spiritual practice in any way that is congruent with who you are. If you are an artist, paint; a musician, sing; a composer, compose; a writer, write; an organizer, organize. First, share within your community of faith. Then, when prompted by the Holy Spirit, move outside your faith community conveying your testimony to those who may not yet know Jesus.

Prayer: Intercede with God in prayer for the concerns of others. Pray for the sick, the emotionally distraught, those who mourn, etc. Pray for them by name. Pray for strengthening of relational circles among families, friends, church, community, nation, and the world. Let God direct the prayer, so that as you pray you learn the concerns that God has for the people and communities of which you are part.

Silence/Solitude: To get connected to your community spiritually, walk the streets of the neighborhood where you live, work, or volunteer. Walk alone and walk in silence. Observe everything: people, places, the condition of property and structures, signs of change, signs of hope, signs of need, interactions between people, services offered, centers of activity. Lift your neighborhood up to God in prayer as you walk, and listen for God's direction as you observe.

Confession: In the sending dimension, confession asserts what one believes with words and with one's life. Tell your seven dimensional faith story when prompted by the Spirit to do so. Just tell the story. Allow your narrative to communicate. To bolster your confidence, you may want to create a personal statement of faith that reflects what you believe about the Father, Son, Holy Spirit, humanity, the church and the lived world. If telling your story prompts questions, this statement may be helpful in clarifying the deeper meaning your story has for you.

Grace/Rhythm: Develop and live your own seven-dimensional rule (rhythm). How to do this is described and illustrated above.

Worship/Celebration: The sentiment, "Preach the Gospel always, if necessary use words," belongs to Saint Francis of Assisi, the 13th century saint and founder of the Franciscans. Worship that glories God in action is the worship of the sending dimension. It is worship that lives the two greatest commandments to the glory of God:

> One of the scribes came near and heard them disputing with one another, and seeing that he answered them well, he asked him, "Which commandment is the first of all?" Jesus answered, "The first is, 'Hear, O Israel: The Lord our God, the Lord is one; you shall love the Lord your God with all your heart, and with all your soul, and with all your mind, and with all your strength.' The second is this, 'You shall love your neighbor as yourself.' There is no other commandment greater than these."
>
> *Mark 12:28-31*

Elizabeth A. Frykberg

Service: Fulfill your calling in unity with the Spirit: Everyone is called to serve. God creates every human being in God's own image for a purpose. Our calling is both general and specific. In general, all are called to live and reflect the love and new life given to us in Jesus Christ; but how we do that, where we do that is specific to the purpose and plan God has for our individual lives. Fulfilling our calling (general and specific) is the service we render for God in the world. That is the calling the seven dimensions of the Jesus Fractal endeavors to actualize in our lives.

Father's Love Letter:
An Intimate Message From God To You

My Child,

You may not know me, but I know everything about you. Psalm 139:1

I know when you sit down and when you rise up. Psalm 139:2

I am familiar with all your ways. Psalm 139:3

Even the very hairs on your head are numbered. Matthew 10:29-31

For you were made in my image. Genesis 1:27

In me you live and move and have your being. Acts 17:28

For you are my offspring. Acts 17:28

I knew you even before you were conceived. Jeremiah 1:4-5

I chose you when I planned creation. Ephesians 1:11-12

You were not a mistake, for all your days are written in my book. Psalm 139:15-16

I determined the exact time of your birth and where you would live. Acts 17:26

You are fearfully and wonderfully made. Psalm 139:14

I knit you together in your mother's womb. Psalm 139:13

And brought you forth on the day you were born. Psalm 71:6

I have been misrepresented by those who don't know me. John 8:41-44

I am not distant and angry, but am the complete expression of love.
1 John 4:16

And it is my desire to lavish my love on you. 1 John 3:1

Simply because you are my child and I am your Father. 1 John 3:1

I offer you more than your earthly father ever could. Matthew 7:11

For I am the perfect father. Matthew 5:48

Every good gift that you receive comes from my hand. James 1:17

For I am your provider and I meet all your needs. Matthew 6:31-33

My plan for your future has always been filled with hope. Jeremiah 29:11

Because I love you with an everlasting love. Jeremiah 31:3

My thoughts toward you are countless as the sand on the seashore.
Psalms 139:17-18

And I rejoice over you with singing. Zephaniah 3:17

I will never stop doing good to you. Jeremiah 32:40

For you are my treasured possession. Exodus 19:5

I desire to establish you with all my heart and all my soul.
Jeremiah 32:41

And I want to show you great and marvelous things. Jeremiah 33:3

If you seek me with all your heart, you will find me.
Deuteronomy 4:29

Delight in me and I will give you the desires of your heart. Psalm 37:4

For it is I who gave you those desires. Philippians 2:13

I am able to do more for you than you could possibly imagine.
Ephesians 3:20

For I am your greatest encourager. 2 Thessalonians 2:16-17

I am also the Father who comforts you in all your troubles.
2 Corinthians 1:3-4

When you are brokenhearted, I am close to you. Psalm 34:18

As a shepherd carries a lamb, I have carried you close to my heart.
Isaiah 40:11

One day I will wipe away every tear from your eyes. Revelation 21:3-4

Elizabeth A. Frykberg

And I'll take away all the pain you have suffered on this earth.
Revelation 21:3-4
I am your Father, and I love you even as I love my son, Jesus.
John 17:23
For in Jesus, my love for you is revealed. John 17:26
He is the exact representation of my being. Hebrews 1:3
He came to demonstrate that I am for you, not against you. Romans 8:31
And to tell you that I am not counting your sins. 2 Corinthians 5:18-19
Jesus died so that you and I could be reconciled. 2 Corinthians 5:18-19
His death was the ultimate expression of my love for you. 1 John 4:10
I gave up everything I loved that I might gain your love. Romans 8:31-32
If you receive the gift of my son Jesus, you receive me. 1 John 2:23
And nothing will ever separate you from my love again. Romans 8:38-39
Come home and I'll throw the biggest party heaven has ever seen. Luke 15:7
I have always been Father, and will always be Father. Ephesians 3:14-15
My question is…Will you be my child? John 1:12-13
I am waiting for you. Luke 15:11-32
Love, Your Dad
Almighty God

Father's Love Letter used by permission
Father Heart Communications ©1999 FathersLoveLetter.com

CHAPTER SEVENTEEN
(PART TWO)
Spiritual Practices for the Seven Dimensions:
Using the Chart and Practices to Grow Seven Dimensionally

What the chart and descriptions of the 49 practices can do for individuals, ministers, priests, and spiritual directors is provide a means of designing a congruent, personalized "rule" that intentionally touches all seven dimensions. A rule, by definition, is a set of practices that help to keep us open to God and spiritual transformation by providing structure and space for growing. In seeking to use this chart to grow spiritually and create a rule, one could move vertically, horizontally, diagonally, or employ a more scattered approach to choosing practices. Horizontally, the practices concentrate on a particular discipline seven dimensionally; vertically, the practices concentrate on one particular dimension across all seven disciplines; diagonally top left to bottom right are the central growth practices of the faith journey as described in the life of Peter. One way of including all seven dimensions and all seven disciplines is to create a cross anywhere on the chart, choosing one dimension and one discipline. Alternatively, one could create, via the chart, a personalized seven dimensional rule for use daily or weekly. For example:

1. Read a passage of Scripture using the method of *Lectio Divina* (as explained in Chapter Sixteen in the section on Spiritual Practices for Empowerment) to hear the passage anew. (For a description see, Empowered dimension/Scripture discipline)

2. Pray with family members. (Community dimension/Prayer discipline)

3. Read Psalm 23 slowly and deliberately listening for the way the Psalm touches the deepest desires of your longing for God. (Listening dimension/Grace-Rhythm discipline)

4. When you do wrong or make a mistake, confess your failing immediately to God, those involved, or trusted individuals. Accept, hope for, but don't insist upon forgiveness. (Graced dimension/Confession discipline)

5. Spend some time in solitude and silence focusing on Jesus Christ's life, death, and resurrection, creating space for God in your life. (Humble dimension/Solitude-Silence discipline)

6. Pray for God to use you for God's purposes in the context of your vocation and in interaction with your colleagues at work, as you lift each of them up to God by name in worship. (Desire dimension/Worship-Celebration discipline)

7. Perform some random act of kindness in God's name wherever you see a need and feel called to respond. (Sent dimension/Service discipline)

Another way of using the chart is to first assess strengths and weakness in present practice. There are 49 questions in the assessment, one for each of the practices in the chart. By taking and scoring the assessment, you will discover which dimensions and disciplines you practice the most and which the least. This assessment is a tool to help you become more seven dimensional in your spiritual practice, to more fully engage the Jesus Fractal.

Spiritual Practice Assessment: Disciplines and Dimensions

Rate the 49 statements below as to how well they describe your spiritual practice using the following scale:

4 — daily practice

3 — weekly practice

2 — monthly practice

1 — annual practice

0 — never or hardly ever my practice

Place the rating in the corresponding numbered box below. Example: If you listen to or read scripture every day place a "4" in the #1 box. If you hear scripture read only at worship each week and you go to church weekly place a "3" in the #1 box, ..., If you don't know what the Bible is place a "0" in the #1 box.

1. I listen to scripture read, taught or preached.
2. When I hear the concerns of my heart for self, family, friends, or circumstances; I lift them up to God in prayer.
3. I spend time alone, listening to God through music, nature and creation.
4. When I hear God loves me, I am touched. I talk to God confessing joyful belief and skeptical disbelief, knowing I am unworthy of God's amazing love.
5. Listening to my deepest longings and desires, I find there is a God shaped hole in my soul.
6. I hear the Word of God read and proclaimed in worship.

7. I seek to act on the Word of God that I hear.

8. I am an active member of a small group Bible Study or spiritual/sharing group.

9. I pray conversationally out loud to God in the presence of other believers.

10. I spend time in meditative silence in the presence of other people.

11. I freely confess my sin to God in corporate prayer; and I reflect and practice transparency in the presence of a small trusted group of believers.

12. I intentionally create space in my life for face-to-face time with God, family, and Christian friendship.

13. I regularly attend worship with a faith community in which I am personally known.

14. I use my spiritual gifts within the faith community.

15. I read and study the Bible.

16. I prayerfully seek guidance in doing God's will.

17. I retreat to my lonely place to be with God and to seek God's guidance.

18. When I feel like I am failing to discern or do God's will, I seek counsel and guidance from mature Christians.

19. The body is the temple of the Holy Spirit; accordingly, I pay attention to my body rhythms. I seek to live a lifestyle that honors my body's needs.

20. I serve in ministry(s) having been commissioned by a group of Christians to serve.

21. I seek to do God's will as I live my life out in the world.

22. I allow scripture to speak to my own experience and admit to God the ways I fall short. I may journal as part of this process.

23. I confess my personal sin to God in prayer or in writing.

24. I prayerfully review my actions (e.g., in an *Examen*), so as to see where God has been active in my life and how I might act more in accord with God's will.

25. I talk with a spiritual director, my small group, or Christian friends about my spiritual life.

26. I give of myself to others in ministry without letting others know about the good I am seeking to do.

27. I participate in worship and prayer services of public confession for issues like poverty, hunger, peace, child abuse, etc.

28. I seek to give of my time, when I have none to give; resources, even when there are not enough; love, when my energy banks are empty.

29. I engage with Scripture in various ways that use my imagination together with my heart and mind.

30. I practice centering prayer (repeating a word or phrase of scripture) or other prayer practices in anticipation of God's presence being experienced.

31. I sit in silence remembering, re-experiencing, and re-affirming in my mind how much God loves me.

32. Aware of my human limits, I experience God working in and through me beyond my capability.

33. I take a Sabbath rest to delight in God, but not necessarily on Sunday.

34. I participate in contemplative worship with others.

35. When seeing someone in need, pain, hurt, or wounded, I respond out of the grace I have received from God.

36. I practice the sacred reading of scripture called the *Lectio Divina*.

37. I am aware, understand, and make use of the spiritual gifts I have been given.

38. I have written and reflect on my faith story; this remembering empowers my spirit in the present.

39. I share with the community of faith from the abundance of what God has given me; I live a simple, frugal lifestyle; letting go of things.

40. I wait (in line, in traffic, for the doctor, etc.) in active anticipation of God using this time for God's purposes.

41. I participate in worship that is celebratory and full of praise.

42. I find my life increasingly filled with the fruits of the Spirit: love, joy, peace, patience, kindness, goodness, gentleness, faithfulness, and self-control.

43. In my own way, I testify to the Good News of who Jesus Christ is to me.

44. I intercede (pray) for the needs of others.

45. I pray for my neighbors and my community, as I walk or drive in my town and neighborhood.

46. I share my faith story.

47. I plan and work my plan for growing spiritually.

48. I live the sentiment: "Preach the gospel always, if necessary use words."

49. I am aware of and am working to fulfill my spiritual calling.

The Jesus Fractal

After listing your score in each box, total the numbers in each column and row.

Answer Sheet

	Listen	Community	Desire	Humble	Grace	Empower	Sent	Total
Scripture	1	8	15	22	29	36	43	
Prayer	2	9	16	23	30	37	44	
Silence/ Solitude	3	10	17	24	31	38	45	
Confession	4	11	18	25	32	39	46	
Grace/ Rhythm	5	12	19	26	33	40	47	
Worship/ Celebration	6	13	20	27	34	41	48	
Service	7	14	21	28	35	42	49	
Total								

Ways to Use The Spiritual Practices Assessment:

Look at your scores and celebrate your 4's. These are your daily spiritual practices. You will find the corresponding practice listed in the corresponding box on the Chart of Spiritual Practices.

Your highest scores on a dimension and a discipline indicate your preferred spiritual style. When you are in need of spiritual nourishment or in a crisis, these are the practices you will find easiest and most constructively beneficial to engage. They are the tried and true ways you connect with God.

Looking at your scores, find the dimension and the discipline where you scored your lowest numbers, mark the "cross pattern" intersecting the dimension and the discipline. Construct a spiritual rule or plan involving the practices from the "cross pattern." This will help you grow spiritually. It will stretch you in ways that may at first feel uncomfortable, but may therefore open you up to God in new and exciting ways.

Where you scored yourself a 0 or a 1 on an item, consider trying or increasing how often you engage in this practice. You will find the corresponding practice listed in the corresponding box on the Chart of Spiritual Practices.

Look at your scores and see if you see any pattern to the numbers? What do these patterns suggest to you about your spiritual life? For instance, are your highest scores on the right hand side of the scoring grid (grace, empower and send) or alternatively are they on the left hand side (listen, community, and desire)? If so what does this say to you about your spirituality? What does it say about the place of the humble dimension in your spiritual life? Have you experienced the grace of being humbled? Or are you defending against honest self-reflection?

Some practices can only be done weekly or monthly given the availability of opportunity. Accounting for this, looking at where you scored yourself a 2 are there ways and opportunity to increase the frequency of these practices? Is there any desire in you to do this?

Scoring: If your score on a dimension or discipline is:

26-28: Celebrate your daily involvement in this dimension or discipline. This is the unachievable ideal, experienced as the gracious gift of God. "Now we see in a mirror dimly, but then face to face."

22-25: If you scored in this range, Mother Teresa is smiling. She isn't a saint yet either, but is well on her way. You are involved in this dimension or discipline weekly. Unless this is one of your lowest scores celebrate the ways God has used these practices to draw you closer. If this is one of your lowest scores, look to engaging more in those practices where you marked a 2 or 3.

15-21: If you scored in this range, there is depth in your spiritual experience of this dimension or discipline, but the best is yet to come. Your spiritual life would benefit from continued intentional development. Look particularly at trying new practices and increasing the frequency of those you do less than weekly.

8-14: If you scored in this range, you are on the journey. Know that God is with you. Be patient with yourself. Try creating more margin in your life to prioritize spending time with God over mere busyness; then choose to increase the frequency of those practices in this dimension or discipline that interest you or you enjoy the most.

0-7: If you scored in this range, your taking this assessment speaks volumes about your desire to know God. Read all the practices in this discipline or dimension and try any that interest you.

Confession

In the process of conceiving and writing this chapter, I discovered something about myself. I discovered that I am more spiritual, and enjoy participating in more spiritual practices than I thought. I pray that as you have read through the specific practices in this chapter that you too have had a similar experience. It became clear to me as I looked over and sought to describe the practices in the chart that the many ways I interact with God are not as haphazard and undisciplined as I had always thought.

I am not the kind of person who wakes up in the morning, opens her Bible and does morning devotions. I am a person who prefers to lie in bed with Jesus on my mind. I don't sit on hard wooden chairs in silence and solitude waiting for God to speak. I walk, play, and pray in nature reciting Scripture from memory (not always with perfect memory), taking in the beauty of God's creation on land and in the sea, amazed at God's creativity. God loves me in my particularity. God loves you in your particularity.

Spirituality isn't form or content; it's a relationship with the love fractal original mediated by the Jesus Fractal original, so we are recreated in *koinonia* in the love fractal image.

Epilogue

Human community, created to reflect and embody the life of the Trinity, doesn't. That is why Jesus came. Jesus the Christ came to restore the Love Fractal.... to enable and empower us to re-form our communities so they reflect and embody the life of the Trinity.... communities that reflect the self-giving quality of life shared by Father, Son, and Holy Spirit.

So how is the Love Fractal restored? The answer suggested in these pages is through the seven dimensions of the Jesus Fractal, a dynamic pattern of relationship, evident in the creation of humankind in the image of God, made manifest in the redemptive work of Jesus Christ, and still accessed in faith today through the sustaining work of the Holy Spirit. We have called this fractal pattern the Jesus Fractal because the pattern can be seen structuring all of Jesus' relational interactions. Jesus listens, participates in community, desires to do the will of God, is humbled, graced by God's love, empowered by the Spirit, and sent into the world. The seven dimensions structure Jesus's life and ministry, as "he humbles himself and becomes obedient unto death, even death on a cross." *(Phillippians 2:8)*

Accessing the Love Fractal through the present ministry of the Holy Spirit is our faithful response to God's love poured out for us seven dimensionally in Jesus Christ. What does this faithful response look like? Jesus Fractal faith is living continually in and out from the seven dimensions.

Let's summarize:

We never outgrow our need to hear the Word of God (*Listening.*) Or the experience of Jesus Christ in community (*Following in Community.*) The desire to live and love like Jesus Christ is the greatest commandment (*Desiring to Do the Will of God.*) Being human, not divine, we are limited, unable to do the will of God that we desire to do (*Humbled in Faith.*) But the fountain of God's amazing grace keeps flowing (*Graced by God's Love.*) Empowering us in the Spirit (*Empowered In the Spirit.*) To go into the world to work with God to restore and live out of the Love Fractal image in which we were all created. (*Sent into the World.*)

My prayer is that the description of the seven dimensions of the Jesus Fractal presented in these pages and the spiritual practices described may be helpful to you as a guide in your seven dimensional life of faith.

APPENDIX A

Characteristics of Persons in Each of the Jesus Fractal Dimensions

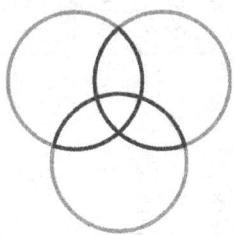

Dimension:	Persona:	Focus:	'I' Statements:	Obstruction:	Moving on:
Hearing the Gospel	Thinker: "I think, therefore I am"	God's story.	I believe.	I don't believe God loves me. (I'm not worth loving or I don't need God.)	Become part of a group of believers with Christ centered leadership.
Following Jesus Christ in community	Relational: "I am my relationships"	Living in relationship/community with Jesus Christ in community with others.	I experience the Spirit of Christ in community (koinonia).	I am a Christian, because I attend my particular church, where we have a particular leader and style.	Wanting to be in relationship with Jesus Christ in every aspect of life.
Desiring to do the will of God—to be like Jesus Christ.	Achiever: "I do, therefore I have value."	Doing the will of God.	I am a productive and purposeful disciple "doing" in the name of Jesus Christ.	God is pleased with all I do for God, because I follow all the rules.	Loss of certainty, experience of crisis, failure, or limitation.

The Jesus Fractal

Humbled in Faith.	Failure: "I am incapable and unworthy."	Facing human limitations and need of redemption in Jesus Christ	I am a sinner, who is unable to do the will of God that I desire to do.	Denial: "It wasn't my fault"; Shame: "I am unforgivable."	Failure is exposed as one's dark side is revealed to God, self, and other Christians.
Graced by God's Love	Beloved: "I am loved and I love."	Experiences of grace, forgiveness, and love.	"I am God's beloved child."	I love people in my church so much and they love me; I have arrived.	Living in and from God's love in every aspect of one's life.
Empowered by the Holy Spirit	Contemplative: "I am spirit and the Spirit of God lives in me."	Intimate relationship with the Spirit of God, who empowers.	I am aware of God's powerful, loving presence strengthening me.	I have the Spirit. I am spiritually empowered. I know what is best, so follow me.	Seeking to do the will of God in humble dialogue with the Spirit.
Sent into the World	Missionary: "I am an empowered servant of the Triune God."	Living the Good News of Jesus Christ.	I am a conduit of God's love, empowered and sent by the Triune God.	I send myself into the world to do the good works, because that is who I will to be.	Union with Christ; living one's calling.

APPENDIX B
Worksheet for Telling Initial Faith Story

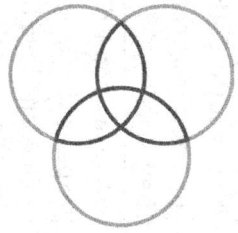

Seven Dimensions	Jesus Christ's Initial Faith Story	Questions to help tell your Initial Faith Story.	Your Initial Faith Story
Hearing the Word of God	Born into Jewish Community, where the Torah is taught. (Luke 1-2:20)	When and how did you first hear the Gospel of Jesus Christ?	
Following in Community	Raised in Jewish family by Mary and Joseph. (Luke 2:21-52)	When and how did you respond to the call to follow Jesus Christ as part of a nurturing community of believers?	
Desiring to Do the Will of God	Found in the Temple at age 12. (Luke 2:41-52)	When and how did you first experience yourself wanting to live and love like Jesus, to do God's will?	
Humbled in Faith	Submits to baptism and "Fulfills all righteousness" (Luke 3:21-23)	When was the first time you remember experiencing failure (limitation) as a disciple of Jesus Christ after wanting and trying to live and love like Jesus Christ in accord with God's will?	

The Jesus Fractal

Graced by God's Love	"This is my beloved son." (Luke 3:22)	How have you experienced God loving and caring for you in spite of or in the midst of your failure (limitation) to love God with your heart, soul, and mind and your neighbor as yourself?	
Empowered by the Spirit	Dove descends. (Luke 3:22)	What is your first memory of experiencing the Spirit in intimate relationship?	
Sent into the World	Temptations in the wilderness. (Luke 4:1-13)	To what ministries have you been called and commissioned to serve? How did this come about?	

APPENDIX C
Worksheet for Telling Ministry Story

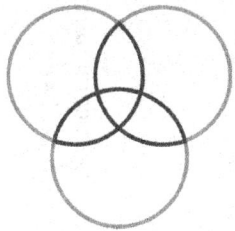

Elizabeth A. Frykberg

Seven Dimensions	Jesus Christ's Ministry Story	Questions to help tell the Story of Your Lay or Ordained Ministry	Your Ministry Story
Hearing the Word of God	Goes to the synagogue, reads Scripture, hears the call to ministry through the Prophet Isaiah. (Luke 4:14-30)	How has your ministry been schooled in the Word of God?	
Following in Community	Calls and teaches his disciples for three years in community. (Luke 4:31-18)	What faith community have you been called to serve?	
Desiring to Do the Will of God	Enters Jerusalem allowing his Messianic identity to be revealed. (Luke 19-21) Submission at Gethsemane, "Not my will but Thy will be done." (Matthew 26:39)	What significant adjustment have you made in order to serve God's will more completely?	

The Jesus Fractal

Humbled in Faith	Submits to death on the cross. (Luke 22, 23)	Where have you been stopped, failed or experienced limitation in your seeking to serve God?
Graced by God's Love	Resurrection (Luke 24)	How and where do you experience God loving you as you serve?
Empowered by the Spirit	Ascends to the Father becoming highly exalted. (Acts 1)	Where are you experiencing God empowering you to serve right now?
Sent into the World	Sends the Holy Spirit at Pentecost. (Acts 2)	How is your service reaching beyond the faith community?

APPENDIX D
Present Spiritual Practice Assessment Work Sheet

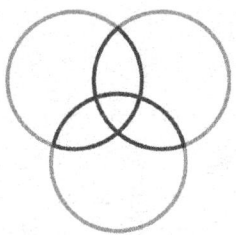

Elizabeth A. Frykberg

Seven Dimensions	Jesus' Spiritual Practices	Questions to Assess Present Practice	Assess Present Practices
Hearing the Word of God	Goes to the synagogue and to the temple where Scripture is read and discussed. He went into the synagogue, as was his custom." (Luke 4:16) His teachings exhibit fresh understanding, "You have heard it said...but I say unto you..."	Where do you engage with Scripture (the Word of God) such that you hear the Gospel afresh and anew?	
Following in Community	Family (Mary) was with Jesus at his birth through his ministry and at his death. Called 12 disciples to travel, eat, sleep, learn, and work with him. Selected Peter, James, and John as a small group within the community of disciples. It was his custom to go to the synagogue when in a town. This was the community center in Jewish towns in the first century. He describes himself in community in conversation with God, saying, "I am in the Father and the Father is in me." He also creates community in conversation with individuals, as seen in John 4, where the story of his conversation with the Woman at the Well is recorded.	What Christian communities are you called and accountable to on an ongoing basis?	
Desiring to Do the Will of God	The Lord's Prayer (Jesus' own daily prayer) states his desire, "Thy kingdom come, Thy will be done on earth as it is in heaven." God's will is Jesus' preaching, teaching, and healing ministry.	How and in what ministries are you called and seeking to do God's will in the name of Jesus Christ (in or outside Christian community)?	

The Jesus Fractal

Humbled in Faith	By living as the incarnated Son of God, Jesus practiced humility. He did not regard equality with God "as something to be exploited, but emptied himself, taking the form of a slave, … he humbled himself and became obedient to the point of death - even death on a cross (Philippians 2:1-11) Humility was an everyday practice for Jesus.	Where do you experience your limitation in being effective in ministry? How do you reflectively and critically assess your spiritual practice and life?
Graced by God's Love	At the transfiguration Jesus shares a "lonely place" experience with Peter, James, and John. God is there and speaks of Jesus, "This is my Son, the Beloved; listen to him." (Mark 9:7) This is evidence of Jesus' experiencing being loved by the Father, as is the intimacy of their relationship as described in John 14-17.	Where and how do you experience yourself being loved by God?
Empowered by the Spirit	Jesus is empowered to teach, to preach, to heal and to perform miracles like healing, the stilling of the storm and raising the dead.	Where and for what are you experiencing yourself empowered by God with excitement and energy for doing God's will?
Sent into the World	Throughout his ministry Jesus relates to the outcasts and the shunned: to the prostitutes, tax collectors, sinners, and Gentiles. He reaches out to the Samaritan and Syrophoenician Woman. (John 4:1-42; Mark 7:24-30; Matthew 15:21-28)	Where are you interacting with people beyond your immediate Christian communities such that your faith is made known to them?

APPENDIX E
Open Ended Questions to Help Assess Present Engagement in the Seven Dimensions

As we continue to mature in faith, the seven dimensions of faith relationship with Jesus Christ are engaged and reengaged over the course of our lives. The following questions will help you assess how you are presently engaged in the seven dimensions of faith. These questions can be used in a small sharing group or in one-on-one spiritual direction:

1. When and how do you hear the Gospel of Jesus Christ proclaimed regularly?

2. What community of disciples do you commune with in your walk with Jesus Christ? What ministries within Christian community are you presently called and commissioned to serve in?

3. How are you serving Jesus Christ in your daily life? Where and how are you experiencing yourself growing in Christlikeness and doing the will of God?

4. Where are you falling short as a disciple of Jesus Christ?

5. How are you experiencing God loving and caring for you?

6. How are you experiencing the Spirit empowering you?

7. What ongoing Christian missions do you support with your time, talent and treasure?

APPENDIX F
Multiple Choice Questions to Assess Current Engagement in the Seven Dimensions

The following questions are also designed to help people discern present engagement in the seven dimensions of the faith journey, as well as, help them to focus energy in their faith development. These questions give specific program possibilities within the church to choose from.

Directions: Please check each statement under each category that applies to you. On the blank lines following the checked responses please indicate the specific activity you engage in regularly. In dialogue with a pastor or spiritual director, use these answers to help you discern how you may become more involved in the seven dimensions of the Jesus faith fractal.

Elizabeth A. Frykberg

1. When and how do you regularly hear the Word of God proclaimed to you in your life?

☐ During worship services

___

☐ During Bible study

___

☐ Watching movies

___

☐ Listening to music

___

☐ Walking in nature

_____

_____

_____

_____

_____

☐ Reading Scripture

_____

_____

_____

_____

☐ Reading devotional literature, theology, or Christian fiction and non-fiction

_____

_____

_____

_____

☐ Attending retreats or Christian camps

_____

_____

_____

_____

☐ Talking to Christian friends and mentors

_____
_____
_____
_____
_____

☐ Family Devotions

_____
_____
_____
_____
_____

☐ On the Internet (Facebook, YouTube, etc.)

_____
_____
_____
_____
_____

☐ Listening to the radio

_____
_____
_____
_____
_____

☐ Watching televangelists

_____
_____
_____
_____

☐ Other

_____
_____
_____
_____

2. What communities of Christian learning and/or serving are you regularly involved in that helps you grow in knowledge and understanding of Jesus Christ?

☐ Worship

_____
_____
_____
_____
_____

☐ Bible study or fellowship group

☐ Sharing or accountability group

☐ Retreats or camps

☐ Ministry team

☐ Mission team

_____

_____

_____

_____

_____

☐ Personal spiritual practices in dialogue with a spiritual director or mentor

_____

_____

_____

_____

_____

_____

☐ Other

_____

_____

_____

_____

_____

_____

_____

3. Where and how are you experiencing yourself growing in doing the will of God?

☐ Caring for family members
☐ Making myself available to talk with friends and neighbors in need
☐ Forgiving those in need of forgiveness
☐ Seeking to understand, not judge others
☐ Stopping to help when I see someone in need
☐ Willing to be interrupted to help someone else
☐   Seek relationally to live out of 1 Corinthians 13: "Love is patient; love is kind; love is not envious or boastful or arrogant or rude. It does not insist on its own way; it is not irritable or resentful; it does not rejoice in wrongdoing, but rejoices in the truth. It bears all things, believes all things, hopes all things, endures all things. Love never ends."

☐ Serve in a pastoral care ministry

_____

_____

☐ Serve in a mission ministry

_____

_____

☐ Visit prisoners

_____

_____

☐ Feed the hungry

_____

_____

- ☐ House the homeless

_____

_____

- ☐ Visit the sick

_____

_____

- ☐ Other

_____

4. How do you take personal inventory of your life including motives and actions? How and to whom do you confess your failure to love sacrificially after the pattern of Jesus Christ?

- ☐ During worship with the corporate prayer of confession
- ☐ In an ongoing mentoring relationship
- ☐ In a spiritual direction relationship
- ☐ In conversation with a counselor or psychologist
- ☐ Praying and confessing in an accountability group
- ☐ Praying and confessing directly to God
- ☐ Paying attention to my inner voice
- ☐ In dialogue with close friends and family
- ☐ Going to Confession
- ☐ Other _____

5. How do you experience the love of God in your daily life?

- ☐ In prayer
- ☐ In worship

- ☐ In family relationships
- ☐ In community with other Christians
- ☐ In community with others who are not necessarily Christian
- ☐ In serendipitous moments during the day
- ☐ In experiences of the beauty of creation
- ☐ Experiencing God working on your behalf through coincidences
- ☐ Other _____

6. When and how are you engaged in intimate relationship with Jesus Christ waiting and/or experiencing the Spirit of God leading and empowering you for ministry in your daily life?

- ☐ In worship
- ☐ In daily prayer practice
- ☐ Sharing and praying with a small group
- ☐ With a prayer partner
- ☐ During mission or ministry experiences

7. What ministries have you been called to serve in the world and/or in the faith community?
Ministry at work

_____

_____

_____

_____

_____

Ministry at school

_____
_____
_____
_____
_____

Ministry in my neighborhood

_____
_____
_____
_____

Ministry in family

_____
_____
_____
_____

Ministry in community

_____
_____
_____
_____

Elizabeth A. Frykberg

Ministry at home

Church officer

Teacher or preacher

Ministry team member

Ministry team leader

Mission team membe

Mission team leader

Other

APPENDIX G
Bible Study: The Seven Dimensions in Peter's Life of Faith

Listening Dimension Bible Study:
1. What do we learn concerning Jesus' ministry from Mark 1:14-15?

2. What does Luke 4:14-21 tell us about the content of Jesus teaching ministry? What does this have to do with the Kingdom of God (the reign of God) from Mark 1:15?

3. What do we learn about Peter's interaction with Jesus in Capernaum from Luke 4:31-44?

4. How is Jesus here ministering in accord with Luke 4:14-21?

5. Imagine that you are Peter or one of the other people encountering Jesus at Capernaum in these scriptures. Have a discussion with your small group regarding Jesus. Talk together about Jesus in light of what you have experienced of his ministry in Luke 4:31-44.

6. What would you assume about Peter's understanding of and appreciation of Jesus at this point?

    a. Peter is skeptical and unbelieving, but listening.

    b. Peter has committed to following Jesus wholeheartedly.

c. Peter is attracted to Jesus and impressed by this new teacher and his teachings.

   d. Peter is using Jesus to get his mother-in-law healed.

   e. Peter is awestruck by Jesus and his healing ministry; he wants to know and learn more.

7. When in your life have you felt like Peter with regard to the teachings of Jesus?

   a. I have always been attracted to Jesus (explain).

   b. There was a specific time when I remember hearing the Good News and being initially attracted (explain).

   c. I am not attracted to Jesus or the gospel (explain).

Follow in Community Dimension Bible Study (Luke 5:1-11):

1. How is Peter feeling when Jesus arrives at the shore?

2. Why does Peter let Jesus get into his boat?

3. Realizing that fish are found in moderate depths and Jesus is asking Peter to put out into the deep waters, how would you have felt (if you were Peter) about responding to Jesus' request in front of a large crowd?

4. Imagine you are Peter. As you start catching fish, what does this feel like? In role as Peter or another person seeing the catch, talk in your small group about Jesus? What do you think about him? Answer and discuss the following three questions in your group staying in role.

5. Why as Peter would you respond, "Depart from me; for I am a sinful person, O Lord?"

6. Why as Peter would you leave your nets to follow Jesus?

7. What are you feeling as Peter, as you leave your nets to follow Jesus? What are your expectations? What are your concerns?

Desire Dimension Bible Study (Luke 9):

1. Disciples of Jesus Christ are called to apprenticeship in Christ-like ministry. In Luke 9, Peter and the others are commissioned to go into the world "as if" they were Christ himself. Short-term mission trips are present day "as if" experiences. Describe a time when you learned something about yourself and Jesus on a short-term mission trip.

2. In answer to Jesus' question, "Who do you say I am?" Peter says, "You are the Christ of God." He discovered Jesus' identity. Who do you say Jesus is? How have you come to this understanding of Jesus' identity?

3. Taking Peter, John, and James with him, Jesus climbs the Mount of Transfiguration (Luke 9:28-36) to pray. While in prayer, the appearance of Jesus' face changes and his clothes become blinding white. A radiant cloud then comes and covers the top of the mountain. While wrapped in the cloud, the disciples become deeply aware of God's presence. A voice comes out of the cloud declaring: "This is my Son, the Chosen! Listen to him." This experience confirmed what the disciples had learned about Jesus while preaching and ministering in the name of Jesus. Imagine you hear a voice saying to you, "This is my Son, the Chosen! Listen to him." What does it mean for you to listen to Jesus? What is he saying to you? How has listening to Jesus the Son of God changed the way you live?

4. Peter grew in his desire to be like Jesus to the point where, he said he would follow Jesus to prison and even unto death if necessary. What kind of sacrifices have you been called upon to make as a disciple of Jesus Christ? Are there limits to what you would be willing to sacrifice?

Elizabeth A. Frykberg

Humble Dimension Bible Study (Luke 22:14-62):

1. Name as many times as you can, when Peter distinguished himself as a disciple of Jesus Christ. Read these verses to prompt your memory: Matthew 14:28-33; 16:13-18; 17:1-8.

2. What is the symbolic meaning of the bread and wine as Jesus distributes them at the Last Supper? What might the disciples thought it meant?

3. How does Peter respond to Jesus' statement that Peter will deny Jesus three times before the cock crows that night? What does this tell you about Peter?

4. Why do you think Jesus predicts Peter's failure, while praying for Peter to experience God's grace, instead of praying to eliminate Peter's failure?

5. Why is it necessary for Peter (for us) to come to understand the depth of our human condition, our sinful nature, our not being able to do what Jesus does?

6. What is the difference in Jesus Christ dying for Peter, a person who sins, as opposed to, dying for Peter a person whose human condition is sin?

7. How is Peter's denial of Jesus a truth-producing error and thereby a step of faith?

Grace Dimension Bible Study (John 21:1-19)

1. What about this scene is familiar and significant to Peter from an earlier event?

2. Why do you think Jesus is cooking breakfast? Why does he ask for some of the disciple's catch to cook?

3. Referencing the other disciples, Jesus asks Peter, "Do you love me more than these?" Peter responds without comparing himself to the others. Why is this significant?

4. There are four different words in Greek that all translate into the same English word "love." The nuances of the Greek have Jesus in his second question to Peter effectively asking, "Simon son of John, do you love me sacrificially, the way I have loved you. Is your love unconditional? Is it *agape* love?" Peter answers using a different word for love, *phileo*, "Lord, you know that my love for you is the love of friendship, the love of one human being for another. I *phileo* you." What does Peter's answer reveal about Peter?

5. The third time Jesus asks the love question, he asks the question Peter has been answering all along. Jesus says to Peter the third time, "Simon son of John, do you love me as a friend? Do you *phileo* me?" Why does this third question hurt Peter? Read John 15:12-14. What is Jesus wanting Peter to understand?

6. The minute Peter fully acknowledges his inability to love sacrificially after the pattern of Christ, Jesus calls Peter to follow him to the cross, to love and glorify God sacrificially, to do the very thing he cannot do. Why would Jesus do that? How has Peter's becoming humble enabled him in a new way?

7. Talk about an experience of Jesus unconditionally loving you that mirrors Peter's experience?

Empowerment Dimension Bible Study (Acts 1-5):

1. During his resurrection appearances, Jesus tells his disciples that they will be empowered by their baptism in the Holy Spirit. Why do they need empowerment by the Holy Spirit? (Acts 1:1-8)

2. Name two ways that Peter emerges as the leader of the disciples in Acts 1:15-26 and in Acts 2?

3. How is Peter's leadership after Pentecost and the resurrection an answer to Jesus' prayer for Peter's faith to not fail him?

4. In Acts 2:14; 4:31; and 5:29, how does Peter prove himself to be a courageous witness for Christ empowered by the Holy Spirit?

5. How about in Acts 2:41, 47, and 4:4?

6. In Acts 2:43; 5:12?

7. In Acts 5:41?

8. In Acts 2:44?

9. In Acts 4:7–22 and Acts 5:18–42?

10. How and why are all of these signs of Peter's empowerment by the Holy Spirit and not just Peter's human striving?

11. How are they evidence of ego transformation from the inside out?

12. What evidence of the Holy Spirit's empowerment have you, or are you experiencing in your life?

Send Dimension Bible Study (Acts 10:1-48)

1. The tanning trade was considered unclean because tanners killed unclean animals, worked in blood, and were in constant contact with things, which might make Jews unclean. Therefore, most orthodox Jews wouldn't stay at Simon the tanner's home. Yet Peter does. What does this tell you about Peter?

2. While on the roof of Simon the Tanner's home, Peter has a vision and then hears a heavenly voice say, "Do not call anything impure that God has made clean." (vs. 15) This happens three times, before the sheet is taken back up into heaven. The vision leaves Peter thinking and wondering about its meaning. What do you think it means?

3. The day before Peter's vision of the sheet coming down out of heaven, an angel of the Lord appears to a man named

The Jesus Fractal

Cornelius, a Roman centurion. Peter and Cornelius are given complementary visions. Why would such powerful "coincidental" evidence of God at work be necessary to help the church proclaim the gospel to a Gentile audience?

4. While Peter is still thinking about the vision, the Spirit says to him, "Look, three men are searching for you. Now get up, go down, and go with them without hesitation; for I have sent them." Why was going with these men a bold move? What evidence do you find in this Scripture for Peter having been prepared beforehand to make this move?

5. When Peter gets to Caesarea, Cornelius explains that he has sent for Peter because a heavenly voice instructed him to do so. Peter interprets the events saying, "I truly understand that God shows no partiality, but in every nation anyone who fears God and does what is right is acceptable to God." This is a remarkable insight. What is it about Peter's whole life of faith that prepares him to be open to God wanting the gospel of Jesus Christ proclaimed to Gentiles?

6. While Peter is speaking, the Holy Spirit falls upon Cornelius and all those listening in Cornelius' home. How is this event similar to the events of Acts 2?

7. Peter in response asks the Jewish Christians who are with him, "Can anyone withhold the water of baptism from these people who have already received the Holy Spirit just as we have?" Why do you think God gave the Holy Spirit to these Gentiles before they were baptized?

8. How is baptizing the Gentiles an act of faith? What does it say about the mission of the church?

9. God sent Peter to Cornelius. Peter fulfills his calling by preaching and baptizing. Where has God sent you? For what purpose were you sent? Where would you like God to send you? For what purpose?

APPENDIX H
The *Kenosis* Passage as Example

Philippians 2:5-11, known as the *kenosis* passage, is another example of the Jesus Fractal at work in the life of Jesus.

Listening Dimension (step one): Christ Jesus did not hold on to equality with God. He relaxed his grip on divine prerogatives and privileges. He **listened** to the Father.

Following in Community Dimension (step two): Christ Jesus emptied himself, putting off aspects of his divine nature voluntarily, laying aside whatever he needed to in order to become human. Nobody robbed him or stripped him of his divinity; he didn't forgo his divine form under protest. He purposefully and willingly divested himself of everything that would have kept him from becoming fully human, kept him from fulfilling his mission of **following God in community with humankind**.

Desiring Dimension (step three): Christ Jesus took on the appearance of a human. In taking on the appearance of a human, Jesus Christ exhibits not just willingness, but **desire to do the will of God**.

Humbled Dimension (step four): Christ Jesus was made in the likeness of humankind, a **humbling** experience.

Graced Dimension (step five): Christ Jesus became a servant of humankind. He came in love teaching, feeding, healing, helping, saving obstinate, arrogant, sinful humanity. He **graced** the world with God's love demonstrating once and for all that God's love for humankind is total and complete. God does not withhold even God's own son for love of humankind. It is realization of this truth—Jesus died "for" me—that humbles us.

Empowered Dimension (step six): Christ Jesus became obedient unto death. Jesus stood toe-to-toe with the power of death and says, "Take me, I surrender." He surrenders not just to any kind of death, but death on a cross. Crucifixion didn't just kill a person. It was torture—a slow merciless death in which every gruesome sensation of dying intensifies. Moreover, while Jesus experienced the physical torture of crucifixion, people walked by laughing, spitting, throwing sticks, hurling ugly accusations, making the hellishness of the situation complete. Christ Jesus started in a position that could be no higher. He ends up in a position that could be no lower.

But the story doesn't end there. Jesus is resurrected. Jesus, by allowing himself to be abused and tortured, by being betrayed and abandoned by those who loved him, by suffering a death of seemingly insurmountable humiliation and personal defeat demonstrates once and for all that God can be trusted, because Christ Jesus is resurrected. "Oh death where is thy sting. Oh death where is thy victory. God gives us the victory through Jesus Christ our Lord." *(1 Corinthians 15:55-56)* In resurrection, Christ Jesus is **empowered by God and** overcomes (destroys) death.

Sending Dimension (step seven): God then exalts Christ Jesus back to the highest place, "giving him the name that is above every name, that at the name of Jesus every knee should bow, in heaven and on earth and under the earth, and every tongue confess that Jesus Christ is Lord, to the glory of God the Father." *(Philippians 2:9-11)*

Jesus in human form trusted God's love for him! And where did it get him? Right back at the right hand of God Almighty, Jesus re-ascended the stairway to heaven. Jesus shows us what happens when one trusts in God's goodness and love no matter what the circumstances. God is the never-ending circle of love that cannot be destroyed.

APPENDIX I
Martin Luther and Having No Shame in the Gospel

Luther was born in Eisleben on November 10, 1483. His father was a copper miner; his mother a hardworking housewife. The gifted Luther received a sound primary and secondary education, before enrolling at the University of Erfurt at the age of 17. From the university, he received a bachelor's degree in 1502 and a master's degree in January of 1505. By May of that year, Luther's father arranged for Martin to begin law school.

One hot, muggy day in July on his way back to school following a visit with his parents, Martin now 21 years of age, trudged over a parched road on the outskirts of the Saxon village of Stotterheim. As he approached the village, the sky became overcast. Suddenly there was a shower, then a crashing storm. A bolt of lightning tore through the gloom and knocked Martin to the ground. Struggling to rise, he cried in terror, "Saint Anne help me! I will become a monk."

Religious training and experience of the *listening dimension* at home, school, and the university had all worked to instill in Martin the fear of God and reverence for the church. So in the moment, as his life brushed death, he knew just what to do. He made an act of contrition and pled for mercy. In the face of death, the only sure course Martin knew was to lay hold of all the help the Church had to offer: sacraments, pilgrimages, indulgences, and the intercession of the saints.

So two weeks after the thunderstorm, Luther enters the Augustinian Monastery in Erfurt following in community, exploring the *community dimension* of the faith fractal. If ever there were a sincere, earnest, conscientious monk, it was Martin Luther. His sole motive and concern was for his salvation. As he began his new life in the monastery, he was given for the very first time a complete copy of the Bible in Latin. Martin read the Bible avidly, exploring the Word of God in *listening dimension* afresh and anew. Month by month the Divine offices moved him through the Psalms, touching the height and depth of every emotion, every mood, every human crisis. Martin committed these verses to memory. At the end of his probationary year, he took his monastic vows; a year after that, he was ordained a priest and celebrated his first Mass.

Ordination should have been a great celebration, but instead, the event resurfaced for Luther in a new form the crisis of his alienation from God. In saying the Mass as a priest, Luther stood for the people of God in the presence of the Holy. For Luther, that was a terrifying thought. When he started to address God with the words, "We offer unto Thee, the living, true, the eternal God," Luther questioned himself:

> With what tongue shall I address such Majesty...Who am I that I should lift up mine eyes or raise my hands to the divine Majesty? The angels surround him. At his nod the earth trembles. And shall I, a miserable pygmy, say, "I want this, I ask for that? For I am dust and ashes and full of sin and I am speaking to the living, eternal, and true God.

Responding to this new thunderstorm, Luther set about the task of earnestly pursuing holiness. The *Desiring to Do the Will of God Dimension* of the Jesus Fractal, became his focus. This was a fairly straightforward goal to pursue, because one of the privileges of the monastic life was freedom from the distractions of the world. Martin obsessively sought to save his soul by practicing the counsels of perfection, not just charity, sobriety, and love, but also chastity, poverty, obedience, fasting, vigils, and mortifications of the flesh. Whatever good works people could do to save themselves, these Luther performed. If ever a monk would get into heaven by his *monkery*, it would be Martin Luther. But there was no peace for Luther, only judgment and condemnation. The problem was not his sin-filled actions, but his sinful condition.

Like Luther, in our Christian walk, each of us must come to understand that we are sinners. We have all missed the mark, "all have sinned and fall short of the glory of God." This is the *Humbled in Faith Dimension* of the Jesus faith fractal. This knowledge is humbling.

Conviction of sin is a necessary moment in time, not an end in itself. It is a bad news moment that prepares the way for the Good News of Jesus Christ. Unfortunately, Luther could not hear the Good News so he became fixated on his depravity. Fortunately, he had a wise and gracious mentor, who sought to shine the light of the Gospel into the darkness of Luther's heart. John von Staupitz was a Doctor of Divinity and Vicar-General of the Augustinian convents in Germany. He directed Luther's attention away from his sins to the merits of Christ, from the law to the cross, from works to faith, from the study of speculative philosophy to the study of Holy Scripture. Staupitz encouraged Luther to pursue his calling to the priesthood through teaching, brought him to Wittenberg to teach, induced him to take the degree of Doctor of Divinity in preparation for taking over Staupitz' own position as professor of Biblical Studies.

Eventually, Luther became the professor of Biblical studies at Wittenberg University, where he gave lectures on the Psalms (1514-15), the Letter to the Romans (1515-16), the Letter to the Galatians (1516-17), and the Letter to the Hebrews (1517-18). It was in the teaching of these courses that he developed a burning desire to understand Paul's Letter to the Romans.

What stood in the way of his understanding was the phrase, "the justice of God." Luther hated the phrase, because he had been taught to understand it philosophically as referring to the justice by which the just God punishes sinners and the unjust. He said:

> I did not love, no, rather I hated the just God who punishes sinners. In silence, if I did not blaspheme, then certainly I grumbled vehemently and got angry at God…I constantly badgered Saint Paul about that spot in Romans 1 and anxiously wanted to know what he meant. I meditated night and day on those words until at last, by the mercy of God,…I began to understand that…the justice of God is that justice by which a person lives as a gift of God, that is by faith…All at once I felt that I had been born again and entered into paradise itself through open gates. Immediately I saw the whole of Scripture in a different light.

In that moment, Luther experienced the love of God, the *grace dimension*, for the first time. The experience of God's perfect love cast out all fear. As a result, when Johann Tetzel, Dominican, inquisitor, sub-commissioner of the Archbishop of Mainz, came around selling God's free gift of grace in the form of letters of indulgence to rebuild St. Peter's in Rome, Martin Luther nailed his 95 Theses to the door of the Castle Church in Wittenberg on October 31, 1517. Later when he was asked to recant or be excommunicated he told the Papal authorities at his inquisition:

> *Unless I am convinced by Scripture and plain reason—I do not accept the authority of the popes and councils, for they have contradicted each other—my conscience is captive to the Word of God. I cannot and I will not recant anything for to go against conscience is neither right nor safe. God help me. Amen.*

Having been graced by God's love, Martin Luther stood up for the grace of God. He had discovered that the salvation he had worked so long and hard to obtain, but couldn't, was his as a free gift from God. Martin Luther worked the rest of his life to help others understand and experience this free gift of the grace dimension for themselves.

A strategic publisher empowering authors to strengthen their brand.

Visit Elevate Publishing for our latest offerings.
www.elevatepub.com

CPSIA information can be obtained
at www.ICGtesting.com
Printed in the USA
FSOW04n2154070316
17607FS